C000089091

Abirami Forbes

and the

Magic Sapphire

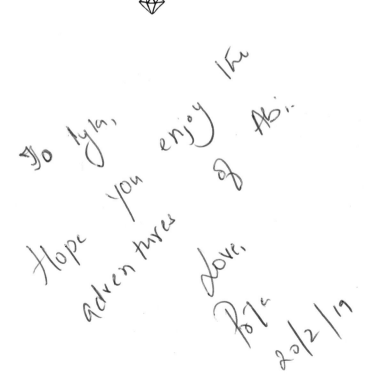

To Tyla,

Hope you enjoy the adventures of Abi.

Love,
Papa
20/2/19

Abirami
Forbes

and
the

MAGIC
SAPPHIRE

Priya
Hunt

Copyright © 2019 Priya Hunt

The moral right of the author has been asserted.

Apart from any fair dealing for the purposes of research or private study,
or criticism or review, as permitted under the Copyright, Designs and Patents
Act 1988, this publication may only be reproduced, stored or transmitted, in
any form or by any means, with the prior permission in writing of the
publishers, or in the case of reprographic reproduction in accordance with
the terms of licences issued by the Copyright Licensing Agency. Enquiries
concerning reproduction outside those terms should be sent to the publishers.

Matador
9 Priory Business Park,
Wistow Road, Kibworth Beauchamp,
Leicestershire. LE8 0RX
Tel: 0116 279 2299
Email: books@troubador.co.uk
Web: www.troubador.co.uk/matador
Twitter: @matadorbooks

ISBN 978 1789017 083

British Library Cataloguing in Publication Data.
A catalogue record for this book is available from the British Library.

Printed on FSC accredited paper
Printed and bound in Great Britain by 4edge Limited
Typeset in 12pt Aldine by Troubador Publishing Ltd, Leicester, UK

Matador is an imprint of Troubador Publishing Ltd

To Appa,
who taught me how to fall in love with writing!

FOREWORD

Most of us engage ourselves passionately in pursuing something that our heart calls out for. We end up investing a huge amount of time and energy on it and then eventually and gradually move towards another passionate call. What we leave behind physically, never ever leaves us emotionally; it kind of settles down in our DNA.

I can see this is exactly what happened to Priya, the author of this book, who as a young teenager would diligently come for Bharatanatyam classes at Ganesa Natyalaya in Delhi. I remember her as an extremely enthusiastic girl committed to the cause of learning the art form. Having completed the course, she moved to England and years later, lo and behold – writes a book on Bharatanatyam dancers, mystical powers and a Gurukul that I would die to go to! Clearly, Priya's passion for dance still remains alive within her.

All the dance stories have been woven into the plot with an on-the-job knowledge that I am proud to see Priya has. The book offers an extensive insight into Indian mythology and takes you on a roller-coaster ride of fantasy, gods, demons and even reincarnation. Human values are presented without you even realising it; the teacher-student relationship is explored beautifully and I was pleasantly surprised to find my namesake as one of the characters!

When it comes to adventure, aren't we all children? This book will hold the interest of anyone who loves a thrill and, of course, anyone who loves India.

Rama Vaidyanathan
Internationally Acclaimed Bharatanatyam Dancer
www.ramavaidyanathan.com

The Start

1

SUMMER VACATION

A bright ray of sunlight danced over Abi's face, waking her up gently. She sleepily pushed away a strand of long dark hair from her face and then woke up with a start as she remembered what day it was. 'Vy, wake up! Our holiday starts today!' she said, pulling her sheets away from her legs and sitting up straight on her bed. She looked across the room towards her sister's bed, expecting to see her snuggled up with her head under her pillows as usual. To her surprise, the bed was empty with the sheets strewn messily over it.

Abi walked up to the study table to check the time. Was she late? Vy was usually the lazy one. The ancient clock propped against her books showed the time to be half past seven. She turned as she heard the sound of voices from the garden. Abi's bed was just by the large window in their bedroom. She opened the window and peered down at their garden below. Their late-blooming magnolia stood majestically in the centre, displaying exquisite white flowers laced with a touch of pink. The garden always made Abi smile. A little blue tit was tapping industriously at the bird feeder, trying to get its beak on a seed of its choice. The flower beds were a riot of colour – begonias and marigolds vied with each other to show off their beauty in resplendent reds and oranges. Almost hidden by a large branch of the magnolia tree, stood Vy, playing with their neighbour's cat.

'You are up early! Why didn't you wake me up?' asked Abi, feeling slightly miffed. She and Vy liked to do everything together – they were identical twins and not only did they look alike, they also seemed to move in tandem. Well, mostly in tandem, except when it came to waking up in the morning, where Abi was almost always the first to get up.

Vy walked away from the tree to look at her sister. 'I would have done, but Ginge here came up to our room with a present that you wouldn't have liked. So, I decided to evict our guest without scaring you.' Vy pointed to a slow worm that was wriggling away on the ground to find shelter while Ginge watched curiously, restrained by Vy from jumping at it again.

'Yuk! Double yuk! I cannot stand slow worms,' said Abi, with a shudder. The thought of a silvery snake-like being on her bedroom floor was enough to make her sick.

Vy gave her a flash of a brilliant smile. Her large dark brown eyes glinted like gemstones – a mix of sunlight and mischief added to their shine. 'Yes, slow worms, snakes, mice, frogs and anything that moves pretty much!' laughed Vy. 'At times, I can't believe you're my twin, given I love all these creatures.'

Abi pulled a face but then smiled. 'Well, better get ready! Let's get some brekky before our long car journey.'

—⚬⚬⚬—

The old grandfather clock was chiming nine in the living room when the girls came down the stairs, dressed up for their trip ahead. They both wore jeans and different coloured t-shirts. Vy was in her favourite purple shade while Abi had selected a white one which complemented her bronze skin beautifully. Both the girls had tied their long hair in a messy plait – they were tomboyish and couldn't understand why their dad would never let them cut their hair short. They entered the bright living room and looked past the sofa to the open-plan kitchen beyond. 'Aha, my sleepyheads arrive, just in time for breakfast. Lay the table, girls. Cluck's laid eggs today – so you're having a very fresh fried egg each with your toast.'
The girls kissed their father and got busy with the plates. The three of them had a lot of practice navigating without getting in each other's way through their tiny but cheerful kitchen, and in no time at all, the table was all set and brimming with food. 'Mm, smells yum, Dad,' said Vy as she looked at the sizzling egg on her plate.

Abi poured out the tea and looked at her father in anticipation. 'What's the plot, Dad? Is Aunty Jo coming over soon? When do we set off for the Lake District?'

Dr Hugh Forbes looked much younger than his forty years, thanks to his slim frame and boyish face. His brown hair was tousled and he was wearing his favourite faded blue cardigan over a checked shirt. He buttered a piece of well-browned toast and smiled at her excited face. 'Jo is coming directly to Windermere. She needs to leave a day early as she needs to meet a visiting scientist who is going to comment on her research. So she decided to get her own car. We can start off as soon as we've had breakfast and given Mrs Perkins the keys. Speaking of her, I noticed that Ginge is bringing more gifts to us nowadays. Vy, stop encouraging him so much,' he said, semi-reproachfully. Vy smiled as she knew her dad loved animals of all shapes and sizes, and the only reason he wouldn't have wanted them all in was due to Abi's aversion towards reptiles and insects.

Abi took a large gulp of tea and frowned as she looked at her father and Vy chuckling at Ginge's antics. 'I must have taken after Mum – bet she didn't like slow worms either.' Dr Forbes smiled wistfully, looking at the painting of a beautiful Indian woman on the mantelpiece. Their mother had died when they were both a year old – so they had no recollection of her. They hadn't even seen any photos of her, and the only things they had grown up with were a couple of paintings that their father had painted years ago. Thirteen years had passed since their mother died, but the girls could see the pain in their father's eyes even now, every time they mentioned her. All they had learnt about their mother was from stories that Aunty Jo told them, though they took them with a pinch of salt as Jo herself had been only seven when their mother had passed away.

'Please keep an eye on the runner beans, Dot,' said Dr Forbes, flashing their old neighbour a charming smile as they handed her their house keys.

'Of course! They are looking rather healthy and I am sure you'll get a bumper crop this year. I haven't been having much luck with my tomato plants, think the deer have been eating them again,' said Mrs Perkins. Abi and Vy exchanged cheeky smiles. Mrs Perkins had a spotless house and was always dressed very elegantly, but her garden was a bit of a disaster zone. Her husband had been the one with the green fingers, and once he died, she'd found it hard to keep the garden in shape. Hugh Forbes and the girls would help out regularly as they loved gardening.

'I'm not sure it's the deer, Dot – I'd buy some slug repellents if I were you. But I'll come and help when I am back,' said their father with a semblance of a smile playing on his lips. They waved their goodbyes to Mrs Perkins and Ginge, her fat and fluffy cat.

2

THE LAKE DISTRICT

Abi sighed deeply with a contented smile as she gazed at the iconic landscape of the Lake District. It was her favourite holiday destination. To be fair, it was also their most regular destination because their father could borrow a cottage that belonged to an old friend of his at very cheap rates. Ivynook cottage was very close to Lake Windermere. It was over a hundred years old; its ancient stone walls were covered by an ivy plant that had firmly taken hold of every nook and cranny of the wall. 'This is the only place that looks amazing even when it's a naff day,' said Vy, admiring the hills and fields shrouded by misty clouds.

Ivynook stood on top of a hill, magnificent in its solitude. The sheep grazing on the hill made it look idyllic. The girls were thrilled to see their aunt's red Mini Cooper already parked by the side of the cottage. 'Jo is early, how unlike her! She must be really looking forward to a break,' commented Dr Forbes with a wry grin. The girls raced each other to the main door, painted bright red and framed beautifully by a climbing white rose bush that had produced a profusion of flowers this summer. The door opened to reveal Josephine Forbes, looking very windswept, with her short dark brown hair flying in all directions. She had large brown eyes that were glinting with good humour and genuine happiness at seeing her family. Abi gave her aunt a great bear hug, nearly squeezing the breath out of her.

'Hey, leggo, you'll squeeze me empty, silly,' said Jo, breaking into a characteristic tinkling laugh. Vy gave her aunt a gentler hug and a kiss.

'You look great, Jo! Though wish you'd brush your hair once in a while,' said Hugh, hugging his sister with one arm as he carried a large suitcase into the house.

———

Days flew by and the family had a wonderful time exploring all the walks in the neighbourhood during the daytime and having delightful meals on the patio in the evenings. They had a cheesy warm shepherd's bean pie on the day they arrived but had moved over to barbeques since. They had been unusually lucky with the weather which had been warm and sunny every day except the day they arrived.

'The weather is changing around the world – it's global warming,' said Vy, reading the papers out loud to no one in particular.

'Well, we can do with some of that,' sighed Abi, basking lazily in the sun.

Hugh Forbes was a great cook and the girls made themselves useful by laying the tables, chopping vegetables and doing the washing-up. After their meals, they would settle down to play board games. Monopoly, Scrabble and Cluedo were the most popular ones, and these were interspersed by Jenga matches, which were hilarious as Jo was all thumbs. 'Jo, I can't believe how badly you suck at Jenga! I would have thought that a chemist would have a more delicate touch,' said Vy, laughing at her aunt's attempts.

'Ah, she's all thumbs because she's distracted. I think she's in love,' whispered Abi. She wasn't soft enough, though, as her father pricked up his ears.

'What's this? Have you got a new boyfriend? Tell me more.'

Jo shook her head, looking rather red and giving Abi a frown. 'No such luck, bro! I spend most of my time with doddery Dr Cogan. No boy in his right mind comes into our chemistry lab.' Hugh Forbes looked into his sister's eyes, not convinced that she was telling the truth.

'Right, who's coming for an evening walk? There is a barn owl nesting in the woods,' said Vy, tactfully changing the subject to save her aunt more blushes.

'Thanks for the save,' said Jo, squeezing Vy's hands as the three girls walked by the woods.

'Abi, you numpty! When will you learn to be more discreet?' said Vy, smiling at her sister. The twins walked next to each other and Jo could only tell them apart by the scar above Vy's upper lip. A scar she wore proudly as she got it while saving a kitten stuck up a tree when she was seven.

The girls didn't press her for any more information but looked at her expectantly, with moonlight dancing in their dark puppy-dog eyes. Jo laughed and shook her head. 'Gosh, you're both little devils. Stop looking at me like that – there isn't much to tell... well, ok. There's a little bit. I have met someone.'

Abi gave a little squeal of delight. 'Who is he? Tell us about him! See, I told you, Vy, that she was being scattier than normal. It's got to be love.'

'Hush! Not sure about love, but it is certainly a big crush. He's of Indian origin – like your mum. Think he's a year younger or two than me, and he is drop-dead gorgeous. But I don't want to tell you any more... not just yet. If things work out, I'll bring him along one day for lunch – if I can gather the courage to tell Hugh.'

Abi pleaded with her aunt, but after ten minutes, she knew it was of no use. Vy had been distracted by the barn owl in the meantime, and the girls spent a few minutes watching the beautiful bird soaring above them, looking for mice.

———

Time flies when you're having fun, and it was soon time for Jo to go back to her university. 'I wish we were travelling back together,' said Abi, feeling sorry that her aunt was leaving a day early.

Jo hugged the girls and kissed her brother on his cheek. 'I am going to be busy for a few days but will come over for Sunday lunch the week after next,' promised Jo.

'Great, I'll make your favourite rosemary garlic roasties,' said Hugh Forbes, smiling at his little sister.

'How about making a curry for a change? You can hardly believe the girls have an Indian mum, given they never seem to eat any spices. I am getting more into Indian food nowadays,' said Jo, winking at the girls as she got into her Mini. They watched her car zip away into the distance.

Abi and Vy felt a bit low after Jo had left. They loved their aunt and her bubbly disposition. She was the closest thing they had to a mother, although she was barely a few years older than them. Hugh spotted the girls moping around and tried to cheer them up. 'Come on, let's go for a walk,' he said, but it was very hot and sticky, and neither Abi nor Vy had the energy for a trek in the countryside. 'What about a drive? There is a really magnificent drive up a hill with fantastic views – come on, girls, it's too hot to sit in the cottage.' Getting tired of saying no to their father, Abi nodded, though Vy still looked reluctant.

'Come on, Vy. A short drive never hurt anyone,' said Abi. Vy smiled as Abi pulled her arm, and joined her family to go for a drive up the hill.

3

THE ACCIDENT

Abi woke up with a start. It was dark and she could suddenly feel the pain in her right leg. She was not sure where she was. She shook her head to try and sort the memories of recent events in her mind. It came back to her – they had been driving down a treacherous slope. A rabbit had bolted across the road – her dad swerved the car and lost control. She couldn't remember anything else.

She sat up and realised that her leg was swathed in bandages. She must be in a hospital! She felt around for a lamp nearby and switched it on. It was as if she was on her own – she could not see who was lying in the neighbouring beds and had no idea whether her dad and sister were also laid up like her. Her throat felt parched. A nurse with a kindly face walked up to her. 'I saw the light,' she said. 'Are you ok? Can I get you some water?'

'Where are Dad & Vy? Are they ok?' As Abi uttered these words, she felt her heart fill with a strange dread.

The nurse wouldn't meet her eyes – 'It is best that the doctor talks to you in the morning dear. You must try and rest some more.' Abi took the glass of water gratefully and sank back into her sheets after drinking.

When Abi woke up again, the sun was high in the sky and the hospital ward looked very different from what she saw at night. The day nurse was busy attending to the three other patients in the room. She heard Abi and smiled brightly at her. 'Dr Jones will be here soon on his rounds,' she said. 'He wants to talk to you.'

Dr Jones looked a lot younger than he probably was. He shook his mop of bright golden hair and smiled awkwardly at Abi. He was accompanied by a burly policeman and a thin middle-aged woman in glasses. A multitude of bad thoughts raced through Abi's head when she saw the policeman's serious face. He introduced himself as Inspector Thomson. 'Do you remember what happened, miss?' He was surprisingly gentle and gave her a small smile of encouragement, asking her to relate as much as she could about herself.

Abi told him what she remembered of the accident. 'My name is Abi Forbes. We had the accident when we were driving down a hill. Is our car ok? Where are Dad and Vy?' asked Abi anxiously.

Inspector Thomson looked grave. 'How many others were with you?'

'Only my dad and my sister. Dad was driving. What's happened to them?' Abi could feel her throat tighten as she said these words. Her breathing grew shallower.

'Do you have any other family we can call, miss?'

Abi could barely whisper Jo's name. 'Josephine Forbes, Warwick University. She's my aunt.'

The woman in glasses gave the policeman a glare, as if to stop him from talking. She pushed forward and introduced herself in a soft, calm voice as Norma Cranford from social services. She patted Abi's hands but by now, Abi was in a panic. 'Tell me... where are they? Please,' she said, fighting back her tears.

'We didn't find anyone. We think the car rolled down the mountain – one of the doors probably flew open and you got thrown out. As for the others...I am so sorry.' Abi stared at the three people standing in front of her, dumbfounded. What had happened to her father and sister? Why were they not in the hospital? They couldn't be...she felt blood rush to her head and fell back, fainting in shock.

—∞—

When Abi gained consciousness, she saw Jo sat in a chair by her side. Her aunt's dark eyes were red-rimmed and her face was tear-stained. Seeing her awake, Jo got up, hugged her tightly and started sobbing quietly. Abi was relieved to see her aunt – the one familiar face in very unfamiliar surroundings. But seeing her in this state just reminded her that what she thought may have been a bad dream was really happening. Abi hoped that Jo could take her home and then somehow, things would get back to normal again.... her father and Vy would miraculously come back home!

Abi's legs took a few days to heal. Luckily, there were no broken bones, but they had to stitch up some deep gashes and keep her under their watch as she had lost a fair amount of blood. Despite having heard what the inspector had said, Abi kept asking her aunt about what had happened to her family. Finally, Jo burst into tears one day. 'The car exploded at the bottom of the hill, Abi. Dad and Vy have joined your mum!' Abi cried so much that night that she thought she would never be able to cry again.

Three days later, Abi held tightly on to Jo's hand as they sat in Dr Jones's consulting room. There were three other people in the room. Abi recognised Inspector Thomson, and Norma Cranford gave them a wan smile. She looked quizzically at the third man. He was around forty years of age and had a very distinguished air about him. He was dark, his skin looked like slightly creased well-polished leather, and his hair was silver in places. He smiled at the girls and introduced himself. 'My name is Akash Sharma. I am your parents' solicitor,' he explained, looking at Abi. 'Dr Jones has kindly agreed to let us use his room to have a word with both of you.'

Dr Jones squirmed uncomfortably in his seat – 'I could leave you alone as you'd probably like some privacy?' he asked Jo and Abi, looking at them directly. Both the girls shook their heads in unison. They'd grown to trust the medical staff in the hospital.

'No, please stay,' said Jo quietly.

Akash Sharma agreed with her – 'Doctor, we need you to release Abi immediately. So I think you'll want to hear what we're saying.'

There was a moment of awkward silence and then Jo spoke up: 'Mr Sharma, I have heard my brother mention you before. Is this something to do with his will? Why can it not wait until I take Abi home?'

'Do you know the terms and conditions of the will, Jo?' Jo shook her head in the negative and Akash carried on. 'Your brother, Hugh, and his wife, Ananya, made this will as soon as the girls were born. The terms are very clear. There is a sum of money left in a trust to take care of all the needs of the girls and to fund your education, Jo, if anything was to happen to both of them. However, there is a strict stipulation. If both parents die, then the girl(s) have to be sent to a school in India, run by a lady called Shakuntala Devi. Your university funding will be held in a trust and paid directly to the college.' Jo and Abi stared at Akash and then looked at each other aghast.

'No, that's not going to happen,' began Jo angrily. 'I am the only family she has! I am not going to let some stranger take her away from me!'

'I am really sorry, Jo, but there's not much that we can do. But Hugh had left a little note for you, to be opened only in these circumstances.' Fighting back her tears, Jo snatched the letter from Akash, tore it open and started reading it. Abi glanced at the envelope as he handed it to her aunt. It was definitely a letter from her father – she felt a pang as she recognised his familiar slanted writing. He'd never be writing to her again!

The anger in Jo's eyes strangely reassured Abi. Whatever the will contained, she was sure her aunt would not let her be taken away to India. Maybe the letter would tell her it was all a bad joke. Jo scanned the letter several times and looked bewildered. She then put her head in her hands and sat silently for a few minutes and wouldn't let Abi see the letter. She looked up at Akash with her eyes swimming in tears: 'What's going on – do you know anything about this?' Her voice quivered as she asked.

Akash nodded gravely. 'Yes, I am afraid this has to be done urgently. We have no choice, Jo.' Abi looked at the two of them with increasing helplessness. What could possibly be in that letter that Jo had now changed her mind? They were discussing her future and it seemed that she was not going to have a say in it.

Jo pulled herself together, wiped her tears and turned to Akash Sharma. 'When does she have to leave?'

'Right away – she needs to pack, and I'll take her to India.'

Abi turned towards her aunt and pleaded. 'Don't do this, don't let me go. I want to stay here with you... please...'

Jo pulled Abi close and gave her a tight hug. 'I am really sorry, Abi – you have to go.' Abi stared dumbfounded at everyone around – in a matter of days, her entire world had come crashing down on her.

4

THE COTTAGE ON THE HILL

It was a lovely sunny day when they reached home. The car journey had been morose and no one had spoken a word. Akash focussed on driving and Jo kept staring out of the window. Abi sobbed quietly – she was really angry with her father, her mother and her aunt. She blamed them for her predicament. She looked wistfully at their little cottage on the hill. Mrs Perkins, their old neighbour, was standing by the door. As usual, she was dressed impeccably – Abi's tears increased in intensity as she was wearing Vy's favourite colour – a neat violet skirt and blouse with a string of pearls, and her grey hair was neatly tied into a small bun at the nape of her neck. She gave them a wrinkly smile. Jo had telephoned her from the hospital to inform her of their plans.

Abi gave her a tearful nod and went into the house without saying a word. Her anger dissipated a little as it was comforting to be in old familiar surroundings. The living room was just as they left it one week ago. The

Sunday papers were spread over the sofa, the magazine left open on the crossword page. She could almost hear her father shout out the clues to her and Vy as they packed for their trip. She glanced distractedly at an article on global warming, the headlines screaming out about floods in Asia. Abi turned sadly and looked at the series of photo frames on the mantelpiece. She hadn't looked at them properly in years – most of the pictures were of the girls with their father and aunt – a fishing trip, Christmas last year and a very special trip to Paris two years ago, with the twins standing in front of the Eiffel Tower. Abi felt her heart would break as she looked at the smiles on her father and sister's faces. She would never see that again! She picked up the photos and hugged them fiercely.

She walked up the stairs, carrying the pictures and a few of her father's books. Dad had been an avid reader and as a naturalist, he had hundreds of books on birds and plants. Her aunt came up and flicked through the books. 'Would you mind if I take this one to remind me of Hugh?' asked Jo, in a soft whisper. 'It was one of his favourites and I always remember him reading out snippets from it about Darwin's expedition to the Galapagos.' Abi nodded and sat up, trying to wipe the tears off her cheeks. She saw her aunt pull a suitcase and start packing some clothes. Clothes to go to India! Abi felt her resentment mounting – she ran out to her dad's bedroom and stared out of the window. She didn't want to help with the packing.

She loved this house. She remembered the times she would wake up early in the mornings just to look out at the countryside and see deer roam about freely nearby. She blinked away her tears and turned away from the window. There was a spectacular painting on the wall that her father had painted. It was a painting of a beautiful girl in white flowing robes, floating towards the sky. The scenery was magnificent – a greenish-blue lake surrounded by dark green trees. The girl had no wings or a halo but she looked like an angel. Vy had been fascinated by this portrait and always thought that the girl in the painting was their mother. Their father had neither confirmed nor denied this.

Abi frowned thoughtfully at this painting, trying to force her mind to produce old memories of her mother, but the truth was that she had absolutely no recollection of her. The girls were barely one year old when their mother passed away. Aunty Jo used to tell them how their father had brought them up with utmost care, love and attention, just as he'd brought her up. Her father, her sister and aunt were her entire world. And now, Abi would have to leave all of them and her lovely home behind!

Abi's sadness gave way to anger as she looked at the beautiful ethereal face in the painting. How dare her mother decide to send her to India – after all, what right did she have over Abi? She had never been there for her! Abi felt the bile rise up to her mouth. For a minute, she wanted to tear down the painting of the angelic woman in front of her and scream at the unfairness of it all. She was raising her hand towards the painting when she heard a soft purr. Ginge was standing on the floor, gently rubbing his body against her legs. 'Oh, Ginge – you must be looking for Vy.' A sob escaped her mouth and she threw herself on her father's bed, crying her eyes out.

Gradually, the tears stopped, and Abi pondered over what she knew about her mother. Very little – except for the fact that she was from India. Every time they'd asked their father about her, his answer would be the same – 'She was an angel, sent to me from the heavens and then one day, they took her back!' She knew her father was saving up money so that one day the three of them could go to India and visit the place where he'd first met their mother. Abi wondered what India would be like – she had heard many things about the country; its colourful culture, its people and its majestic mountain range – the Himalayas. Her dad was very keen to go and explore the mountains there and examine the flora and fauna. To Abi and Vy, India was just another holiday destination, as Paris had been a few years back. As they remembered nothing of their mother, they could not really associate anything with her, and although there was some curiosity about the country and excitement about a holiday, they had no other burning desire to go to India.

A gentle hand touched her back and woke her out of her reverie. Jo was looking at her with worry written on her face. 'Are you ok, Abi? I have done some packing for you – but you may want to check if you need anything else.' Abi walked listlessly behind her aunt into her room. A set of clothes were folded neatly and lay on the bed. There were shoes, some cosmetics and a first aid kit next to it. 'Just let me know what else you would like and I'll pack it all away,' said Jo, pointing at the empty suitcase lying with its mouth wide open on the bed. Abi shook her head – she didn't want to even think about what needed to be packed. She wanted to stay here. She stood there staring blankly at the case on the bed.

Finally, Jo gave up and packed it herself and gently ushered her downstairs. 'Abi, come and have some tea, dear.' Mrs Perkin's gentle voice brought Abi back to the present. There were steaming mugs of tea on the roughly hewn wooden table in the kitchen. A large sponge cake with cream and jam and cucumber sandwiches sat next to it.

'Come, you must be hungry. Abi, you know I don't want to let you go – I have to – please don't be angry with me.' Jo looked anxiously at her, almost trying to read her mind. Abi took the cup that her elderly neighbour handed her and turned her attention to the food. The sandwiches were soft and fresh and the cake was moist and delicious.

The hot tea and food made Abi feel less resentful. Food always made her feel better. She took a large gulp of tea and shook her head at her aunt. 'I am upset but I know it's not your fault really.' Abi stared at her knees. 'Whatever was in that letter... I guess you feel you're doing the right thing.' She looked up hopefully, wondering if her aunt would show her the letter now, but Jo only nodded. Abi bristled. 'I just don't get it.' She threw her teacup on the table and it splashed the mahogany tea all over the sandwiches. She didn't care. 'How could you do this to me?' She was shouting now. 'I never knew Mum. I've never been to India. Isn't it bad enough to have lost Dad and Vy? Do I have to lose my home, too?' She collapsed in her chair and put her head in her hands, sobbing violently.

'Abi…' Jo began, hesitantly.

'I hate you – how could you let them do this to me?' said Abi fiercely, lifting her face towards her aunt.

Jo just stood there for a few moments and then reached out to her slowly. 'Abi,' she said again, 'there are reasons – I cannot tell you them right now, but one day you'll understand. This is not easy for me either, darling.' Jo's face looked totally despondent. Abi let her aunt wrap her in her arms.

'I don't hate you, not really.'

'I know you don't, darling. Things will work out, I promise.'

'And I don't hate Dad either.'

Mrs Perkins came back into the kitchen. Abi had never even noticed her leaving. She must have left when Abi started yelling at her aunt. She had just tidied away the tea and sandwiches when Akash walked in. 'We have tickets on the flight to Delhi. It leaves tonight and I am afraid we have to leave for the airport within the next hour. Abi – please check that you have what you need. You don't need much as you will get clothes to wear, books, etc. at school. Just make sure you have your essentials.'

Abi walked back up the stairs and listlessly checked that she had her toiletries in the case. Akash came up to the room. 'I'll take the suitcase to the car,' he said, leaving her alone in the room to have a few moments of contemplation.

As he left, Abi could not fight back her tears – she did not feel like calling or writing to her school friends and saying goodbye. She ran downstairs and found Jo clearing up the kitchen. 'Would you let my school and my mates know that I'm going to India? Please let them know that I'll contact them when I get there.' Jo nodded silently and led her to the car outside.

Akash looked thoughtfully at them as they walked towards the car. 'Abi, do you know any Hindi at all? The teaching medium in Gurukul is English, but I am sure the girls also speak to each other in Hindi.'

Abi nodded. 'Dad was a genius with languages and he used to speak Hindi. He insisted on teaching us – he said it should connect us back to India in some way. So, I can speak and understand it quite well.' Abi turned her face away from him to hide the tears that threatened to come out when she spoke about her father. They all stood there for a moment – no one wanted to break the silence. Everyone stared at their feet.

This was it – a final goodbye to her home of fourteen years. Abi looked around her – she could see the fields stretched below and clumps of trees in glorious green colour at a distance. In the winter, the hill would get snowed under and the girls would play with the snow, sledging down the slope and building snowmen in the back garden. She looked out wistfully at the apple trees – why did she have to leave her lovely home, her school, the countryside and even the country and go to a place that she'd never been to? And why had her father and Vy left her alone to face this?

She looked at everything around her, letting the last memories of her home etch into her mind. She needed something that would remind her of this haven, of her family, of the wonderful times they'd had – something that would connect her back to England when she was alone in new surroundings. Suddenly she knew what she needed – she ran upstairs to her father's room and picked up the portrait of the angel that Vy used to say was their mother. She didn't fully understand why she was doing this – but something told her that she needed to take this with her. Her Indian mother would be the link back to her English home and family. She ran back to the car, opened the boot and started fumbling with the suitcase to try and get this in. It just about fitted. She heard a soft chuckle and looked up to see Akash smiling at her. He looked strangely smug, as though he had expected her to do this. Abi looked angrily at him – who was he to judge her and what could he know about how she felt? He wasn't the one who was being uprooted from everything and being banished to a land far away. She turned away from him angrily. Akash closed the boot.

Abi heard a sob behind her. She turned back and gave Jo a tight hug. 'Write to me, please! And do try and come over when you can,' said Abi, without much conviction. She knew that her aunt was an easy-going, carefree person without any head for money and that she would never be able to save up enough to visit India.

She walked up to Mrs Perkins and gave her a quick hug and thanked her. 'Don't you worry, my dear. I will look after your garden and your lovely home for when you come back,' said her old neighbour. Abi gave her a sad smile. She knew that the future of the house was uncertain, and Jo would have to take a decision someday soon about whether it needed to be sold. She tried not to think about it as she looked at the house longingly for what may be the last time.

Abi and Akash got into the car and drove off down the hill. Abi put her head out of the window and waved sadly to her aunt – 'I'll miss you! Take care of yourself.'

5

THE MYSTERIOUS MAN AT THE AIRPORT

Abi had never been to the airport before. Her father could not afford train or air travel, and they'd always gone either by car or coach on their holidays. Even their Paris holiday was by car. She looked forlornly at the shiny new terminal at Heathrow. Vy was always fascinated by architecture and she could almost feel the excitement her twin would have experienced, had she been there. There were great big video screens with colourful images on them and modern kiosks where people seemed to be printing their tickets.

Akash led her to one of these kiosks and punched in a few details to print out two sheets of paper. 'This is your boarding card,' said Akash.

Abi looked at the boarding card – it had her full name on it – Abirami Forbes. 'How do you know my full name?' asked Abi curiously. All her friends always thought that

Abi stood for Abigail and Vy stood for Violet. In reality, both girls had Indian names – Abirami and Vydehi.

'I had your passport,' smiled Akash. 'Also, I had suggested these names to your mother when she gave birth to both of you.' Abi looked at him in surprise – she didn't know what to make of him. She wanted to know how he knew her parents and wanted to hear more stories of his time with them.

'So, how do you know them?' she asked, almost bracing herself for the answer. Talking about her father hurt.

'A tale for the flight – no time now! Come, let's go through security,' said Akash as he walked towards a short queue of people.

Abi felt close to tears all the time but did not want to cry in front of Akash. He seemed so cold and judgemental. She decided to play a game to occupy herself, where she could talk to her absent sister, quietly in her mind. By doing that, Abi suddenly found the airport more interesting – there were so many people to watch and shops to look at. Akash bought her a bar of chocolate to eat that Abi took gratefully – the tea-sodden sandwiches at home were a distant memory. She started describing the scene to her twin without speaking. There was a plump old man in a very tight striped suit, hand-in-hand with a young, beautiful model-like girl walking by the shops. Two policemen in full gear were on patrol and gave her a smile and a nod as they walked past her. A harried mother with three kids was trying to find her passport or some other paper while her kids were trying to escape from her. A businesswoman was walking up and down the shops, talking loudly on her mobile. Abi knew Vy would have admired her smartly cut suit and shiny high heels. A bunch of college students with backpacks were staring unblinkingly at the flight information screens, possibly trying to figure out where their flight was departing from. Abi took pleasure in describing everybody to her sister and imagining her response.

Suddenly she saw him – he was tall, dark and had a glossy moustache and a wisp of a goatee. He must be in his late teens but was dressed like an older man, in a very expensive-looking brown suit and a hat. There was something captivating about him, like he was out of an old movie. He had startling green eyes that seemed to stare right into her, although he was very far away. He seemed to be looking straight at her but suddenly put his hand out to catch one of the toddlers that had escaped from his mother. The child would have fallen in the way of a man pushing a stream of small trolleys. The harassed-looking mother gratefully took back the child. Abi could not tear her eyes away from the scene – the young man seemed so special, so intriguing.

She was still looking at him when she realised that she was being ushered to the boarding gate by Akash. They boarded first and Abi turned around to find no sign of the green-eyed man. It was only then that she noticed that Akash seemed to be turning around and looking for someone, too. 'Is something wrong?' she enquired.

'No, let's find our seats,' said Akash with a forced smile. Akash seemed to be very tense and kept straining and looking around even after they found their seats. It was only when the stewardess announced that the door was closed and they were about to take off that he visibly relaxed and stopped squirming. After a few moments of silence as the flight took off, he turned around to talk to her. 'So,' said Akash, 'do you know the meaning of your lovely name? It is another name for goddess Lakshmi, the wife of Lord Vishnu. Do you know anything about the Indian gods?' Abi shook her head to the negative. 'There are three main gods in Indian mythology,' Akash went on – 'they are Brahma, the creator; Vishnu, the preserver and Shiva, the destroyer. Besides these three, there are other lesser gods such as Indra – King of gods and the god of thunder, Vayu – god of the wind and so on. Each of them has their own consorts, meaning partners, vehicles and weapons. You will learn a lot of this in your school.' Abi looked out of the window – mythology did not interest her in any way. She had been taught a bit of Roman and Greek mythology in school, and she was sure that Indian mythology would be equally confusing and pointless.

After the seatbelt signs had gone off, Akash put his hand on her arm and said kindly, 'I am sorry that so much is going on in your life. I want you to know that your parents have arranged this in your best interest. I knew both of them really well. You mother was the most amazing, beautiful and talented woman I have ever met. And your father was my best friend and luckiest man in the world.' Abi looked at him in mild surprise. She had never heard her father mention Akash, yet he spoke as though he were best friends with both her parents. 'The school that you are being sent to is very special. Shakuntala Devi is extremely capable and will look after you well. She taught your mother after all.'

'How do you know my parents?' enquired Abi hesitantly.

'Your father and I were classmates in university. We went backpacking to India together, and I was with him when he first met your mother.'

In normal circumstances, Abi would have been very interested in knowing more about her parents and how they met. But just hearing that little snippet about her father made her want to cry. She wanted nothing more than to stare aimlessly out of the window and cry secretly to herself. Akash seemed totally oblivious of her emotional state and carried on – 'Your mother was a fantastic dancer – she could absolutely mesmerise the audience with her brilliant performance.'

'Yes,' said Abi, perking up slightly, 'she was an Indian classical dancer, wasn't she – Bharatanatyam, I think.'

'Good, you know about Bharatanatyam,' said Akash. 'You'll learn it soon.' Abi looked at him in surprise – she always thought that one had to start young to become a dancer. She and Vy had never learnt dance at school – both were too involved in sportier activities, like tennis. Tennis reminded her of her father again. His visage floated into her mind – he was dressed in his usual jeans and a crumpled jumper that had leaves and twigs stuck on it as he often hid in the bushes trying to study birds or collect some botanical specimen. She thought wistfully of his disarming smile – she could not help wondering how someone so down-to-earth, like her father, could be good friends with someone as posh and formal as Akash.

Soon Akash stopped talking and channelled his energies towards polishing off several small bottles of cognac. Abi ignored him and looked out of the window. They had gone above most of the clouds, and she could no longer see the scenery below. It was getting darker and quieter – she felt that they were riding into a storm, but as this was her first flight, she could not be sure. Suddenly she could see several streaks of lightning outside – their plane was surrounded by dark, ominous clouds. Abi looked around her to see if her fellow passengers had started panicking yet – she did not want to appear cowardly in front of Akash. Akash was still focussing on his cognac, and it did not seem like he had noticed anything. Most of the other passengers seemed asleep.

The stewardess walked past casually and gave Abi a smile – 'Can I get you anything, miss?'

'No, thanks,' said Abi. She thought to herself that this must be normal during a plane trip and tried to look unconcerned, but now the plane had started rocking in the clouds. The seatbelt sign went on – Abi fastened hers again and put her head close to the window – it was very dark outside – she could hardly see anything. Then she saw the strangest sight that she had ever come across in her life!

She could see the outline of what looked like a white elephant between two clouds. Abi strained her eyes to see better – she was helped by another streak of lightning. In the flash of light, she saw a man dressed elaborately in silk, wearing a gold crown, sitting on top of the white elephant, which looked like it had more than one trunk. He was looking directly at her and smiling. Abi rubbed her eyes – she must be either dreaming or maybe the fumes of cognac were having an effect on her! There was a roar of thunder in the distance and then it became very dark once again – the elephant and the man with the crown had disappeared.

Abi kept her eyes peeled for even a shadow of an elephant outside – the storm seemed to have passed, and although the sky was dark, Abi could see the lights of distant cities down below clearly. She frowned to herself and wondered if she should tell Akash what she saw. She shook her head – he'd probably give her his irritating know-it-all smile and tell her that she was imagining things and needed to sleep. Sleep was the last thing she wanted but decided to give it a try anyhow. The tiredness took over.

By the time she woke up, the lights were on in the cabin and Akash was munching his way through an elaborate breakfast. 'Have a roll', he said, passing her a bread roll and some butter. 'We should be landing shortly; there won't be time for you to have a full breakfast. Don't worry, we'll get some nice lunch when we go to the hotel. We'll be spending the day in Delhi and then travelling overnight to the mountains.'

<hr />

Abi found her mental game of talking to her sister was the only thing that kept her sane and stopped her from crying. She started describing the new city to Vy in her mind. Delhi was a riot of colours – Abi had never seen such a hustle and bustle in any other city before. There were people everywhere – beautiful women in colourful saris, street vendors pushing carts with fascinating eatables, brown street children selling magazines at every traffic stop and a chaotic maze of traffic that weaved in and out between vehicles, cows, goats and people. Their taxi took them to an old imposing building surrounded by greenery in the city centre. 'It's one of the best hotels in the city. This is my little treat for you, Abi. It's the least that I can do,' said Akash. 'I would like to take you around to see a few things – especially the old city. I know your dad would have wanted me to show you Delhi, and it will take your mind off things.'

They checked into their rooms. Abi wished Vy was there to see her luxurious room – she had never seen anything like it. There were silk cushions on the magnificent bed, lots of lovely old paintings of the city on the walls, a large TV and a beautiful balcony that opened out towards the garden. She was even more excited by the bathroom with an enormous roll-top bath and a separate shower. She took her time in the shower, painstakingly describing all the various potions, creams and salts to her sister, and then changed into her jeans and t-shirt. As she stared at herself in the mirror, she could see Vy smiling back. Was she slowly going mad? Talking to someone who was no longer alive? She took a deep breath and went down to meet Akash in the lobby. He looked much more relaxed and almost handsome, in blue jeans and a colourful Indian shirt. 'Come, we will first see "Jantar Mantar". It is a sundial built by an ancient king – it's wonderful. Then we'll go into Old Delhi.'

Jantar Mantar was a collection of pink buildings, each meant to be a sundial or perform other astronomical functions. Again, Abi wistfully remembered Vy's fascination with architecture and pretended her sister was still with her. Akash explained the function of each of the buildings and instruments in there. Then they took an auto-rickshaw ride to Old Delhi. The auto was a curious contraption on three wheels. It looked much less stable and less safe than a car, and their driver was clearly in a hurry to get to his destination. Windblown and out of breath, both Akash and Abi stepped out into Old Delhi.

Quaint little streets, narrow precarious buildings, street vendors selling all sorts of savouries and sweets, goats, dogs, bicycles, cycle-rickshaws and a sea of people making their way calmly through all of this activity awaited them. Abi remembered the stories her father had told her about India. She could have stood there and studied the scene around her forever. They walked slowly through all the chaos and finally stopped at a little cafe where Akash bought her a few savoury snacks that Abi enjoyed, wishing her father and sister were next to her to share the unusual concoction. It was spicy and tangy and cooling at the same time. She was used to samosas and onion bhajis in England but had never come across such enjoyable fare. 'You've just tried a *raj kachori*, *aloo tikki* and *papri chaat*,' said Akash, tucking into a plate of chaat himself. They spent some more time wandering through various old-fashioned markets that sold spices, tinsel, paper and a huge variety of other items that Abi could not even recognise.

'Dad always wanted to bring both of us to India,' she whispered.

Akash smiled sadly. 'Hugh loved India – in some ways, he left part of himself here when he went back to England.'

Soon, it was time to get back to the hotel, pack and make their way to the railway station. They found their train on a crowded platform. There were wooden berths inside their compartment – Akash put their bags under two of the berths and asked her to take a seat by the window while he went out and bought some crisps, water and a magazine to read on the train. The train started on time – the sky was already dark, and as they sped up, they left the twinkling city lights far behind. As Abi stretched out on her berth, the colourful city of Delhi flashed through her mind. Despite the heartache that was now part of her, she had had a reasonably good day, which was hopefully a sign of times to come in her new school. Her heart beat a little faster when she thought of what would be her new home – she would have to make new friends, what would the teachers make of her, would she be taught the same subjects as she was in England? Not knowing the answers, Abi drifted into sleep – she looked forward to waking up to a new day and sharing more of what she saw with Vy, who seemed to have now taken permanent residence in her mind.

6

GURUKUL

It was nearly three o'clock in the afternoon the next day when they arrived at the school. It had been a long and arduous journey. After the train ride, they had to take a spiralling car ride up the mountain. After three hours of being in the car, they met up with two guides with horses and mules. The horse ride felt really long and painful. There was a sudden roar of thunder and Abi looked up at the darkening sky with apprehension. 'It's normally much drier, but we've had a lot of rain this year,' explained one of the guides, as their horses splashed their way through puddles. They stopped for a short while to eat a bite of fruit and drink some tea. Luckily, despite the thunder and lightning, rain stayed away.

The next stage of the journey was on foot. One of the guides stayed with them and they were accompanied by two mules carrying their luggage. Abi was breathless, cold and tired. They had been climbing higher and higher up the mountain. The views were spectacular and if Abi had not been exhausted, she would have appreciated the loveliness around her. 'How much further?' she panted to Akash.

'We're here – welcome to Gurukul! It is a school like no other, based on an ancient Indian tradition. In the old times, royal children were often sent away to learn arts and sciences from a guru. During this time, they had to be totally devoted to him and follow each and every command. In India, a guru is treated no less than a god. Just wanted you to be aware of this as you will find things a bit different here from the UK,' said Akash, with a smile.

Gurukul, the school, was nothing like Abi imagined it to be. There were scattered buildings of mud and straw hidden between a profusion of flowering shrubs. As they climbed further up the winding path, they started seeing people. Young girls, dressed in colourful sari uniforms, were carrying baskets of flowers and fruits. Abi looked at the girls and felt a pang of jealousy. They were beautiful – each wearing a sari in red, green or yellow with a pair of matching tights underneath. They had dark black plaits and some were wearing flowers in their hair. All the girls had a big red spot *bindi* on their foreheads. They moved very gracefully and quietly. Some of them glanced at her as they passed by. Abi felt very self-conscious. Her jeans were muddy, her shirt was very crumpled and her hair was coming down messily from her plait. At the top of the path stood a beautiful archway made of mud with a roof of red tiles. They stepped through this doorway to enter a large, clean and simple courtyard. Abi felt that the large open space in the centre of the courtyard could contain more than a thousand people if need be – it seemed enormous. There was a brightly coloured amber dais on one end and there were two girls dancing on it. They were watched by a number of students and teachers sitting down on straw mats below the dais. Abi looked around the courtyard. The central space was surrounded by a number of uniform rooms built in a rectangle – there must have been thirty or more rooms. There were a number of beautiful trees standing at each corner of the courtyard. Behind these buildings, you could see the Himalayan Mountains rising up with their snow-capped peaks shining in the sun. The setting and the beauty of the place was breath taking!

⸎

Abi felt the apprehension rise as she stared at her new unfamiliar school. Akash thanked and bid goodbye to the guide and gently guided Abi towards a room that was directly opposite the arched doorway but on the other end of the courtyard. There were tiny terracotta lamps filled with oil that had been lit up on the floor on either side of the door to this room. Abi felt intimidated and a little in awe as they entered the large, dark room. It took her a few minutes to adjust her eyes to the absence of bright light. In one corner of the room, there were a number of pictures of Indian gods adorned with fresh flowers. There was a large brass oil lamp throwing soft light on the pictures. There were a number of parchments and portraits stacked in front of the lamp. Near the window, there was a low table and mats. Behind the table sat an old lady wearing white robes. She seemed very tall and very well built. Her completely silver hair was plaited with white flowers. She was wearing a very large red *bindi* on her forehead and her lips were red – not coloured with lipstick, but probably from whatever she was chewing. Abi looked into her kohl-rimmed eyes. They were a strange grey colour – very deep and intense. Abi felt a shiver run down her spine as the grey eyes looked into hers.

Akash seemed to share her sense of awe as he almost whispered his greetings to the old lady. 'Guruji, I present Abirami Forbes, daughter of Hugh and Ananya.'

So, this is Guru Shakuntala Devi, thought Abi to herself. She had been expecting a sophisticated, grey-haired, well-dressed principal, but this lady looked more like an old dancer gone to seed. Yet there was something intimidating and awe-inspiring about her – maybe it was her dramatic appearance or the subtle lighting in the room. 'Welcome, Abi – is that what your friends call you?' said the old lady in a surprisingly soft, melodic voice. Abi nodded – she was fighting tears – this place was even more alien than she expected, and she was dreading being left here alone. 'Don't worry, you won't be alone. There are a number of girls your age out here, and I am sure you will make some very good friends.' Abi stared at the old lady – how did she know what she was thinking?

'While you are here, you need to understand our rules and practices. I run this place and all the girls call me "Guruma" – it literally means teacher-mother. The girls' quarters are outside the courtyard and your luggage will have been placed in your room. There are a number of boys in the school, but they are mostly part of the orchestra – either learning how to sing or play musical instruments. Your classmates are a really wonderful bunch of bright and talented girls. You will learn a number of subjects in school – many differ from what you learnt in England. The main subject would be Indian classical dance – Bharatanatyam. Besides this, you will also learn the sciences, arithmetic, a number of different languages, Indian mythology and an elective subject. Most girls your age will choose their own elective subject – but as you are new here and are coming mid-term, I will choose your subject for you. It is an ancient form of Indian martial arts. Besides studying, you'll also do yoga and meditation. All girls have to strictly follow the instructions that any of the gurus or teachers give them. There is no scope for dissent or misbehaviour in our school,' said Guruma in a stern tone. 'But,' she added kindly, 'I am sure you will be fine as your mother has chosen this place as the safest and best place in the world for you. I need to talk to Akash, so please say your goodbyes to him and I will call one of the girls to take you to your room.' She went out to call for a girl and Abi and Akash were left alone in the room.

'Well, thank you for everything,' began Abi awkwardly.

Akash gave her a warm hug and a dazzling smile, flashing his suspiciously perfect white teeth. 'You'll be fine here, Abi – I'll write to you and keep in touch. Take care of yourself and please do everything that Guruma tells you, even if it seems strange in the beginning.'

Guruma returned with a young girl in a red sari uniform. 'This is Sumathy – she will be your roommate and friend. Sumathy – please take Abi to her room, get her to freshen up and change and I will see you at dinner.'

Sumathy gave Abi a shy smile as they walked outside the room. 'The girls' rooms are further up the mountain. We have to go out from a different doorway and then walk up the narrow path between the rhododendron bushes,' said Sumathy in a gentle voice. She was very slim, probably a year or so younger than Abi and had very long black hair that had been plaited tightly and hung behind her, touching her waist. She was a few inches shorter than Abi and had just escaped being beautiful because of her front teeth that slightly protruded, giving her a rabbit-like appearance. Abi felt that she liked her instantly. They made their way up a narrow and steep path and found a large number of mud huts scattered among the flowering bushes. 'Ours is the one on the left,' said Sumathy. Abi entered the hut with some trepidation – her living quarters were very basic – it was an airy room with large windows and two beds in the centre. There were two tables and chairs near a window each and two cupboards by one wall. In the corner stood a mud pot and a couple of glasses – it probably contained water. Sumathy had put up an old fading photograph on the wall above her bed. 'Those are my grandparents,' she said. 'I never met my parents – they died in an accident and I was brought up for a few years by my grandparents before coming here. They are no more now. How about your family?' she enquired.

Abi felt a pang as she replied, 'All gone – they're no more – my mother died when we were young, and I lost my father and sister in an accident, too.'

Sumathy squeezed Abi's hands – 'don't fret, you will find peace here. Come; let me take you to the stream for you to freshen up.'

Washing and dressing by the stream was a novelty for Abi. It was deserted but she felt very self-conscious as she tried to get into her new red sari. 'Here, let me show you how,' began Sumathy, taking the folds of material from Abi's hands.

'So the new girl has no clue on how to tie a sari,' said a sneering, loud voice from behind the bushes. The voice belonged to a girl, probably around sixteen years of age. She was wearing a yellow sari, a yellow flower on her dark, oily hair and long garland made of flowers. Her face was round and fair and would have been pretty but was spoilt by the contemptuous expression that she was wearing. 'Don't see her doing much dance either, do you?' she smirked.

'I am sure she'll be very good,' said Sumathy loyally. 'Abi, meet Pooja – she's one of our top dancers in the school.'

Abi stretched her hand towards Pooja who was staring at her with narrowed eyes. 'We greet people by folding our hands in a Namaste – not shaking them like westerners,' she scoffed, and walked away.

Sumathy shrugged her shoulders and asked Abi to ignore her. 'Pooja is conceited but she is a great dancer. Every two years, Guruma selects a dancer to dance at the Sun Temple Festival. It is a great honour and we think Pooja will definitely go next year. It's particularly special next year as it's the twelfth year – there's a myth that the Sun god comes down to watch the dances once every twelve years, and he grants a special wish to the best dancer in the festival. She's so fortunate,' sighed Sumathy. 'She's bound to get a special wish.' Abi hitched her sari up thoughtfully, not knowing whether to laugh at Sumathy's floral language and strange stories or cry at the strangeness of it all.

Dinner was a sociable affair – everyone sat on straw mats in the great courtyard. A simple dinner of rice, lentils and beans was served to them on banana leaves. No cutlery was provided – Abi watched Sumathy scoop up the rice along with some gravy and vegetables. After a few messy attempts, Abi managed to do the same. The girls chatted while they ate. All the teachers sat on one side and ate their meal in silence. Abi looked around her to try and absorb as much of her new surroundings as possible. She could see Pooja throwing her evil glances periodically. At the end of the meal, Guruma got up and walked towards Abi. 'You look lovely in your sari – just like your mother!' Abi looked at her in surprise – she had not seen her reflection in the mirror yet.

Almost reading her mind, Sumathy whispered to her, 'I'll take you back through the make-up room that has a mirror – you can see yourself.'

The make-up room was well-lit. It had a number of mirrors, costumes strewn on the floor and baskets containing pots of make-up. Abi looked at herself in one of the mirrors in astonishment. The red colour contrasted beautifully with her bronze skin. Her long black hair had been tied into a single plait with a bunch of white flowers on one side. The red *bindi* on her forehead and the kohl that Sumathy had applied to her eyes completed the look. Abi could see a distinct resemblance to her mother's portrait. She went to her room and unpacked her father's painting and hung it up on the nail above her bed. 'You were right, Vy. This is our mother's painting,' she murmured to herself. As she lay down to sleep, she thought of all the events of the day – maybe it wouldn't be as bad as she imagined. If this was where her mother grew up, maybe she could get used to it, too. She shook her head doubtfully and closed her eyes, trying to fall asleep.

5

LIFE AT THE NEW SCHOOL

Abi felt as if she'd barely gone to sleep when a pair of hands shook her awake. Disoriented, she rubbed her eyes and looked up at a plump, grey- haired lady in white teacher's robes shaking her. 'Wake up, all the girls have got ready and started – you're late on your first day!' Abi got up in a rush and looked around her. Sumathy seemed to have folded her bed sheets neatly and disappeared. Abi felt a slight pang of resentment that Sumathy hadn't bothered to wake her up. The teacher smiled at her kindly. 'I am Guru Usha – I will be teaching you natural science and will also introduce you to all that needs to be done as part of schoolwork. Normally, you need to wake up by five in the morning, go and have a bath by the stream, change and come to the courtyard by five thirty. It's already past five – you're late, hurry.'

Abi scrambled over to the stream, had a quick wash and change of clothes and ran down to meet Guru Usha at the doorway of the great courtyard. Guru Usha smiled as she adjusted Abi's badly tied sari and handed her a broom. 'Your task this morning is to sweep the southern half of the courtyard clean. Come on, hurry.' Abi looked at her in surprise – she had no issues with manual work but found it really odd that students were expected to clean the school. Guru Usha must have understood her expression as she grinned and said, 'A bit different from the English schools, isn't it? Gurukul is run like schools were run in ancient India. You live with the gurus and share all the household work. You will also be cooking, washing and cleaning. There's plenty to learn – and it's not just dance and academics. Everyone participates with all the work – even the teachers. Come on, what are you waiting for?'

Abi saw another girl sweeping the northern half. She nodded at her and started doing the same to the other half of the courtyard. Once she had finished, a couple of other young girls came over with wet mops and wiped the courtyard clean. Then Sumathy appeared and walked to the centre of the courtyard and started drawing an elaborate design with a white powder. 'This is called a *kolam* – a South Indian design that's drawn on the floor each morning with rice flour. I'll teach you how to do this soon,' whispered Sumathy as her hands flew, creating complex and intricate patterns on the floor. 'I am sorry I didn't wake you up this morning, I had to get up extra early as I had some other work, and you were sleeping so peacefully that I didn't want to disturb you,' she said. 'But I will make sure I do from tomorrow.'

All the girls were then made to assemble by the dais. Guruma climbed on the dais and uttered a few lines in an unknown language in her melodic voice. The girls repeated the words. 'It's a Sanskrit *shloka* – bet you've never ever heard it before.' Abi heard a sneering voice behind her and knew Pooja was standing close by. The prayer was followed by a series of complicated yoga sequences that Abi found very hard to follow, despite the teacher's instructions and much to Pooja's amusement and sniggers. Guru Usha walked up to her at the end of the sequence and said that she needed to take extra classes on yoga to catch up with the other girls.

'Right, next task for you today is to fetch drinking water. We give the new girls easier tasks. You will graduate to picking flowers for the prayers, drawing the *kolams*, washing, chopping vegetables and finally cooking for the entire school. Every month we have a cooking competition – two sets of girls are made to cook and the teachers will judge the winners. It will be your turn in the next few months,' said Guru Usha, grinning as if it were a big treat. Abi rolled her eyes and picked up the large pots that she had to use to carry the water. Guru Usha led her to another stream that was at a lower level to the school. 'We ensure that the water for drinking, bathing and washing is all kept separate,' explained Guru Usha as Abi filled the large pots and struggled to carry them. 'Place one on your head and another balanced by the side of your waist. Here, let me demonstrate,' said Guru Usha, trying to stop Abi from spilling all the water. It was a long, slow walk up to the kitchen – a large building that stood on the left-hand side of the courtyard. Abi's pots kept splashing water all over her, but she finally got there in the end.

The kitchen was a flurry of activity. Some of the girls were chopping vegetables, some cooking and others washing banana leaves to be used as plates. 'We have a wonderful cook – but all the girls and teachers help out in preparing the food.' Breakfast was served in the courtyard. All the girls sat on straw mats on the edge, as they had done for dinner. Abi had never eaten such soft rice cakes and spicy gravy before and she enjoyed it. However, she wasn't sure she could do this every day for breakfast and felt that she would start yearning for her cornflakes and oats soon. She thought wistfully about her father's breakfast treats and blinked away a tear.

Breakfast was followed by several classes where Abi learnt natural science, arithmetic and Indian mythology. She found the first two subjects similar to what she had studied in England and liked them. Mythology bored her and she struggled to keep up with the complicated tongue-twister names of the Indian gods and demons. Mythology was taught by an old, bearded male teacher called Guru Mahesh. He spoke in a very monotonous drone, and Abi was sure that this added to her boredom and growing dislike of the subject. The next lesson was dance – Abi had been looking forward to this ever since she'd seen the girls dancing when she first walked into the school.

The girls were made to stand in groups based on their proficiency, and Abi felt a bit ashamed to be standing with a group of eight-year-olds. The senior dancers were allowed to dance on stage. Abi watched Pooja enviously as she danced to the beat of Indian drums and cymbals. She moved with incredible energy and a feline grace.

Guruma was teaching the senior girls – she taught them some complicated steps that only Pooja was able to pick up on the first go. Abi's own dance lesson was much less exciting. The girls were taught how to bend their legs in the classic dance pose, and most of the lesson was around practising this while their teacher moved about correcting their posture. Abi was amazed at how difficult it was to hold such a seemingly simple pose steadily for even a short period of time. They were then given a book containing dance poses, terms and their explanations. 'Your homework is to read chapter one and memorise all the terms to describe the hand gestures. Also, you need to practise your pose. You will be tested on all this tomorrow,' said Guru Uma, their young dance teacher. She was a dark-haired, tiny woman but seemed to radiate power when she demonstrated the dance moves. She had a young baby that gurgled in a little hammock next to her in every class.

⚬⚬⚬

The next few days were a blur to Abi. She woke up early every morning and had to learn and complete a new chore. The day was filled with activity – chores, lessons, dance, yoga; and meditation in the evenings. Abi barely coped with the chores and found the days too long for her liking. Although she liked some of her theory lessons, she found it hard to concentrate and had to make a real effort to keep her eyes open through the mythology classes. The classes were in English, but the girls did talk to each other in a mixture of different languages. Abi could luckily understand and speak in Hindi, but she was a bit hesitant as some of the girls had initially found her accent very funny. Dance was going slowly and Abi found it impossible to ignore Pooja's snide remarks while she struggled to learn her new steps with the younger girls in her group. She was yet to start her martial arts elective but she was sure that she would find it as challenging as the rest of her lessons. Abi started getting more and more despondent in her new foreign surroundings. She missed her lovely home in the UK and thought often of her school friends. She tried not to think of her father in order to avoid crying, but the absence of Vy was like a constant ache that filled her being and gnawed at her. She stopped talking to Vy in her mind, as she had nothing positive to tell her.

One day, everything went badly from the start. Abi was assigned to collect water from the stream but broke a pot on the way back. She had to then make the journey twice to complete her assignment. Breakfast was a bit lacklustre as Abi yearned for porridge and maple syrup that day but had to cope with spicy rice pancakes called *dosas* instead. The lessons were absolutely disastrous. Guru Mahesh decided to hold an impromptu quiz in the class and Abi could not answer any of the questions, much to her embarrassment. Abi thought things could just not get worse – but she was proved wrong by her dance class. She floundered in the class and did not remember the steps that she had been taught previously. Most of her younger co-dancers seemed to be doing much better than her. Guru Uma was annoyed and Abi could sense her frustration. To add insult to injury, Pooja decided to come and watch the performance and Abi felt even more self-conscious each time she heard peals of laughter emanating from the audience. At the end of the lesson, Guru Uma made Abi stay back and practise and also gave her more homework to do.

When Abi got back to her room in the evening, she was exhausted, humiliated and depressed. Gurukul was even more alien than she imagined. She had always been a good student in the UK and had performed well in sports. To be at the bottom of almost every class out here really pained her. Abi felt a surge of tears and hid her face in the towel hastily as Sumathy entered the room. Sumathy seemed preoccupied and barely noticed Abi. She put her books away and just as she was about to leave the room, turned around and asked Abi if she was coming for dinner. 'You carry on; I am not hungry,' said Abi, with her face still carefully hidden in the shadows. But she needn't have worried – Sumathy did not look at her at all and walked off out of the room.

Abi felt even more upset when she was left alone. She wished she could talk to her aunt but she wasn't sure how to. There was no internet connection in the school and so she had not been able to write an email to her. And Abi had not had the time to write a letter. She started sobbing and bemoaning her fate. *Why have these things happened to me? I was so happy in the UK with dad and Vy – why am I being subjected to this cruelty? Not only have I lost my loving family, I am far away from my home and my friends and hate this horrible place where no one cares for me...* Abi started crying and it made her more depressed and upset than before. After a while, she stopped sobbing and made a decision. She was going to run away from this awful place. As soon as she thought about it, she felt better. Yes, she now had a plan. She'd run away to the town in the valley and find a way of getting back to Delhi. She could then go to the hotel where she had stayed with Akash and see if they'd allow her to contact the UK. Then she could call her aunt and find a way of getting a ticket back home.

The more she thought of it, the better it seemed to her. She avoided thinking of her father's letter and her parents' will and convinced herself that if she made a break for it, there would be a way to get back to her real home. Sumathy came back after dinner but did not speak to Abi. She collapsed into bed and in some time, Abi could hear her gentle snores. Abi quietly got up and packed a little bag with some essentials. She checked that she had some money on her. Akash had changed some pounds to rupees and had given these to her during their journey. Abi took a few essential items and left most of her other belongings behind. At the moment, her only thought was to get as far away from Gurukul as possible. She slipped out of the room into the dark night. Freedom beckoned!

6

PLAYING TRUANT

Abi started her long trek to the town in the valley, aiming for the railway station. When she had come to Gurukul with Akash, they had covered the distance between the railway station and the school by car, horseback and by walking the remaining distance. Abi had no car or horse at her disposal. She started trudging downhill uncertainly – night had fallen and the hills looked very unfamiliar to her. She had been walking for nearly an hour without knowing whether she was even going in the right direction. 'Are you lost, miss? Where are you going?'

Abi was startled to hear a voice close to her. She turned around to see a man on a bullock cart. She had seen him before – he supplied vegetables and fruits to the school. He had a kindly but not a very clever face. Abi hoped that her luck would hold out and he turned out to be as dim as he looked. 'I am going down to the town to catch a train. I am on an important mission. Unfortunately, the guide sent a note to say the horse has gone lame, and I don't quite know what to do except walk all the way.' The vegetable vendor looked aghast.

'What! Walk all the way to the town in the valley? That will take you two days if you're lucky. But wait – I can take you halfway there and then you could get the night bus from where I leave you. You will be safe with me – you know me, don't you? I am Mani from the village.' Abi nodded, secretly relieved at the offer.

'Yes, I know you. That is very kind of you. I will come with you – please drop me at the bus stop,' said Abi.

———

Mani's cart took a long time winding its way down to the halfway point. Abi nodded off to sleep, and when she woke up, they were by the side of a road, half way down the mountain. 'Here's where I have to leave you. Will you be all right? There's a bus that operates at night – but it is not very frequent. I hate to leave you alone here, but I have a long journey to make to the village and my wife is about to deliver a baby. Please don't wander away from the stop – the bus should be here soon.'

Abi yawned, stretched and jumped down from the cart. 'Thank you, Mani. Good luck with your baby. When are you going to go back to the school?' she asked, wondering when he would leak the story of her truancy to her teachers.

'Not for a few days. They have all the supplies they need for a week, but I should be back there with more fruits and vegetables next week. You have a safe journey back.' She watched him go back silently. She felt very lonely and vulnerable, standing in the middle of nowhere, waiting for a bus that may or may not arrive.

———∞∞∞———

Abi sat by the side of the road hugging her knees to keep warm for what felt like an hour to her. The night was chilly and dark. She could hear various sounds of insects all around her. She kept hearing rustling and footsteps; but after a while, having seen no one, she realised that these were most probably her imagination. Abi heard an owl hooting in the distance. She started feeling a bit scared – here she was, in an unknown country, at an unknown bus stop, with no human being for miles around her. 'How stupid could I be? Was it really so bad?' she chided herself quietly.

But her luck held through once again – in a short while, a dilapidated bus rumbled along and stopped close to her. The conductor looked at her in surprise. 'Are you travelling on your own? It is not safe! Particularly at this time of the night!' he said, as he issued her a ticket.

Abi put on a brave face and a contemptuous expression. 'I know how to look after myself, thank you. When will we get to the railway station in town?'

'About four thirty in the morning. The first train only arrives there by six,' said the conductor as Abi settled herself in a seat. The bus rumbled downhill – there were only three other passengers and they all seemed fast asleep. Abi nodded off once again for a short while, and when she woke up, they were just pulling into the railway station in town.

Abi stepped off the bus and looked around her carefully. At this time of the morning, the normally bustling railway station was almost empty. The sky was still dark, although it was lighter than before. Abi picked up her bag and walked up to the platform. There was no one there – she put her bag down and sat on top of it, looking at the filthy platform around her. There was a bundle of rags left near a pillar – it looked incredibly grimy and dirty. Abi frowned, wondering who would have left such a bundle of rags behind when it moved. She gave a high-pitched squeal, without meaning to. The bundle of rags unfolded into a scrawny little boy. 'What are you screaming for? You gave me a fright!' he said in Hindi, rubbing the sleep from his eyes. Abi looked at him in horror – it looked like he had not bathed in years. His skin was very dark, but Abi was not sure whether that was his complexion or if it was a thick layer of grime on his skin.

'You gave me a fright, too,' said Abi indignantly as the boy looked accusingly at her. 'Why are you sleeping on the platform? It is so filthy,' said Abi, wrinkling her nose.

'Ha! So, the platform is filthy for the princess, is it? Well, I sleep here as I have no other place to go. This station that you're turning your nose up at actually happens to be my home!'

Abi looked at the boy with a mixture of pity and revulsion. He was indeed the filthiest creature that she had ever seen. His hair was standing up on his head, matted with dirt. His eyes had white discharge around them; his nose seemed to be bleeding – or at least, she hoped it was only blood! His clothes were torn and extremely dirty and he had no shoes or slippers on his feet. She tried avoiding looking at his face and spoke to him gingerly, as if afraid of angering him again. 'What is your name? Do you not have anyone – parents? Other relatives?'

She shuddered as the boy snorted. 'Parents? Na, long story. Myself Raju. Your good name?'

'I am Abi. I don't have any parents either. I know what it must be like for you!' said Abi, suddenly relating to the boy.

Raju sat down on his haunches and scratched his head. He felt around his torn shirt and found what he was looking for – a local hand-made version of a cigarette, called *beedi*. He lit it up and blew little wisps of smoke thoughtfully. 'I doubt if you can even begin to imagine,' he said. 'Do you not get enough to eat? Do you worry about where your next meal is coming from? Do you think about how to hide any money you earn from crooks around you? If you do any of this, then maybe you can understand what my life is like.'

Abi looked at him in shock – she had seen street children in Delhi but had never thought about how hard their lives must be. She felt really sorry for Raju and her eyes betrayed her feelings. Raju's voice became a bit gruff. 'Enough about me, let's talk about you. What is a young schoolgirl doing, travelling on her own, in the middle of school-term? You running away?' said Raju, shrewdly sizing her up. He could see a fleeting flash of fear in Abi's eyes when he said that. He smiled a charming smile. 'Don't worry; actually, I am not going to rat on you! But why are you running away anyway?' This was the first time in many days that someone had asked Abi about her life. She was overwhelmed and it all came blurting out. She told him about her life in the UK with her father and sister, the freak accident in the Lake District, how she was sent to India against her wishes and all the hard work that she had to do at school.

Raju was a good listener. He heard everything she said and his forehead furrowed in a deep frown. 'I still don't understand why you're running away from school. Clearly, there was a reason why they've sent you to India. How can your running away actually solve anything?'

Abi got a bit defensive. 'Do you have to say *actually* in every sentence? You have no idea what it's like. They expect me to get up early in the morning and clean and cook. Then they have all these boring lessons. Then the horrible dance classes. The girls there make fun of me because I don't fit in. I hate it there! I have no freedom to do as I wish, no familiar surroundings, nothing.'

Raju finished smoking his *beedi* and threw the stub on the railway track. He looked at her steadily and said: 'You are actually a coward.'

Abi was scandalised that a little twerp of a boy whom she'd barely met would judge her so harshly. 'Oh yeah? And you're very brave? You don't even go to school.'

Raju sighed. 'Yes, I wish I could, though. I have always wanted to study. At times, when I rummage through dustbins, I get hold of some books. I try and read them by the street lamps at night. I am pretty good at maths.'

Abi still looked mutinous at being called a coward. 'Well, you don't know how it is when your family disappears overnight and you're sent to an unknown, unfamiliar place.'

Raju flashed a grin. 'You think I don't know about that? My parents were actually killed by a mafia don over a feud, and my elder brother, baby sister and I were thrown out on the street. Overnight, we went from having a roof over our heads and a normal life to being street children who had to scrounge around for food. My brother decided to take to petty crime. I was actually totally against it – so he left me behind and took our baby sister with him. I decided to try my hand at honest work – so I would clean shoes, try and do little jobs for shopkeepers, etc.' Abi listened to his story with rapt attention – it was unimaginable for her to think that small children had to go through such a hard time. 'But I don't actually resent it,' said Raju. 'Life is what you make of it. I have friends in the streets, manage to make ends meet by doing hard work all through the day. If I am lucky, I get to read a bit.'

'What about your brother and sister?' asked Abi.

Raju gritted his teeth and looked away before answering. 'My brother got involved with some hard core gangsters. Things went from bad to worse actually – he got involved in all sorts of mafia feuds. To get back at him, one of his rival gangs killed our little sister.'

Abi gave a gasp of shock. 'No! Oh, Raju, I am so sorry. What about your brother?'

Raju gave her a wry smile. 'He's in jail. At least there, he can't actually get into more mischief.'

Abi had tears in her eyes. Raju's story made hers sound like a fairy tale. 'How can you not be bitter and angry?' said Abi.

'Well, how is my being bitter and angry actually going to help me? It won't bring back my sister or my parents. Life throws things at you. Your best option is to catch what it throws and do something with it. I want to work hard – I am desperate actually to go to school – but I can't afford to. So, maybe if I work hard, one day, I can make enough money to go to school. There are many children like me – hopefully, someone will set up a school for kids like me somewhere.'

Abi sat down and pondered about her own plight in silence for some time. Surely her situation was not that bad! She was being sent to the school where her mother had learnt to dance. She knew that she was not making much of an effort to learn. She wondered if she was making a big mistake by running away. Almost as if he'd read her thoughts, Raju piped up: 'You know what – I think you'd be much happier with yourself actually if you go back. Make a real effort to know the people around you – you'll make friends. Plus you'll never forgive yourself if you give up too soon. And what if they send you back again? It will be even worse to come back.' Abi stayed silent – she knew he was right, but going back would mean that she'd have to go back to her routine – something she hated.

'Raju, how do you manage to cope with your life? You sleep here, have to get up early and try and find work and food. You probably have to work all day. How do you manage this routine day in and out?'

Raju flashed a tiny grin. 'The mind does as it's told actually. I tell myself that I will enjoy the day. I actually enjoy everything I do. Yes, it's not as wonderful as I want it to be – but that's no reason for me to be morose and make it worse than it is. Try it – it really works. And then, maybe one day, you will actually become a great teacher and will set up an institution for poor kids like me.'

Abi got up and looked at him with new respect – the young homeless kid in front of her had taught her a valuable lesson in life. 'Yes, you're right. I will take the next bus and make my way back to school. Thank you, Raju. I hope one day, your dreams will come true.' Abi handed him some of the money she had, but he refused to take it. Abi had a sudden brainwave. In her bag, she had packed a storybook for the journey – she pulled it out and gave it to him.

His eyes shined brightly as he flicked through the pages. 'Thank you – I will really treasure this.'

7

ABI SETTLES IN

Abi thought a lot during her bus journey. Raju was right –
she had not even made the effort to know her classmates
or make friends. Sumathy, her roommate, seemed a nice
girl, but Abi had barely tried to be friendly. She spoke to
Vy in her mind after what seemed like ages. *'I promise I
will try my best.'* She knew that some girls, especially Pooja,
would continue to be mean to her. But now the trick was
to learn to ignore that and concentrate on the ones who
were nice. *'Maybe one day, I could learn enough and build this
institution where children like Raju could be comfortable.'* And if
*I continue to talk to Vy when things get rough, maybe they will
get easier,* she thought to herself.

It was a long journey back and it was mid-morning by the
time she was standing at the bus stop in the mountains.
The bus turned and carried on – she knew she had to

take the un-metalled path up the mountain – only horses and bullock carts could go up here. She started walking uphill slowly. This was going to be painful.

It was a long, steep climb. Abi trudged along without seeing anything or anyone on the path. After an hour, she sat down to rest for a while. She was almost falling asleep when she heard a rustle. She sat up straight and looked around her. There was no one to be seen. Her heart was beating faster; she was sure she had heard something. Then, in the bushes, she saw a shadow. It looked as if someone was hiding there. She got up uncertainly – was she imagining things or was there someone dressed in black, crouching behind the foliage? She turned with a start when she heard the clip-clop of horses behind her.

To her astonishment, there were two horses just behind her. Guruma sat majestically on one with Sumathy's face peering from behind her back. Kaliram, the school caretaker, a large, muscular man with a very gaunt face, sat on the other horse. Sumathy was nearly squealing in delight. 'I am so glad we found you, Abi. I was feeling so guilty.' Abi smiled perfunctorily at her as her eyes were really only watching Guruma's reaction.

Guruma got down from the horse and put a hand on her shoulder. 'You were climbing back up?' she enquired, guessing as much from the direction in which Abi and her bag were pointing. Abi nodded silently. Guruma smiled. 'I am glad you decided to come back. I am sorry that we did not make you feel more welcome.'

Abi shifted her feet guiltily. 'It is my fault, too – I did not make the effort.' Kaliram climbed down and helped get Abi onto his horse. Guruma was back on hers and looked steadily at Abi.

'Abi, Sumathy was distraught when she woke up early morning and found that you'd left. She woke me up and we have been searching for you for a while. But don't worry, none of the other girls in school know about it. They'll probably think that you were ill or something,' said Guruma, correctly interpreting the look of worry on Abi's face.

———

Abi had forgotten about the crouching figure when they got back to school by early evening after walking the last few miles. Guruma avoided going through the courtyard and led the girls to their room through another path. 'I am going to have some food sent up to your room. I would suggest both of you rest. You're exhausted – both physically and emotionally.' The girls nodded and went into the room. Guruma popped her head in through the door and looked at Sumathy. 'Sumathy, thank you very much. You were brilliant.'

Sumathy blushed and smiled coyly at the principal. She then turned towards Abi. 'Abi, welcome back! We really do care for you and want you to be here with us. I hope we can make you feel part of the school soon.' She left before Abi could say anything.

Sumathy walked up to Abi and gave her a quick hug. 'Abi, I am so sorry that I did not try and be a good friend to you. I have been a bit preoccupied – it was my grandmother's death anniversary and I was very close to her. So, I was in a world of my own, thinking about old times. I didn't mean to – but I know I ignored you. When I found out you were gone, I ran to wake up Guruma. She was so upset – I think she took it as a personal failure that you felt bad enough to leave. Will you forgive us?'

Abi was silent for a while. She felt terrible that she had caused so much grief to both Sumathy and Guruma. She gave Sumathy a watery smile. 'I am sorry, too. I did not really make a proper effort. I will try now. I am sure things will be fine.'

Abi settled into the school routine much more comfortably after that. No one had realised that she had played truant and so no one asked any awkward questions. She did feel that the teachers were now making a greater effort to get her participation in class – or maybe that was her imagination! She practised her lessons in her head every time she spoke to Vy, and things seemed a little easier. Guruma kept an eye out for her – she watched Abi's performances in her dance class from far away and gave her an encouraging smile when she messed up. Before long, Abi started her martial arts elective and found that right up her alley. She was very sporty and this subject gave her the necessary physical exercise – she found that she enjoyed it much more than dance. *I lack the grace and fluidity needed for dance,* thought Abi while watching one of Pooja's brilliant performances. Pooja continued to be her mean self, but this bothered Abi less now as she had made other friends.

Sumathy was of great comfort – she taught Abi how to draw intricate *kolams*, introduced her to other friendly girls in her class and also helped her practise her dance steps in the evening. Kala, Arundhati, Sita and Vasundhara were good dancers. Anushree and Jayalakshmi were very studious and quiet girls. Most of the girls were friendly and kind with the notable exception of Pooja. Even the young boys in the orchestra were friendly and patient when Abi made mistakes in her dance. However, Abi still missed her family and friends from England. She missed Vy most of all and found it hard to fill the void with Sumathy or any of the other girls. She shared that special twin bond with her sister – they used to almost read each other's minds and had always stayed together through all sorts of trouble at school. Gurukul was now a happier place for Abi – but the pain of losing her father and sister still bothered her a lot. She wondered if she was going mad, speaking to Vy in her head all the time.

She developed a strange bond with Guru Uma's little baby who had now learnt to crawl. Her name was Vidya and Abi shortened it to Vi to remind her of her sister. The baby had a little birthmark on her lips that looked like the scar on Vy's face post the cat-saving episode. This only endeared the child to Abi even more. Vi felt a great affinity to Abi which was unusual as she had never really bonded with any babies before this. Abi started talking to Vi, much the same way as she spoke to Vy in her head. She hoped that taking to a child seemed slightly less deranged than talking to a dead sister.

⸺⟨⟩⸺

One evening, when Abi was missing her family more than ever, she decided to take a walk by the stream. Sumathy had been tasked with helping with the post-dinner clear-up and so Abi was all alone. As she walked through the woods towards the flowing water, she looked around her and admired the serene beauty of the mountains. The sun had set but there was still a bit of residual light – she could see the stars slowly appearing one by one in the sky. There was a gentle breeze blowing and it carried the pleasant scent of evening blooms. Abi sniffed appreciatively as she found herself a seat on a rock. She could hear the tinkle of flowing water splashing over pebbles and there was no other sound. She sat in silence for a long time with many thoughts racing through her head. She found this new school life enjoyable in parts and distressing in other parts. She disliked some of the classes and the fact that her dance lessons seemed to be moving just one step at a time. She really felt the absence of anything familiar in her life at the moment. She was contemplating whether she should write to her aunt when she heard a faint rustle of leaves. She looked up and realised that the sky was now an inky blue and many stars were shining on it – night had fallen. She heard the noise again and suddenly began to feel a bit scared. 'Who's there?' she demanded as bravely as she could and got up to try and make a run for it. She could not see anyone nearby, but the light had faded and she did not have a torch with her. What if there was a dangerous animal close by? The girls had told her stories of panthers in the mountains. She had a flashback – the figure in black, crouching behind the bushes when Guruma found her. Fear gripped her heart.

Abi was still thinking of the best course of action when she saw Guruma walking towards her. She knew that the rustling had nothing to do with Guruma's appearance and that the creature causing it was still close by – so she ran quickly towards the old principal. Guruma's eyes were wary and watchful as she held her hand out to Abi silently. Maybe it was because she was dressed in all white – a light seemed to emanate from her. She looked around her and said quietly to Abi, 'You should not be out here in the dark. The mountains are not safe. That's why I was so worried about you when you left school a few days back.' Abi was grateful that Guruma did not call it "running away" and gave her a little smile. Guruma led her back to her room; and before letting her go in, she looked deep into Abi's eyes and held her hands. 'Abi, I know this is difficult for you. You miss your family and everything is new. Your mother was a great dancer – and I am sure you will be, too. You are a very brave girl to come back and to settle in. I am very pleased that you've now made new friends – keep them close. And please promise me that you will not go off wandering in the dark.'

'Yes, Guruma,' said Abi, thrilled that Guruma thought she was brave.

Guruma suddenly gave her a smile and said, 'Oh, pay more attention to your mythology classes, will you? There are creatures that grow strong in the dark. And I wouldn't want you to come across any of them while you are not prepared.' With a mysterious smile, she glided away. Abi stood in her doorway watching her disappear and then went to lie down and get some sleep before another busy day ahead.

8

FRIENDS AND FOES

The next few days were gone in a whirl of activity. The girls got one day off every week, but Abi used this time to learn how to cope with the daily chores. Although she had always given her father a hand with household chores, the work in Gurukul was very different. It seemed more manual in India as there were no dishwashers or washing machines, and cooking on firewood was very different from bunging a roast in the oven. Sumathy was amazed at the amount of interest that Abi took in learning and performing these activities. Abi often thought of Raju and how he had trained himself to enjoy work, and she taught herself to do the same. And now she found that hard work was one good way to forget the dull pain that the absence of her fond ones was causing her.

Unfortunately, the lessons were not engaging Abi in the same way – Abi found mythology exhausting and struggled with the new Indian languages. She was not interested in learning new terms and seemed to be lagging behind her eight-year-old dance group, much to Pooja's amusement. Once a month, the dance groups had to perform all that they had learnt that month in front of an audience of teachers and students. Things came to a head for Abi on the day her group had to perform. Although they were a beginner's group – they had learnt several basic dance steps and terms – they were expected to demonstrate these steps in unison on the dais followed by a discussion of the dance terminology. Abi had not rehearsed at all – she had even skipped their group rehearsals on the pretext of some chore or other. She was nervous and unprepared. As the group took their positions, Abi tripped over something and fell face forward on the stage. Some of the other girls and the orchestra members helped her to her feet, but by now she was feeling even more anxious. The entire sequence of steps was a disaster – Abi forgot most of the steps and tried to copy her classmates but made several mistakes. The girls took turns to explain various dance terms. When it was her turn, Abi could simply not remember the meaning of her word. At the end of the humiliating experience, Abi rushed down and ran past everyone in a hurry to get away from it all. But she could feel hundreds of eyes focussing on her – some smiling in derision and others dulled by disappointment.

Abi was badly shaken by the incident. She blamed herself totally; and even when Sita, one of her classmates, told her that she heard Pooja gloating about tripping her up on her way to the stage, Abi shook her head. 'No, it was my fault that I did not practise. People trip and fall all the time but they get up and recover. I have to take responsibility for my own failures – I cannot blame anyone else for it.' For the first time since she had returned to school, she felt that she had let herself down.

Disappointed, Abi got back to her room to find a letter from Akash Sharma. She had completely forgotten about him. It was not a very long letter and contained the usual enquiry about school life and health. The second paragraph was more interesting. It read:

Abi, I am sure you are missing your family and friends. And you're probably struggling with some of your lessons. When I struggled in school, I learnt a "mantra" or a magic verse that really helped me. It is in Sanskrit and reads as follows:

**Udhyamena hi Sidhyanthi Kaaryani Na
Hi Manorathai hi
Na Hi Suptasya Simhasya Pravishanthi
Mukhe Mrigaha**

It means that all great things are achieved through hard work and not through dreams alone – just like a deer will never voluntarily enter the mouth of a sleeping lion. (The lion has to get up and work to get its prey!) Hope it helps you.

With love, Akash

Abi stared at the letter for a while. She was touched and a bit surprised by the relevance of the *shloka* in her life, now more than ever.

The dance incident and Akash's mantra gave Abi a steely determination to improve her dance – she spent every minute of her spare time practising. She was not afraid of hard work and repeated the Sanskrit *shloka* several times a day for inspiration. Sumathy was very impressed with the progress that she was making and helped her every evening by teaching her a few extra steps without anyone else knowing about it. Abi now started enjoying her dance practice – she found that the more she practised, the better she got. She would often perch baby Vi on a seat as her audience as she danced – the baby gurgled with happiness, which elated Abi. She woke up early every morning and practised for an hour on the porch outside her room. She stayed awake late at night to learn new terms and more about the history of dance. She found that learning Sanskrit, one of India's oldest languages, helped her in understanding dance and yoga even more. Soon, she was doing so well that her teacher moved her to join a more advanced group of girls for her dance classes. Abi's passion and focus extended to the studies as well – she started paying a bit more attention to mythology classes and tried really hard to practise her newly learnt language skills with the other girls. She progressed well in the martial arts lessons and was now working with a stick – which was quite advanced. Life was slowly settling into a nice rhythm.

As part of their natural science classes, Guru Usha would often take the girls deep into the forest to identify, draw and learn from the flora and fauna. They were almost always accompanied by the caretaker Kaliram. They often went up to a waterhole in the middle of the forest. It was full of lotus flowers and reeds – the water was greenish-blue in colour and when the sun threw a diffused light through the trees, it looked incredibly beautiful. Many animals came up to the hole to quench their thirst. The girls would stay hidden in the bushes and watch for a long time. Abi really enjoyed these practical lessons.

On one such trip, they came across a magnificent herd of spotted deer. Without thinking, by instinct, Abi walked out of their hidey-hole and silently went up to the deer. To everyone's surprise, the deer welcomed Abi to their midst – a young foal actually nuzzled up to her. When the other girls tried to walk out, the deer became wary and walked away into the forest. Abi was cheered by most of her classmates except Pooja who seemed to sulk in the corner. This attraction to animals was not new to Abi – she remembered that squirrels, deer, badgers and even birds would come and play with her and Vy in the UK. Vy had an affinity with all creatures, including frogs, snakes and insects that Abi avoided. But she was great with birds and animals and had often fed birds perched on her palms. She attributed it to the fact that her father was a naturalist and had a great passion for wild life. She and Vy had clearly inherited his genes.

⊶⊷

News of the deer incident soon spread among everyone in school, and Abi became more popular than she had ever been. Abi enjoyed her new-found popularity and mingled more with everyone, making more friends.

Her teachers were happy with her as she studied hard, practised dance & martial arts very diligently and accepted new chores without ever complaining. Guru Uma often entrusted her with looking after baby Vi, much to Abi and Sumathy's delight.

⸺※⸺

Many days passed – it was soon Abi's turn to participate in the cooking competition. Abi was really looking forward to this – she had learnt much about Indian cuisine from the cook and some of the other girls who were fond of cooking. She had always admired her father's creativity in the kitchen and hoped that she could prove to be a worthy daughter by winning the competition. The competition was organised once a month; and two girls had to share cooking the feast for all the teachers. The teachers would taste both sets of meals and then declare a winner. Abi was pitted against her classmate Dhanya. Dhanya was a plump curly-haired girl with a real passion for food, which gave her a natural advantage. But Abi felt quietly confident – she thought that being an underdog would actually help her pleasantly surprise everyone. She thought of recipes and recited them to baby Vi, hoping that the child's tinkling laughter meant approval of the winning formula.

⸺※⸺

The day arrived and both girls started cooking with gusto. Abi made a complex vegetable stew with coconut milk, spicy lemon-flavoured rice and almond fudge for sweet. She was very pleased with the way everything looked – the girls were not allowed to taste their cooking, but Abi was sure that it would taste as good as it looked. She had faced a mini-crisis when she found the salt cellar empty in the middle of making the meal – but help came in the form of one of the girls who brought her a jar of salt and ran off before Abi could properly look at her or thank her.

The teachers sat on the dais, as was the custom during these competitions. They were all served both sets of meals in different banana leaf plates. Abi was sure they would appreciate the delicate spices and flavours that she had pulled together. To her horror and dismay, she found that most of the teachers made a face when they put the first morsel of her meal into their mouths. There was a hushed silence as Guruma called out to Abi: 'Please come here and taste your food.' Abi put a spoonful of stew into her mouth and nearly spat it out in distaste. It was full of sugar! The fudge on the other hand was salty. She was mortified; the jar had contained sugar and someone had swapped labels… a mean trick had been played on her. Her eyes brimmed with tears as they sought out Pooja in the crowd. And she was right; Pooja was gloating in the corner with a malicious gleam in her eyes. Abi murmured her apologies to the teachers, who then declared a beaming Dhanya as the winner.

Abi walked determinedly away from the rest of the girls towards the forest. She wanted to be alone – she was furious with Pooja and wanted to think of the best way to retaliate. She walked up to the waterhole and sat by the banks plucking at reeds absently, sobbing slightly. 'Why are you crying?' A childlike voice echoed over the water. A young boy – probably around five or six – was standing next to her with a wooden flute in his hands. He had nut-brown skin, beautiful brown eyes and a curly mop of black hair that nearly reached his shoulders. He had plump cheeks that dimpled beautifully as he smiled at her. He was wearing a weather-beaten pair of shorts and an old crinkled shirt.

Abi was really drawn towards him, and although she had not felt like talking to anyone about it just a moment ago, she felt the sudden urge to tell him everything. She blurted out the entire incident in a few words. 'It was Pooja – she has always hated me. And she tricked me by swapping the salt with the sugar when I was not looking. She is horrible. I will pay her back!'

The little boy gave her a puzzled look. 'Why do you think she hates you?'

Abi frowned – she had never really thought about that. 'Well, my friend Sumathy thinks it is because Pooja is jealous of me. She probably thinks I am better in some way, though I don't know what.'

'Well,' said the boy, sounding much older than his age, 'if she is worried that you are better than her, isn't it better to continue being even better at what you do instead of wasting your time playing tit-for-tat? After all, that will annoy her even more. Is there anything that she does better than you?'

'She is a better dancer,' said Abi. 'She's fantastic – she is bound to be selected to dance for the school at the Konark Festival next year.'

The boy sat down beside her and gave her a solemn look. 'Well, if I were you, I would practise so hard that I get selected for the festival instead of her!'

Abi stared at him in dismay. 'That can never happen – I am just a learner and she has been dancing for so many years.'

'So what – if you put your mind to it, you can do it. I am sure of it. I can see that in your eyes. But it is up to you. If you'd rather play silly tricks, go for it.'

Abi smiled in spite of herself. She was amused at the wise words coming out of the little boy. 'Who are you? What's your name? What are you doing here?' said Abi.

'My name is Krishna but you can call me Krish. My parents live in the village beneath the school. I often come here to see the deer and play my flute.'

Abi smiled and held her hand out. 'I am Abi. Krishna is a nice name – why have you shortened it to Krish?'

'The same reason as you – I am sure your name is not just Abi, is it?' retorted Krish. 'Besides, it is a popular name in Hindi cinema now.'

Abi chuckled – she had heard that the villagers were obsessed with Bollywood and the Indian film industry. No doubt there was a film or an actor named Krish. 'Well, thank you, Krish, for your words of wisdom.' Abi's anger and disappointment melted at the child's innocent advice. 'I am going to really practise my dance and try and improve it – let us see if I can do well.'

Krish nodded at her: 'Good idea. But I'd go with a more positive attitude. Also, when you dance, you should just lose yourself in it – don't worry about the surroundings, the audience or anything else. That's how

I play the flute!' He played a couple of notes that echoed over the still waters beautifully.

'That's amazing, play some more...' pleaded Abi.

'Not today; it's getting late and my mother says it's dangerous to stay out late nowadays. Good luck with the dance and see you soon.'

Abi was very quiet and thoughtful on her way back to the room. Her hatred and anger had vanished thanks to a child's clear thinking and honest words. But they had now been replaced by a fierce determination in her heart. She was going to improve her dance – she was going to give Pooja a real run for the Konark Festival position and she had less than a year to do it in. Sumathy met her outside their room – she had a troubled look on her face. 'I know how much you wanted to do well in the cooking, Abi. I am sorry that Pooja mucked it up for you. I went and confronted her later on and asked her to confess to the teachers but she refused. I am afraid you won't be given cooking duties for several weeks.'

'That's fine, Sumathy,' said Abi. 'What I want to do now is to focus on my dance. I want to learn more than Pooja has in the last few years. I want to get that place at the Konark Festival.'

Sumathy looked at her, startled for a moment. It took her a few moments to digest Abi's words and she looked searchingly into her eyes. Abi held her gaze with confidence. Sumathy broke into a wide grin. 'If anyone can do it, it's you. I have seen that determination in your face. Yes, I'll help you, and so will some of the other senior girls. I can also help you get fit and ready for this. What a great way to pay her back! Come, let's go and practise.'

When Abi went to bed that night, she was exhausted as she had been dancing all evening. As she closed her eyes, she thought of Krish – the boy with the beautiful eyes and wise thoughts. She thought of the Konark Dance Festival and imagined the glory of being a dancer in such a prestigious location. There was a new purpose in her life – life was not going to be monotonous anymore.

9

A Diwali Present

Abi lost count of days and weeks – she now had an all-consuming purpose – to improve her dancing so much that she could give Pooja some real competition. She practised night and day and her teachers noticed her dedication and hard work. However, she didn't feel she was dancing as well as some of the others, particularly Pooja. One day, when she sat down after two long hours of practice, Guruma walked up to her with a glass of water. 'You are working very hard, my child. You must rest for a while.'

Abi took the water gratefully. 'I feel frustrated – I am doing my best but don't seem to be making as much progress as I'd like. My friend Krish, the little boy from the village, says that I should lose myself in my dance, but I don't quite know how to.'

Guruma smiled. 'Ah, Krish. You would think he's a wise old man, the way he speaks. Let me put an idea to you. All our dances have a story and a central character.

As soon as the music starts, stop looking around you, at the audience, the orchestra or anything else. Imagine that you are this central character and really feel for them. Imagine their pain or pleasure, based on the music you're dancing to. Ignore everything else. Try it.'

Abi decided to try Guruma's tip that evening. When the music started, she started to imagine that she was the character in the story – a princess who was getting ready to meet her consort. She forgot about everyone around her and imagined what it would be like to be the princess. She felt a mix of haughtiness and self-admiration course through her veins. She was transported to an imaginary palace where the princess was getting ready with her friends and maids. She got so lost in the act that she only realised that she had been dancing when the music came to an end and there was spontaneous applause from the girls and Guru Uma who had come to watch her dance. She blushed and said a grateful thanks in her mind to Krish and Guruma who had given her a winning formula on how to lose herself in her art.

⁂

Abi went from strength to strength, and her teachers and friends were amazed at the progress that she seemed to be making. Her self-confidence also improved greatly, and she was able to put the embarrassing episodes of disastrous dancing and cooking past her. Besides Sumathy, Abi made other friends and she became quite fond of Kala and Sita, thanks to their sense of fun and their skill at dance. For the first time in many days, she felt at peace with herself.

She did miss her home and family – but now, she had friends to share her life with. Guru Uma beamed with pleasure at Abi's progress, and baby Vi cheered her up every time she gurgled and laughed after a performance. Abi's life took on new meaning and purpose and she really enjoyed the company of her friends, particularly Sumathy but also little baby Vi, who seemed to be attached to her like a limpet all the time. Guru Uma was delighted to have someone look after her baby. Abi often wondered who Vi's father was as it didn't seem that Guru Uma was married or had a family. Most of the married women in India wore vermillion, a red powder, on the centre parting of their hair. Abi knew that people were very old-fashioned in India about certain things, and having children out of wedlock was one of them. She never questioned Vi's parentage but satisfied herself in the company of the good-humoured child. Vi filled part of the void that Vy had left in Abi's world. She still missed her sister and her father, but it felt easier to think of them now. Abi felt finally at home in the mountains of India.

One day, Guru Usha was in a rare charitable mood and decided to skip lessons and tell the girls a story. Abi listened entranced as Guru Usha brought alive the tale of a lonely princess who was in danger due to evil enemy forces. A handsome prince was in love with her and decided to dedicate his life to protect her. However, as he knew that her father would not approve, he never showed himself to the princess. He simply followed her and kept her away from danger without her knowledge. It was a beautiful yet poignant tale as the prince died in the end to save the girl he loved. Most of the girls were misty-eyed when Guru Usha finished the story. That evening, Kala, Sita, Abi and Sumathy sat up on their porch after dinner, discussing the romantic story. 'Wouldn't it be wonderful to have a man who loves you so much that he gives up his life to protect you?' said Sita, with a sigh.

'Do you know anyone like that?' asked Kala of the other girls. Abi was lost in thought while the other girls chattered away. She started thinking of the mysterious man with those wonderful green eyes whom she saw at Heathrow Airport. She let her imagination run wild that he was a mystery prince who was trying to protect Abi from some unknown danger. Her mind was spinning a very romantic tale when she was brought out of her reverie by the girls saying goodnight to each other.

As they went to bed, Sumathy dreamily said: 'Abi, hope we find princes like that. That would be so nice!' Abi smiled as she laid her head on the pillow. She felt that she already had!

The winter chill was falling on the mountains and the evenings were growing darker. The school was gearing up to celebrate Diwali, the festival of lights. Abi had heard of it in the UK and knew it was one of the main festivals in India. The school really took it seriously. The girls spent long, happy hours decorating the courtyard in readiness. There were flowers and lamps everywhere, and the cook had organised the most elaborate meal that Abi had ever eaten. As the morning of Diwali dawned, the girls woke up as usual but had no chores to do. Instead, they gathered in the courtyard to watch the lighting of special noiseless but colourful fireworks. 'Diwali is very noisy in the towns and cities, but in Gurukul we are mindful of the wildlife around us,' said Kaliram, the caretaker, as he lit sparklers and handed them around the girls.

After a glorious breakfast, the girls were all given new robes to wear and spent some time getting ready. The morning was filled with impromptu dance performances that Abi really enjoyed. Even Guru Uma took to the stage and delivered a spectacular performance. Abi watched her teacher in awe – it was clear that she deserved to be a guru. The girls exchanged little gifts – some of the girls had collected colourful bunches of flowers to give to each other; others had used coloured paper to make various crafts and paintings. There was a lull post-lunch as the girls rested, in preparation for more festivities in the evening.

In the afternoon, Guruma sent for Abi. Abi entered her room in some trepidation – she was so in awe of the principal. She had only spoken to her once or twice since the cooking debacle – the disappointment in Guruma's eyes still burnt in Abi's mind. 'Come, my child – don't stand in the doorway!' Guruma's melodic voice rang clear. Abi walked shyly up to her. 'I believe you are making incredible progress with your dancing. I am really proud of you and so very happy. Your mother was the best dancer that I have ever had the good fortune of teaching. And you're now ready to receive her gift.' Abi looked at her in pleasant surprise. She had seen Guruma watching her practise silently from a distance on a few occasions – but had not appreciated that her progress had been duly noted. She smiled at her teacher, but Guruma was now rummaging in an old box. She pulled out an old velvet anklet case. Once the dancers reached a certain level of proficiency, they were allowed to wear anklets for their dance rehearsals. Anklets were a crucial part of the dancer's attire. When a girl was ready, the teacher would hand over a set of anklets that she could now keep. They were normally brass beads and bells sewn on a colourful pad of cloth with buckles that could be strapped on before dancing. But the anklets that Guruma held were much more beautiful. They looked like they were made of gold and had a divine shine – the pad of cloth was made of an exquisite yellow silk material, and there were semi-precious stones stuck around the borders. The buckles seemed to be made of gold as well. Abi gave a gasp as she saw them – she had never seen a more beautiful pair of anklets. 'They belonged to your mother – you are now ready for them. Use them well. Happy Diwali!'

Abi couldn't wait to try her new anklets on at the practice that evening. And yes – they caused a bit of a flurry. All her friends couldn't stop admiring her new possession, and Abi was pleased to notice the envy in Pooja's eyes. The girls had a great time lighting up some more silent fireworks and singing and dancing all through the evening. The cook had surpassed himself, and the evening meal was one of the finest that Abi had ever eaten. There were mounds of steaming rice, beautifully cooked vegetables laced with coconut and chillies in a stew called *avial*, large crunchy poppadoms, another tangy gravy called *sambar* that was poured on the rice, a selection of delightful pickles and finally, a most tantalising array of sweets. Abi surprised herself by eating more than she thought she ever could. 'Dad was a great cook but we never ate food like this. It is funny how I have got used to the spiciness of Indian food – I thought I'd never do that,' said Abi to Sumathy who was also tucking in happily.

'Spice is good for you – keeps the colds away,' said Sumathy, her mouth full of *burfee*, an Indian milk-cake that tasted like fudge.

That night, Abi felt very happy – she had had an amazing time with her friends, but what touched her most were her mother's anklets adorning her feet all evening.

The next day, Abi got a letter from her Aunt Jo. She read it with a sense of guilt – she had not written or even thought of her aunt for a while. The letter was an elaborate one and described what her aunt had been up to in university. Apparently she had finally officially hooked up with the young man she fancied. Given the long paragraph that she'd written about him, it seemed quite evident to Abi that her aunt was smitten. She had enclosed a picture of herself and Varun inside the card. Varun was in his late teens, probably of Indian origin – dark with long flowing hair, a small goatee and moustache. His high cheekbones made him look gaunt, but there was a mischievous glint in his eyes. Abi stared at his photo as if in a trance – where had she seen him before? She gave an audible gasp when she remembered. His startling green eyes brought it all back – he was the man she had seen at the airport on her way to India.

Abi sat staring at the photograph for a long time. All these days, she had been generous with her imagination to create a wild story on the mystery man episode at London Airport. In the past, this had been like an exciting spy chase where he was a secret agent coming after her for some mysterious reason and she escaped in the nick of time. Although she was not sure whether he was friend or foe, she had often thought about him in a very romantic way, even then. Since Guru Usha's fairy tale, she had started imagining that he was her secret admirer prince – someone who would even die to save her life. She had built up this image of him in her mind – he was her one true love! It was a silly thing to do but it gave her a lot of pleasure to ruminate about him. She never imagined that he was a "real" person and that she would ever have to socialise with him. That would be awkward. 'Ah well, that will probably never happen as Jo is never going to have enough money to travel to India!' Abi murmured to herself. Then, the last lines in her aunt's letter caught her attention: *Abi, do write to me and tell me what you want for Christmas. PS: Varun & I hope to be travelling to India on a backpacking holiday in a few months' time. His father is loaded – and has agreed to fund our air tickets. I am saving up for the rest of the journey. I will write to your principal closer to our travel dates and arrange things. How exciting! See you soon.* Abi read this part around three times with apprehension and excitement – so she would get to meet the mystery man after all.

10

THE BIRTH OF A DANCER

Abi found Gurukul a much nicer place to live, now that she had good friends and enjoyed her lessons more. Before she knew it, the year was about to end and it was Christmas already. The school did not really celebrate Christmas in a big way, unlike Diwali – but the doorways to the courtyard were decorated with floral garlands, and the dais had a small, glittering Christmas tree on it. When she looked at the tree, Abi thought wistfully of Christmas at home. Her father used to always make a big effort and decorate the house with an enormous Christmas tree. He also used to make a wonderful, rich Christmas pudding with loads of cherries, sultanas and other fruit, which the girls helped assemble. Aunty Jo would come round, and they'd spend hours playing silly games and nibbling at lovely snacks. Some years, it would snow; and then everyone would go out to try and make a snowman with a carrot for a nose and pieces of coal as eyes. Then they would sit around the table to eat a glorious meal.

After dinner, it was time to open presents. Their presents were mostly small and inexpensive, but they were always thoughtfully selected and carefully wrapped. Abi blinked away a tear when she thought of those happy times – they would never come back again!

The day brightened up a little when a parcel arrived for Abi. She ripped it open with a lot of excitement and found a small battery-operated CD player with tiny built-in speakers. She ran and got a dance music CD to play on this and then looked into the rest of the package. Aunty Jo had sent the present with lots of love. Abi smiled as she remembered her aunt fondly. She knew that Jo did not have loads of spare cash – she must have really saved up to buy Abi a present. It was an old model and she probably bought it cheap and second-hand, but to Abi, it looked priceless. Abi decided to spend the day away from the school and took a walk with the CD player in her hands. She thought she might go away into the forest and listen to her dance music by herself. It was hard for her to spend the day normally with her school friends when it had meant so much more in the old times.

Old memories kept resurfacing and she walked through the forest in a daze without really noticing where she was going. Suddenly she found herself in unknown territory; the trees were thinning down, and as she made her way through them, she found a large ledge at the edge of the forest. The ledge was rocky but wide and even and stretched out towards a chasm – the chasm was surrounded by mountains, some snow-covered and some bare and bereft of any vegetation. It was a most beautiful location. As Abi walked up on the ledge, her footsteps vibrated on the rock, wakening her with its energy, and it gave her a great idea –what if she used this area to practise her dance! She would have an audience of the sun, clouds, breeze and the mountains; and it would be absolutely perfect.

She placed the music player on the side and started to slowly dance to the music. It was surreal – the breeze played with her hair while her footsteps reverberated on the rocky ledge. The sun came out from between clouds and shone on her. She was completely alone, yet she felt that she was dancing to an amazing audience on stage. *This is my own private little practice spot*, thought Abi.

———

After that day, Abi went to her ledge every day to practise her dance. She did not tell anyone else about her secret spot. She noticed one day that as she danced, a number of animals and birds had actually collected around the edge of the forest – as if they were watching her dance. Abi was slightly awed by this but soon ignored it as she was immersed in her own routine and lost in the sound of her music and her anklets. She could actually feel her steps improving. Although there was no mirror to see how well she was performing, she thrived in her unusual surroundings.

———

Abi's routine, consisting mostly of hard work and practising her dance, consumed her completely; and before she knew it, it was spring. Sumathy was spending a lot of time making sure Abi ate well and added a lot of fruits and nuts to her diet. 'You need energy as a dancer, and nuts will give you protein and good fat,' said Sumathy, taking on the role of a nutritionist to the dancer. In spring, the mountains were a riot of colours, and her secret stage was even more beautiful than before. Sometimes, along with the animals, young Krish would come to watch her dance. At times, after much persuasion, he would play the flute while she whirled around the stage. Abi's dance had improved beyond all recognition – she felt her feet move totally in tandem with the music beat, and Sumathy told her that she was now dancing more gracefully than most of the dancers in the class. A lot of this was a result of her hard work – but she knew that some of this came from deep within. She loved dancing – it was in her bones, in her blood, in her heart. It felt right.

—◦◦◦—

Early spring was also the season for exams – Gurukul had a very unique system, one that Abi was totally unfamiliar with. There were some traditional exams where they had to answer questions in an examination hall. However, their practical exams were really unusual. One of the practical exams was that the girls had to use everything they'd learnt to perform on stage – both dance and martial arts, for those who had this elective. Besides this, when they reached Abi's year, they also had a second level examination. They had to teach what they had learnt to at least two young students. The girls were allowed to select their students from nearby villages or town. The girls had to do some research on the schools and children nearby and request the teachers in these schools to allow them two days in which they would teach the children. Marks were given based on how well the children were able to pick up and perform what the girls taught them. Most of Abi's classmates had selected the nearby village children as their students. Some had opted for a school in town. 'Town children are very smart and will pick up dance or martial arts quickly – at least, that's what everyone thinks,' said Sumathy to Abi. But Abi had another idea. She wanted to see if she could teach Raju, the urchin she met on the station when she ran away from school, and some other street children.

As part of her research, she went down to the town and met up with Raju. He was delighted to see her. He looked much the same, though Abi suspected that he was grimier than before. He loved her idea – two days of studying were like heaven to him. 'I will find other street children who would be interested. You see, not all of them would like to learn – so leave it to me to pick the right ones. But where would you teach us?' asked Raju. Abi had that planned out, too.

She went to the main school in town and met up with their principal. She explained what she wanted to do. The principal, Mr Basu, was a middle-aged man with black-rimmed glasses, suspiciously black hair and a bushy moustache. He knew of Gurukul's examination practice – in fact, some of the girls had selected students from his school. He looked at Abi in mild surprise. 'There are many good students in my school. Why do you want to pick the street children?'

Abi was expecting the question and had her answer ready. 'Sir, many of the other girls will pick your students. However, for these street children, this is an unusual treat. I don't care if they don't learn too much or perform as well as your students. These couple of days will mean a lot to them. If you can lend us your school hall after hours or at the weekend, I can persuade my teachers to come down with me and conduct my examination on those days. Please, sir – this means a lot to me.'

Mr Basu looked at Abi's eager, sincere face and smiled. 'Ok, we can open the school one weekend if you can get your teachers to conduct your exam then.'

Guru Uma looked a bit surprised and doubtful when Abi told her about her plans. However, Guruma smiled benignly and gave Abi permission to teach street children. 'What will you teach them?' she enquired gently.

'I thought of martial arts – they would probably find that more interesting and useful than dance,' said Abi. Some of the other girls sneered at Abi's choice, but baby Vi seemed to approve as she clapped with delight when Abi talked to her about her plans. This convinced Abi that she was doing the right thing.

On the first day of the exam, Abi went down to the town, along with Guruma. Normally, one of the other teachers would have gone down to examine her, but Guruma was quite fascinated by Abi's project and decided that she wanted to see this. Abi was a bit nervous about the kind of kids that Raju would have selected. At the appointed time, Raju met her along with four other street children. There was one other boy and three girls. The girls were all uniformly thin and were wearing tattered frocks. The other boy looked a bit healthier but had all sorts of bruises over his hands and legs. When Abi enquired about these, he just shrugged his shoulders and said he had a little accident.

Abi sat down with the children and explained why they were there and what she was going to teach them. She asked them what they would like to learn and how. Martial arts struck a chord with them, as expected; but before teaching them anything, Abi got a bucket of soap and water and made them all scrub up and clean themselves. She had brought some spare clothes from the school that her classmates and members of the orchestra had donated. The street kids wore these and looked cleaner than they had done in ages. They were interested and eager and easily picked up the steps that Abi taught them. To Abi's surprise, Mr Basu had also come to school and was watching the proceedings quietly. He offered everyone a simple but welcome lunch and stayed until the evening when the classes finished. The kids arrived promptly the next day, eager to learn more and demonstrate their learning. Abi was delighted with their attitude and aptitude, and at the end of their demonstration, she joined Guruma and Mr Basu in giving them a standing ovation.

Raju walked up to Abi and gave her a great big smile. 'Abi, I really appreciation what you've done for me and for the others.' Abi smiled at his broken English and felt warm and fuzzy that she was able to do something for them.

'I only wish I could give you the ability to study somehow,' she said.

'Well, if they are eager to learn, I can do them a special class every weekend,' said Mr Basu, who had overheard their dialogue. 'I am very impressed and touched by what you've done for these street children – you have taught me something, Abi. And their interest in learning is heartening. Children – would you like to come to this school every Sunday to learn some elementary things like maths and English?' asked Mr Basu, addressing the street children.

Raju looked a bit unsure: 'We don't have any money, sir,' he said.

'Well, the only fee you have to pay is to turn up on time and pay attention. Would that be possible?' The children looked incredulous but delighted at the offer. Abi looked gratefully at Mr Basu – she was not sure how she had fared in the exam but she did not care. This was better than she had ever imagined. Happy and content, she made the journey back to school with Guruma.

——

Abi breezed through the other exams. She was so engrossed in her dance performance during the dance practical exam that she didn't even notice that the audience were up on their feet and giving her a standing ovation until she had stopped dancing. Guru Uma commended her as the most improved dancer and praised her to all the other teachers and students. At the end of all the exams, Guruma called Abi to her room. 'The exams will be marked later, but I wanted to talk to you about your second level practicals. Abi, I think you did a marvellous job with those children. Not just by picking street children but also the manner in which you taught them. You have impressed Mr Basu so much that he is now teaching them every weekend. I wanted to congratulate you – well done!'

Abi gave her principal a beaming smile. 'It's thanks to you and to my friends here. You have helped me truly understand what Gurukul is all about – and also, I appreciate the fact that you've never mentioned my running away from school. I want to be a good student and make you proud.' Abi blushed with pleasure as she left Guruma's room – she felt a great sense of achievement.

11

AN APSARA'S DAUGHTER

After the exams, Sumathy suggested that they go to a nearby village on market day to explore and have some fun. Abi took a break from practice that day and went off with Sumathy and a few other girls. The village market was spectacular – there were hundreds of little stalls selling various produce, clothes, trinkets and crafts along a steep hill outside the village. It was a very remote location, but the market was buzzing with people who had come from far and wide. Sumathy and Abi walked leisurely, enjoying the sights. As they stopped by a trinket stall to examine some pretty earrings, a wizened old woman hobbled close to them and said, 'Would you like me to read your fortune, my pretty young things? I am a great seer and can tell you many things about the future.'

Abi looked doubtful but Sumathy was very excited. 'Oh yes, come on, Abi, we must try this.' Reluctantly, Abi tagged along as Sumathy followed the old woman to a wooden table and two chairs placed in a strategic location, away from the hustle and bustle of the market.

She examined Sumathy's hands first. 'You are a brave young girl – lost your parents and brought up by your grandparents, weren't you? You have many secret ambitions and dreams, but at the same time you don't feel that you have the capability to realise them.' Sumathy had a look of shock on her face. 'You must believe in yourself – you are more capable than you give yourself credit for. You will be drawn into an adventure very soon. And you will come out shining.'

The old woman then moved towards Abi. 'Come on, I want to see your hands.' Her coarse hands grabbed Abi's softer ones and she pored over them. Both girls looked at each other and waited expectantly, but the palm-reader wouldn't say anything.

Finally, Abi nudged her. 'So, what can you see?'

The old woman looked fearful. 'Nothing. I cannot read your hands. Please go!'

Abi was intrigued – she started following the old woman who was now hobbling away from the girls. 'Why can't you tell me? You see something – what is it?'

The old woman increased her speed; for a crippled old lady, she was incredibly quick. Abi almost ran after her. Sumathy was trailing behind. Suddenly the old lady turned around and whispered to Abi, 'You are the daughter of an *apsara* – why didn't you tell me?'

Abi stared at the woman in shock. 'What—' she began.

The old woman snapped at her: 'Your mother dances in Indra's court. I cannot read the hands of a celestial being. You must be careful. There are many dangers around. And if I stay near you, I will get into danger, too.' Abi stood there, perplexed; and before she could recover herself, the old woman had disappeared in the crowd.

Sumathy caught up with Abi, but they'd lost their hand-reader. 'Don't worry, she was probably ranting anyway, though I am not sure how she knew about my parents! She was accurate in what she said about me,' said Sumathy, staring into the distance.

⟨⟨⟨⟩⟩⟩

Abi was very thoughtful on their way back from the market. She hadn't told Sumathy what the old lady had whispered to her. Could it be true? Could she be the daughter of an *apsara*? Abi knew from her mythology lessons that *apsaras* were celestial dancers. They danced in the court of Indra, the King of Gods. There were many myths and stories about when *apsaras* had come to Earth, consorted with a human being and had given birth to semi-celestial children. The poet Kalidas had written a play about Shakuntala, one such daughter of a celestial nymph. *No, it can't be! That's a myth. There can't be any apsaras,* thought Abi fiercely. She looked at her mythology book and flicked through the sketches idly. She came upon a sketch of Indra, the King of Gods. He was dressed in fine silks and had a golden crown on his head. He was riding a white elephant and carried a bolt of lightning in his hand. Abi stared at this picture – it brought back some memories; what was it? She sat up in shock – this was the vision she saw out of the window of the plane when she travelled to India. Indra had come to see her on her way here!

The old woman's words kept ringing in Abi's ears and she decided that she needed to investigate further. Her teachers often said that her brilliance at dance was inherited from her mother. Now, that would make perfect sense if her mother had been an *apsara*. After debating it in her head several times, Abi decided to confide in Sumathy. After all, she was a good friend and she needed someone to discuss this with. To her surprise, Sumathy found it much easier to accept. 'Really!' she exclaimed, 'but of course! That makes sense, Abi. You're such a brilliant dancer – and you've learnt it all faster than any other girl I know. That must be because you're an *apsara's* daughter.' Abi reckoned that having grown up in India with grandparents who probably told her mythological stories at bedtime, Sumathy found it much more natural to accept. In contrast, Abi's western upbringing stubbornly refused to let her believe it totally. Then Sumathy had a thought: 'Do you remember Guru Mahesh had spoken about the *apsara* portraits that are in Guruma's room? He said that once in a blue moon, with the help of a magic gem, a human being gets a chance to go to heaven. An artist called Dev once had the privilege to go there and he had painted a series of *apsara* portraits. Guruma has the entire collection.'

'What about it?' wondered Abi. 'How is that going to help us?'

Sumathy clicked her tongue impatiently. 'Keep up, Abi. You have a painting of your mother. If we go through Guruma's collection and there's a painting that resembles her, then we've proved that you are indeed an *apsara's* daughter!'

—⚬⚬⚬—

The girls hatched their plans carefully. Abi did not want anyone else to know what they were searching for – so they would have to find a time to get into Guruma's room and go through all the portraits when she was not around. Abi was sure that the portraits were stacked with the parchments in the little temple corner in her principal's room. One of them would have to keep watch while the other looked through the portraits. At times, Guruma went on little overnight trips with one or two teachers. The students never really knew where she went, though there were rumours that they visited a sage up on a snowy mountain for his blessings. The only people who knew about these visits beforehand were the kitchen staff as they'd pack food for the teachers. Sumathy spoke to the cook and managed to find out the date of the next visit.

—⚬⚬⚬—

When the day came, the girls put their plan into action. They waited until the evening meal was finished. As most of the other girls made their way to their rooms, Abi and Sumathy casually walked across the courtyard to Guruma's room. Sumathy was carrying a large bowl of fruit. She dropped it on purpose in front of the doorway and then got busy trying to collect the fruits. Abi slipped into the room – it was dark except for the soft light from an oil lamp near the pictures of the gods. She could see the portraits stacked near the lamp – there were many and it was too dark to see in this light. She picked up the whole stack and hid them awkwardly in the folds of her sari and hurried out. Sumathy was surprised at the speed of her return. 'Let's go,' hissed Abi. 'I'll tell you later. We need to get to our room and then get back here in the morning.' The girls got back to their room without bumping into anyone. However, as soon as they got back, Guru Mahesh, who was on patrol duty, knocked at the door and told the girls to turn their light out and go to sleep. It was too difficult to go through all the pictures at night. They would have to wait until morning.

∽∾∿

Abi had a restless night – they were so near yet so far. Finally, before the first light of dawn appeared, the girls ran to the stream and washed and dressed before dawn broke. They ran back to the room and eagerly went through all the portraits in the first light of the morning. Abi couldn't help admiring the talent of the artist. The portraits were beautiful – they were old, drawn on papyrus, and the paint was fading. However, the expressions, beauty and grace of the girls that they depicted took Abi's breath away. 'These girls look divine – they must be *apsaras*,' whispered Sumathy. They went through nearly thirty portraits without seeing anyone remotely similar to Abi's mother.

Abi picked up the next portrait and held it near the window to see clearly. It was the picture of a beautiful girl, wearing a flowing white sari and white flowers in her hair. She seemed to be floating towards the sky. Sumathy held Abi's hand excitedly. They looked at each other with shining eyes – this was an almost exact replica of the painting Abi's father had drawn. Abi had hung her dad's painting on the wall next to her bed. They took it down and examined both the pictures. They were definitely of the same girl, although the setting was different. 'Yes, this is it – this is her!' Abi said breathlessly to Sumathy, who nodded in agreement. They had found her mother – she was indeed an *apsara*.

In their excitement, the girls had forgotten the time. They realised that they were late for all the morning work. They had the task to draw the *kolam* in the courtyard. Reluctantly, Abi gathered all the portraits and hid them between the folds of a blanket. 'I will pretend that the blanket needs to go to Guruma's room and then return the portraits,' said Abi. They ran down to the courtyard – most of the other girls had finished their share of work. Sumathy hurried around to start the *kolam* and nudged Abi to disappear into Guruma's room.

Abi ran into the room and had just replaced the portraits in their original place when she felt a hand on her shoulder. 'Did you find what you were looking for, child?' Abi froze as she heard Guruma's melodic voice.

She slowly looked around and was relieved to find Guruma smiling at her. 'I knew you would come to check one day,' she said.

'Did you know that my mother was an *apsara*? Why did you not tell me?' said Abi, finding her voice.

'Would you have believed me? There is a time for everything, and there are some things in life that can only be learnt and not taught.'

'Please tell me about her –who was she, how did you know that she was an *apsara*? Is she still in Indra's court?' The questions flowed freely out of Abi's mind.

Guruma led Abi to a seat. 'Your mother was entrusted to me by the gods. She had decided that she wanted to spend some time in human form, and I was to protect her during her time on Earth. She met your father here, fell in love and married him. I don't know much else about what happened. After giving birth to twins, she must have returned to Indra's court – I don't know why – something must have compelled her to leave you and your father.'

Abi looked at Guruma in amazement. 'Does that mean she's alive?' she asked breathlessly.

'Child, *apsara*s are not mortal – she cannot die. She is in her heavenly abode, as we speak. But while on Earth, she and your father have entrusted you to me. My role is to teach you all I can to enable you to develop into the wonderful girl that you are turning into.'

'Can I not meet her?' asked Abi longingly.

Guruma looked very solemn: 'No, child. Human beings who have pure hearts and have committed pure deeds can go to heaven after their mortal life is over. You need to concentrate on discovering yourself and living your life to its full, not thinking of death and going to heaven. If you kill yourself, we believe that is a sin – and therefore you will not get your passage to heaven. Go, eat breakfast and get ready for your studies.' Abi recognised the dismissal and made her way back to Sumathy.

She was in a mutinous mood – it was very hard to know that her mother was not dead and yet she could not see her. She told Sumathy the whole incident in whispers during breakfast. The first lesson was with Guru Mahesh – mythology. Sumathy had another brainwave. In the middle of class, she raised her hand and asked Guru Mahesh a question – 'Sir, you told us the other day that the artist Dev went to heaven and painted the portraits of the *apsaras*. If the portraits are back on Earth, that means he would have come back to Earth. How is that possible?'

Guru Mahesh smiled an enigmatic smile and said, 'In very rare circumstances, it is possible for some gifted individuals to visit heaven in their mortal form. They need to be able to complete tasks that will take them up the seven magic steps to heaven. And they need the light of a special gem to provide them entry through the doors of heaven.'

'Where can this gem be found, Guruji?' Abi could hardly contain her excitement as she asked the next question.

'I have no idea – and you need to concentrate on our next lesson – that is about Vishnu and not about *apsaras* and heavenly trips.' The rest of the lesson carried on in Guru Mahesh's monotonous drone about one of Hindu mythology's main gods.

12

THE MYSTERY MAN

Abi & Sumathy tried hard over the next few days to get more information about the seven magic steps to heaven but had no luck. Luckily, Abi had her dance practice to distract her from the obsession with her mother. Each time she felt frustrated, she would go away to her secret ledge and dance her heart out.

The summer holidays were due to start soon. Unlike in the UK, many of the girls stayed back in school during the summer holidays. Some, like Pooja, needed to practise to get ready for the dance festival trials in the coming year. Others, like Sumathy, had no place else to go. Many of the teachers and Guruma stayed at the school – although it was not operational in full force, there were plenty of people around.

One evening, Guruma called Abi to her room and gave her some great news. 'Your aunt will be visiting you shortly, Abi. She's coming over here with a friend and will be camping out by the river. I have invited her and her friend to join us for lunch. After that, you can see her and spend some time with her. They will be around for the Festival of Holi as well. I think your aunt's visit will work wonders for you – I know you have missed her much!' Abi couldn't believe her ears – she was overjoyed to hear about her visitors.

She almost bounced back to her room to tell Sumathy. 'You will love Aunt Jo – she's really cool and such good fun.'

Sumathy watched Abi's excitement in some amusement and asked, 'So, who's her friend? Is that the boyfriend you mentioned?'

Abi felt her heart skip a beat – how could she have forgotten about the mystery man! 'I don't know for sure – I suppose it would be…' she replied nervously.

———

That night, Abi could just not contain her excitement – she would meet her aunt tomorrow. She tossed and turned in bed, long after Sumathy had gone to sleep. The next few days would be a real adventure! She longed to tell her aunt all about school, dance, her secret hiding place in the forest, the animals and about her mother. She was sure that Aunty Jo would not have known about the magic and intrigue surrounding her mother – the question was whether she'd believe it. Abi was also quite excited about meeting the boyfriend. She would get to know him finally – and he was probably quite boring and ordinary in real life and nothing like the romantic, dangerous and powerful mystery prince that she had imagined him to be.

Abi woke up very early the next day and went to her secret hideout to practise her dance. She knew that she would not get much time later on in the day. Later, she took real pains in getting ready. As she looked at her reflection in water, she was surprised to see how much she resembled her mother's painting now. By midday, she had run to the courtyard three times to keep an eye out for her visitors.

It was nearly lunchtime before Jo and Varun arrived at the school. They looked very suntanned, tired and dusty. Jo put down her backpack with a thump and ran towards Abi to give her a great big hug. After a warm embrace, Abi looked at her aunt – she looked much the same, although a bit browner than usual. The twinkle in her eyes matched the wide smile that danced on her lips. Jo turned towards the young man accompanying her. 'Varun, I want you to meet my most favourite person in the world – my niece Abi.' Abi turned an enquiring face towards Varun – he did not look like what she remembered of the man at the airport. He had long brown hair that had become tousled and dusty in the climb to the school. He was wearing sunglasses – so she couldn't see his eyes.

He gave her a million-watt smile and shook hands with her – 'I have heard so much about you – Jo could not stop chattering all the way here – she is so excited to be here – and so am I!'

Abi lead the twosome to Guruma's room. Guruma welcomed them warmly and led them to the stream for a quick wash before they could all have lunch. When they arrived for lunch, they looked much cleaner and nicer. Abi introduced Sumathy and they all sat down to eat. Guruma was sitting diametrically opposite them. They were in the middle of lunch when Abi noticed the strange look that Guruma was giving her aunt and her boyfriend. 'I wonder if she disapproves of a girl travelling with her boyfriend,' Abi whispered to Sumathy, who nodded sympathetically. Varun had taken his glasses off. Abi herself found it hard to stop staring at his gorgeous green eyes.

After lunch, Jo and Varun spent a few minutes in Guruma's company and then went off to pitch their tent near the stream. Abi and Sumathy gave them a hand. Jo was in fantastic spirits and Varun seemed to be great fun – he cracked lots of jokes and was very strong and capable. He had nailed the tent down in no time and started a small fire to boil tea. They had a fabulous tea and munched through some cakes and biscuits that Jo had brought from the UK. The two girls had a wonderful afternoon, and Abi felt more content than ever. She had not had such a great time in recent memory.

'Tell me about the Festival of Holi,' said Varun, looking at both Sumathy and Abi for an answer. Abi was not sure herself and she looked at Sumathy for help.

Sumathy sat up straight, only too delighted to be asked. 'Holi, like most Indian festivals, is about the triumph of good over evil. There was a demon king who had a kind son called Prahalad. Prahalad was a big devotee of Lord Vishnu, much to his father's annoyance. The demon king became so angry with him once that he asked his sister Holika to enter fire with Prahalad in her lap. You see, Holika had a gift – she could not be harmed by fire. However, when she did that, their ruse backfired.' Sumathy paused and looked around to make sure that they had understood her pun and humour around "backfire". Varun laughed and encouraged her to go on.

'Prahalad was a very pure soul – so nothing could destroy him. Holika got burnt instead. But actually, nowadays, no one thinks of the mythical origins of the festival. Most people use it as an excuse to socialise with friends. It is my favourite festival – it is celebrated in spring or to mark the beginning of summer; we splash each other with colour and water and have a great time! It is a bit later in the year than usual this time.'

Jo thumbed her travel guide book thoughtfully. 'It says in here that the festival can be a bit boisterous and can take unwary tourists by surprise.'

Sumathy shook her head: 'That's probably in the cities where people get a bit carried away. It is really nice out here. We only use herbal colours – there are no chemicals. I mix the colours myself, using some of my grandma's secret recipes. Plus we sing and dance and have a great time.'

Abi kept thinking about Varun all through the evening – he seemed such good fun and he was so handsome. She tried to avoid it, but Guru Usha's fairy tale kept coming back into her mind all the time. She was so preoccupied through dinner that she did not notice that Sumathy was not sitting by her side as usual. She was sitting with Guru Mahesh and talking excitedly to him.

That night, Abi retired early to bed – she was not in the mood to talk to anyone. Sumathy had been busy with her grandmother's books for a few days, trying out new ways of creating make-up and cosmetics using ancient recipes. She came back that evening with a little lamp and a silver cup. 'I am making kajal using Granny's recipe. But I need your help. The lamp has to burn in moonlight and we need to turn the cup over it a couple of times to catch the soot or lamp black. Would you be ok to wake up once in the night, say midnight, and I'll do the second turn? You need to move the lamp and cup to where the moonlight falls.' Abi wasn't keen to argue and nodded unenthusiastically.

Around midnight, Abi woke up as planned and went outside to the porch to turn the silver cup that had been left poised over the lamp. Something moved in the forest – she looked around to see what it was. Was it a noise that she'd heard? Her heart gave a massive jump as she saw a green light far away and heard the very faint strains of a musical instrument. In the distance, she saw a dark figure. She stood hesitantly for a while and tried to get her eyes used to the darkness. The figure stood in the forest for a long time, but Abi could not make out who it was. She went back to bed and tried to sleep but tossed and turned for most of the night.

In the morning, she had just nodded off when she was woken up by an excited Sumathy. 'Wake up, Abi – I want to show you something special!'

Abi woke up bleary-eyed. 'What… where?'

Sumathy had already scrambled up on Abi's bed and pulled down her father's painting off the wall. 'There must be a clue in this painting. I didn't want to wake you up last night. I spoke to Guru Mahesh about the magic gem…' Abi gave her a blank look. 'You know, the magic gem – the gem you need to climb the seven magical steps of heaven,' said Sumathy impatiently, trying to pore over the painting.

Suddenly Abi felt very awake. 'What did he say?' she asked breathlessly.

'He said that the gem is very hard to trace. However, the story goes that whenever an *apsara* leaves Earth to go back, she drops the stone in a secret place if she wants someone to find her.'

Abi looked bewildered. 'What has that to do with the painting?'

Sumathy's eyes were shining. 'I reckoned that your father painted this when your mother left. This looks like an *apsara* reaching for the skies. So, I thought, there may be a clue in here…' Abi picked up the painting and took it towards the window.

There was a lot of detail on it. The *apsara* was higher up than the earth below her – she was clearly floating or flying up towards the heavens. Beneath her, there was a lake with sparkling water and lotus flowers. The lake was surrounded by a forest of dark green trees. You could see deer moving in the forest as well as birds perched on the trees. Abi was amazed at the amount of detail that she had never noticed before. It was probably because her eyes were almost immediately drawn towards the angelic girl. She had never looked carefully at the rest of the picture before this. It was exquisitely painted – the trees, the lake, the flowers, the birds and animals were very realistic. The deer looked like they were actually moving, and Abi marvelled at the cleverness of the painting. The whole scene looked very familiar. Abi looked at the greenish-blue waters of the lake and gave a startled cry of recognition – 'It's the waterhole! Sumathy, look – this is the waterhole where we often go to spot the deer. It's full of lotus flowers and the trees –no wonder this place looked so familiar…'

The girls were bursting with excitement now. Sumathy agreed with Abi that this looked almost exactly like a scene from the waterhole. 'It makes sense – that's why your parents wanted to send you here… maybe so that you could discover this secret and make your way to heaven…' said Sumathy in a hushed whisper. Abi was not so sure about that but continued to scan the painting with troubled eyes. The water in the lake was really shining – the sunlight reflecting off its surface.

Abi squinted at the lake, looking at the lotus flowers. 'There seems to be something at the bottom of the lake. It's quite dark and I'm not sure; can you see it, Sumathy?'

Sumathy said, 'Yes, but it's not clear. Let's take this out to the porch and look in the sunlight. Mind the kajal – it needs to be kept going for a few more nights.'

When they went out, the sun shone on the picture – and as if by magic, the lake became much clearer and came alive. They could see the beautiful lotus flowers blooming in abundance on the lake. They could also see the fish and reeds beneath the flowers in the greenish-blue waters. The muddy bottom of the lake could also just be made out. There seemed to be a blue light emanating from the centre of the bottom of the lake. The sun threw a bright ray of sunshine on the picture and the girls gasped in unison. 'That's it – the gem. It's at the bottom of the waterhole!' Abi and Sumathy looked at each other, their eyes shining with the light of adventure.

'Hey, girls... good morning! What are you doing with your dad's painting, Abi?' The girls looked up to see Jo and Varun standing in front of them, wearing amused expressions. Abi hastily moved the painting aside. Was she imagining it or could she see Varun's green eyes focussing on the lake?

'We were just admiring the craftsmanship,' said Sumathy in a feeble lie.

Luckily, Jo and Varun seemed to have other things on their mind and did not press any more. 'Isn't it Holi today? Happy Holi!' said Varun to the girls.

Sumathy slapped a hand on her forehead. 'Of course! I forgot – come on, Abi, we need to get to the courtyard or we will miss all the celebrations. But before that, we need to prepare.' She looked at Jo and Varun's clothes. 'You both better change into older clothes – ones that you don't mind spoiling. And I'll give you some oil. Apply this generously over your body, face and hair – then the colours will wash off easily.'

Abi and Sumathy applied oil and changed into old robes. Jo and Varun did the same and walked back to the girls' room – the four of them then went to the school courtyard together.

The courtyard was a riot of colours. There was singing and dancing and almost everyone was multi-coloured thanks to the red, yellow, green and blue coloured powders being thrown around. Everyone was carrying a *pichkari*, a type of tube with a piston – you could fill the tube with water, and as you pushed the piston in, you could spray others. The four of them joined in and had a splendid time playing with water and colours. After a while, Kaliram, the caretaker; and the cook walked around distributing glasses of *kanji* and almond milk. Kanji was a drink made out of fermented carrots and was an acquired taste. Sumathy seemed to devour glass after glass while Abi, Jo and Varun stopped after one sip.

'It's really musty!' said Abi and helped herself to a delicious glass of saffron-flavoured almond milk instead. The whole morning carried on in this vein.

Lunch was an informal affair and once again, Abi marvelled at the variety of goodies that the cook had produced. 'Indian food is so diverse,' she said to Jo, who was clearly enjoying trying all the new things. There was a lot of dancing later on and Abi found herself dancing with Varun for most of the time. She was really enjoying his company, but after a while, she realised that Jo was not on the dance floor. She stopped guiltily and started looking for her aunt. She was relieved to notice that Jo was having fun at another end of the courtyard. Abi felt slightly puzzled as to why Jo and Varun were not spending much time together.

After an exciting day, Varun went back to the tent. 'I am tired and want to crash for a long time. Jo would like to stay back with you, Abi.' Abi nodded enthusiastically – she would love to have a long chat with her aunt.

Jo, Abi and Sumathy had a very pleasant evening; they sat up on the porch outside their room after dinner and talked about anything and everything. After a while,

Sumathy retired to bed. When alone with her aunt, Abi casually brought up Varun's name in the conversation. 'How serious are the two of you?'

Jo gave a little laugh. 'Not very. Actually, we split up before this trip, but then everything was planned and both of us really wanted to be here. So, we're more like friends on this trip rather than boyfriend and girlfriend.' She had a mischievous glint in her eye. 'Why, Abi? Do you like him?'

Abi blushed beetroot red. 'Oh no, nothing like that… just wanted to know if he was going to become a relation.' Jo did not look very convinced but then changed the topic and both the girls talked of other things for a long time. Somehow Abi could not bring herself to talk to Jo about her mother's magical roots. It seemed so unreal and silly to talk about heaven and *apsaras* when Jo was recounting the latest fashions in the UK high streets.

<hr />

It must have been past midnight when they got up to go to bed. A night owl called out in the forest. Abi turned and looked at the trees before closing the door. She could feel someone's eyes staring at her from the distance. *It's probably just a creepy feeling,* thought Abi. *I must stop obsessing that Varun's staring at me wherever I go!* She chided herself as she lay in bed. It had been a long, exciting and tiring day.

13

THE MAGIC SAPPHIRE

The next day, Jo got up early and went back to her tent. It had rained heavily in the night and it was very windy in the morning. The girls got dressed and went to the courtyard to get breakfast. Abi was surprised to see Guruma walk up to her – 'Come with me, child. I want to talk to you.' Abi followed her to her room. 'What do you know about *asuras* and such?'

Abi was a bit puzzled by the question but rattled off what she remembered from her mythology classes. 'They are the antithesis of devas, the gods. They are deities, too – but are consumed by their thirst for power and \riches. I am generalising but many are supposed to be evil and sinful.'

Guruma nodded sagely and said, 'I suppose you know about *danavas*, *yakshas*, *rakshasas* and so on?'

'Yes, I do. *Rakshasas* are terrible creatures – magical shape changers. *Danavas* are a type of *asura*. *Yakshas* are spirits – they could be good or bad.'

Guruma took Abi's hands in hers. 'What links these creatures – what's common in all of them?'

Abi wondered if this was some kind of informal test but replied confidently, 'They are attracted to wealth, riches – they are often greedy. And they grow stronger at night.'

'Excellent,' said Guruma with a smile. 'I want you to remember that, especially now. I do not think you should visit your aunt and her friend at night. And be careful, Abirami… please remember what I've told you.' She wouldn't say any more and dismissed Abi with a smile.

Abi left Guruma's room in a bit of a daze. What did she mean by her words? What was the connection with *asuras*? Was she indicating that Varun was a magical creature? She was sure that Guruma wasn't talking about her aunt! She had noticed at lunch the other day that he had hypnotic green eyes, but did that mean that he was dangerous? She was cross and wished that Guruma would just tell her things openly instead of hinting at them vaguely.

After breakfast, Abi was still lost in thought when she saw Jo and Varun walk up to them. 'We're going for a walk in the forest – join us?' asked Jo. 'Surely you're free to do as you wish during the holidays?' Abi nodded and both the girls went to change, inform the school and join Jo and Varun in their exploration.

Varun had a map that they were following. To Abi's consternation, it seemed to lead straight to the waterhole. She tried to divert them towards another route – 'I'll show you my secret stage, where I practise.'

'Another time, Abi. I want to see this waterhole – I believe that spotted deer can be seen there. I want to get some good photos in the morning,' said Varun, tapping his beautiful camera. Sumathy and Abi gave each other an apprehensive look. They had no choice but to walk to the waterhole.

As he hoped, Varun was able to get some good shots of deer. Abi kept looking at him to see whether he was staring at the lake, but there was nothing obvious. He gave her a big smile. 'Come on; let me take a picture of you by the lake.' As he clicked many photos, Abi could look at him openly. He was very handsome. He had an angular face with high cheekbones. His long, wavy hair had been brushed back and fell softly on his shoulders. He had the most spectacular green eyes – they absolutely arrested Abi's attention when he looked at her. He was probably only a few years older than her, but he was very poised and confident. And he had a million-dollar smile.

Abi brought herself out of her reverie – *What are you doing, Abi?* she said to herself. *I know he's not Jo's boyfriend anymore, but he is not yours either!* Guruma's words about *asuras* and suchlike rang in her ears. But she could not help looking at his green eyes with a pang in her young heart.

⸻

They had a great day once again and were tired when they got back to their room that evening. They had already eaten and were quite ready to go to bed when Sumathy walked up to Abi seriously. 'I am a bit concerned about the gem, Abi. I think we should try and get it out before someone else does. What do you think?'

Abi nodded in agreement. 'When we didn't know about it, it was ok. But now that we do, I agree that we must act really quickly. Maybe tomorrow?' The girls had just started planning when they heard a knock on the door. *Who can it be at this time?* wondered Abi, apprehensive thanks to Guruma's dire warnings.

Sumathy opened the door to reveal Jo standing with a sleeping bag. 'Varun had a problem with his camera. He's going down to the nearest town to sort it and will be back tomorrow. He thought he'd travel at night to save time, and I thought I'd join you girls again tonight. Is that ok?'

The girls smiled and nodded; but that night, as her aunt and Sumathy slept peacefully, Abi started wondering about Varun. *Why has he disappeared at night? He did see us pointing at the gem in the painting. And now, he knows the way to the waterhole. Could he be after the gem himself?* It was a long, uncomfortable night for Abi; and when dawn broke, she was only too glad to get up.

That morning, Jo left them after breakfast and went back to her tent. She was planning to spend the morning sorting out some travel plans and was not going to meet the girls for a while. Abi and Sumathy were just waiting for an opportunity to be alone and start planning how to get the gem out of the waterhole. 'It is not going to be easy. I can't swim at all – and for one of us to go right to the bottom of the lake… how are we going to breathe underwater for that long?' wailed Sumathy.

'I am a good swimmer and I'm sure I can go down to the bottom of the lake. But I am not sure how long it will take for me to get the gem out of the ground or how I am going to breathe underwater, and it will be really cold at this altitude. I wish I had a scuba diving kit of some sort!' said Abi wistfully.

Then Sumathy said something unexpected. 'Abi, I am sure the gods can do things like this without scuba diving kits. Maybe they'll gift you their powers for a short while and you can retrieve the gem?' Abi looked at her friend as if she were mad. This was one of the major differences in being brought up in the west – Sumathy, who had been brought up in the mystical east, seemed to be ever ready to believe in miracles and magic. Abi found it very hard to do so. 'Come on, Abi. The gods know you're the daughter of an *apsara*. They love you anyway… you're such a good person. I am sure you can ask. After all, how will it hurt?' Sumathy was very persistent.

'Hmm, if I can ask them for something like that, why can't they just give me the gem?' demanded Abi sceptically.

'That's not the same. You have to work to get some things, but this is just a little extra help on the way. Come on, Abi, give it a go, and trust me, what's the worst that can happen?' Abi finally agreed despite misgivings.

Both the girls made their way to Abi's secret stage. 'This is the best place to see the sun and feel the breeze on your face,' said Abi, leading Sumathy through the forest. 'I can ask the Surya, the sun god, and Vayu, the god of wind, if they would be able to grant me the ability to stay warm underwater and breathe there for a little while.'

Sumathy clapped her hands in delight. 'I am sure they will agree. Perform a little prayer dance and then ask them for a boon.' Abi thought this was really silly but didn't want to hurt her friend by pooh-poohing her idea. Abi had carried her CD player. She put on the dance music and got ready to do *pushpanjali*, a prayer dance.

The weather had changed thanks to the unexpected rain showers in the night. The sun was hidden among the clouds, and it was a very gloomy and windy stage that Abi stepped on. As the music began, Abi started to dance and, as usual, she quickly lost track of her surroundings and could hear nothing else. Sumathy watched in amazement – she had not seen Abi dance like this before and was entranced by the sight. She was joined by a number of little birds, squirrels and deer – it seemed that the forest had collected to watch the *pushpanjali*.

In a few minutes, the clouds moved away as if to make way for the sun god to come and see the dance. The sun shone brightly on Abi, and the breeze played with her hair. When she had finished, Sumathy nudged Abi. Abi reluctantly joined her hands in prayer and addressed the gods – 'I wish to come and visit my mother in heaven. The only way that I know is to find the gem at the bottom of the waterhole and then make my way up the seven magic steps. Getting the gem will be the first challenge. The water is cold and I can't breathe underwater for long. Please grant me the power of staying warm underwater and being able to breathe for at least an hour so that I can bring the gem up.' Both the girls looked up to the sky in anticipation. The sun still shone brightly and the breeze was very pleasant, but there was no response of any kind. Abi felt very stupid standing there waiting for a sign of some sort. Sumathy looked eagerly towards the sky. Not wanting to hurt her friend by belittling the episode, Abi quietly linked her hand through Sumathy's and walked away from the ledge, towards the waterhole.

'Do you think they would have granted me the power?' Abi couldn't resist the doubtful words.

'I am sure they have. The sun was so bright and the wind died away and became a pleasant breeze. I bet that's a sign. I wish you'd asked for this power for more than an hour, though,' said Sumathy.

'If I don't do it in an hour, I doubt I can do it at all. There's never any point in asking for anything more than what you actually need,' said Abi wisely. 'Come on, let us go and try. If I can't breathe underwater for long, I will know very soon and I will come back out. We will need to find another way then.'

Both the girls made their way to the waterhole and stood on the bank taking in the scene. The greenish-blue waters were really calm. Diffused sunlight fell on the lake, and clumps of beautiful lotus and lily flowers floated lazily on the water. 'It is such a beautiful lake. I'm going in now,' said Abi, taking off her bangles and removing her sari. 'I'll keep some clothes on – but I may be cold when I get back. Sumathy, I think you should go back to the school and make some excuse for where I am to both the teachers and to Aunty Jo. Then bring me a towel and some fresh clothes. By that time, I'll have either been successful or if not, I'll come back immediately.'

'Are you sure you'll be ok on your own?' Sumathy looked very unsure.

'Oh yes, it is daylight and I have been here loads of times. My little friend Krish may come wandering around here soon. Go on...' urged Abi. 'And Varun has gone down to town – I don't think he'll be back until the evening,' she added secretly to herself, watching Sumathy walk back through the forest.

Abi said a little prayer to the sun and wind gods and dived into the water. She doubted she had any special powers but thought she could hold her breath for a little anyway, and she wanted to give it a go. She was surprised to find the water pleasantly cool. She was holding her breath in anticipation – she was amazed that she could see underwater without much trouble. Did that mean her prayers had been granted? Hesitantly, she exhaled and gingerly tried breathing underwater, prepared to splutter and come up to the surface any minute.

To her astonishment, she found that she was able to breathe normally. She felt her nostrils and open mouth act as gills and work with water instead of air. Her prayers had been answered! She didn't quite know how to feel but remembered that she only had an hour at her disposal. The water was quite dark and murky. As Abi swam towards the centre of the lake, things got a bit clearer. Maybe it was due to the diffused sunlight falling on the lake. As her eyes got used to the darkness of the water, she started seeing reeds and fish around her. 'I wonder if there are crocodiles or any other dangerous creatures in here... oh, I must stop worrying about it and focus on the task at hand.'

As Abi dived further down, she found that the lake was much deeper than they had originally thought. She could not see the bottom of the lake. She navigated her way through the reeds and fish. Was she imagining it or could she see a great big snake coiled up at the bottom of the lake? Abi blinked a few times to try and clear her eyes. She could see the outline of a dark snake-like being at the bottom at a great distance below her. She could not be sure, but it seemed that the snake had five heads! Cold terror gripped her heart – what sort of creatures inhabited this lake? Then she remembered her mythology class. Guru Mahesh had taken great pains to describe Vishnu, one of the three main gods of the Hindu religion. His words rang in her ears – *Vishnu the creator is the most benevolent of the gods. His abode is at the bottom of the ocean. He stretches out on a five-headed snake and is often seen in the company of his wife, the goddess Lakshmi.* Abi stared at the dark figure – could this be the god Vishnu? Was she going mad thinking he could exist? But then, here she was, breathing and swimming underwater with no trouble. If this was Vishnu, she was not in danger... he was actually here to help her. Abi dived deeper and deeper, but the figure seemed no closer than it was when she first saw it. Finally, when Abi's hands touched the sandy bottom of the lake, she could not see the figure any longer.

She found that she was able to stand at the bottom of the lake. As per the laws of physics, this did not make any sense. So, this must be the power that the gods had bestowed upon her. She couldn't believe this was happening, but she had no time to marvel at the miracle. *I only have an hour in total. I must hurry…* thought Abi and started feeling around the bottom with her hands to see if she could see or feel anything. After several minutes of splashing about in the bottom, Abi stood up in despair. *This is not going to work. I am disturbing the water, and it's getting murkier than before, and I can barely see anything. Think, Abi… think. There must be a better way.*

Abi closed her eyes and thought of her father's painting. The gem had started shining through the water when sunlight had fallen on it. *That's it!* thought Abi triumphantly. *It must be the sunlight.* She closed her eyes again and prayed to the sun god. The clouds parted high above the lake and the sun came out. As if by magic, a ray of light fell through the water to a spot some distance away. Abi started swimming towards this spot. As she reached the spot, she could see a bluish glow at the bottom of the lakebed, joining the sunlight. Abi knew she was on the right track. She was now trembling with excitement as she made her way to the bottom again. At the bottom, there was a rock that seemed to be glowing blue. Abi lifted the rock with some difficulty to reveal the brightest and the most beautiful blue sapphire that she had ever seen. She picked up the egg-sized gem with care, and it shone with a magical blue luminescence in her hands. Her eyes gleamed victoriously. She had done it… she had overcome the first challenge!

14

THE UNDERWATER BATTLE

Abi was overjoyed – she turned the gem in her hands and admired its shape and brilliance. *It's like a piece of the moon in my hands,* thought Abi excitedly. She had never seen a jewel of this size, and it was almost as if she could not take her eyes off it. After a few wonderful moments of staring at the sapphire, Abi decided to make her way back. First, she had to find a way of safely carrying the stone back to the surface. She was still wearing the leggings that all the schoolgirls wore under their sari. She always carried a few spare safety pins tucked in there. She wrapped the stone carefully in her handkerchief and pinned it to her leggings. It was not great, but hopefully it would be secure enough until she reached the surface.

As she started making her way to the surface, she felt the water rippling around her as if some enormous creature was swimming through it. Fear gripped her heart. She knew that she was taking a risk, coming to the lake on her own despite Guruma's warnings and her own misgivings. She had sent Sumathy away as there wasn't much her friend could have done standing on land while Abi was deep underwater. She turned her head left to right in a panic to see what was causing the water to heave so greatly. She could hear her heart thumping loudly. As she strained her eyes, she saw a monstrous outline of a great big fish.

The fish was more than three times her size and was making its way straight towards her. Abi panicked and was frozen to the spot – she could see a gigantic serrated jaw with great big fang-like teeth. The fish had greenish-blue iridescent scales that shimmered in the water and large green saucer-shaped eyes. *Green eyes!* Abi stared at the fish in shock – she had seen those startling green eyes before – this was Varun! *Guruma was right – he is a shapeshifter… and he wants to kill me. Oh my God, I have to move…* Abi started swimming up desperately, pushing the water down to try and move up faster.

The size and speed of the fish meant that it could catch up with her in no time at all. Abi saw the great jaw open wide as the fish tried to swallow her. She ducked and moved below the level of its jawline. Although the fish was very streamlined while swimming, its great size meant that it could not manoeuvre easily. This bought Abi a few moments and she kicked her legs to try and get to the surface again. She was struggling for breath – she realised that her one hour had probably run out and she must get back to the surface or else she would drown. The fish was now swimming up towards her again. Abi tried to weave from side to side, but the fish was too fast and wide. She closed her eyes in despair – she knew this was the end. A moment or two passed – Abi should have been inside the fish by now! She turned around to see what was happening. The monster was being pulled back towards the bottom of the lake by a gigantic snake!

Abi watched in wonder – this was the clash of the titans. The snake was larger than a python – she had heard of an "anaconda", a huge snake that could swim in water, but surely that was native to South America! This creature was unlike any that she had seen before. It was larger than any snake she had ever read about, had green and yellow markings on its large, sleek body. Then Abi realised that it had five heads – this really was Vishnu's snake! Its heads were unusual for a snake – two horny bits of skin on each head, large eyes and great yellow fangs that were trying to sink into the fish. It had wrapped its tail around the fish's tail fin and was pulling it fiercely away from Abi. But the fish was an equal match – its jaws snapped at the snake and the two monsters went round and round just below Abi, churning the water of the lake into a whirlpool. Abi could hardly breathe – she had to get back to the surface. She found it really hard to swim up; it was either due to the movement of water caused by the great fight, or it was because she was now completely unable to breathe underwater.

Abi could feel her legs give way below her. Lack of oxygen was sapping all her strength – the lake was looking darker, and she could not keep her eyes open any longer. Just as she felt her consciousness drifting away, she saw a rope fall into the lake a few yards away. *This is my last chance,* thought Abi. With what seemed like an impossible amount of effort, she caught the rope and was dragged up to the surface. The water below her was moving fast – the great snake and the great fish were still fighting each other below the surface. Abi could not see who her saviour with the rope was as she did not have enough energy to even open her eyes. She held on to the rope and was dragged towards the bank. She felt two pairs of little hands grab hold of her and carry her to the grass.

<hr />

When Abi came to her senses, she was shivering uncontrollably. The water had been cold, and while she had managed to stay warm thanks to her boon from the sun god, her one-hour time had run out due to the attack. She looked around for her saviours – Krish and another young boy were sitting on the bank, building up a pile of logs. Krish smiled at her. 'Are you ok now, Abi? We are trying to build a fire to warm you up.'

Abi gave him a watery smile and asked him through chattering teeth: 'What happened? How did you know I was underwater? How did you save me?'

'I could see the water churning in the centre and knew something was wrong. I saw your sari on the bank and thought you may be caught in reeds or something and you were trying to get back up to the surface. I had a rope – with my brother Bal's help, I threw the rope in the centre of the lake to see if you grabbed it. I felt a tug… we struggled to pull you out, but as there were two of us, we managed.'

Abi thanked both of them profusely. 'I would have died

in there if you hadn't found me. I cannot thank you enough.'

'Abi, are you all right?' Sumathy came running towards her with a towel and clothes. 'I was detained at school. I told Guru Usha that you were with your aunt, and I told your aunt that you were taking some extra lessons. But it was my misfortune that the two of them met and started talking to each other. They came to find me and I had to make up another story about your dance practice before I gave them the slip and ran back here. What happened?' chattered Sumathy while Abi towelled herself dry.

'I'll tell you, let me just change.' The boys had built their little fire. Abi went behind a bush and got rid of her wet clothes. As she removed her leggings, she finally remembered the gem. 'Oh, lord, I hope I haven't lost it in the fracas…' Luckily, she found it still pinned to the leggings. She removed it and tucked it away in the folds of her sari. Abi got back and started warming up by the fire. Krish and Bal were sitting at a distance – Krish was trying to teach Bal how to play the flute and was clearly struggling to succeed.

'Did you find the stone?' whispered Sumathy.

'Yes, but I got into trouble. Sumathy, I think Varun is a shapeshifter, an *asura* or a *rakshasa*. As I tried to come back to the surface, I was attacked by a monstrous fish. It was huge and had the same startling green eyes as Varun. I was lucky and was saved by a great snake that started fighting with the fish, or else I would have been swallowed alive!'

Sumathy looked at her friend in concern. 'Are you sure that the water isn't affecting you and you're not having hallucinations? Why should Varun try to kill you?

And how can he turn into a fish? That sounds ridiculous.'

Abi looked at her friend angrily. 'It is usually me who finds it hard to believe these things. No, I am not hallucinating. I know what I saw! And I know that it was Varun!' said Abi mutinously.

Sumathy still looked a bit sceptical but quickly changed the topic and asked to see the stone. Abi turned around to see the boys still focussing on the flute and then slowly took the jewel out, hiding it from their view. 'Wow! That's breath taking...' said Sumathy gazing at it in wonder. Abi looked down on the stone and her anger melted away – it was the most beautiful thing that she had ever seen. It glimmered in the sunlight, and both the girls sat and stared adoringly at it for a while.

'Right, we must be off,' said Krish, walking towards Abi. Abi quickly hid the gem away and thanked him once again for saving her. 'The life of a friend is more precious than all the riches and gems in the world,' said Krish importantly. The two girls stared at each other – did he know they had a precious stone?

Bal walked up to Abi and held out his hand. He was taller than Krish, skinny and had shoulder-length black hair. He was wearing a loose white *kurta* and white *dhoti*, typical villager attire. He gave Abi a shy smile and said, 'Hope you feel better soon. You should go and get something warm to eat or drink. Turmeric milk is ideal, Mother says.' Abi waved the boys goodbye and started walking back slowly to the school. As she got up, she turned back towards the waterhole. The water was still churning... the fight was still on!

She would not speak to Sumathy on the way back.

All sorts of thoughts raced through her head. Strangely, she had accepted that Varun was a shapeshifter easily enough. Maybe this was due to the fact that Guruma had asked her to think about *asuras*, *rakshasas* and so on; but Abi really struggled to understand or accept that Varun wanted to harm her. Before she met him, she had created imaginary romantic stories in her head about the green-eyed boy she'd seen at the airport. When he arrived in India, she had very quickly warmed to him and really enjoyed his company. When her aunt confided in her that they were not seeing each other any longer, she had become infatuated with him. And now she had to accept that he was an enemy and wanted to harm her. The joy of finding the stone had been lessened by the shattering of her romantic dreams.

15

THE START OF A NEW TERM

When Abi and Sumathy reached Gurukul, there was a great deal of commotion. It looked like the teachers had mounted a search for them. Guruma was the first to spot them. She had an unusually stern look on her face when she walked up to them. 'Sumathy, I am really disappointed in you. We were all so worried about Abi, and then you disappeared. What have you two been up to?' Her eyes fell on the bundle of wet clothes in Abi's hands. 'How are your clothes wet? Where have you been? After all the warnings I gave you…'

Abi was still shivering and her teeth chattered so much that she could not reply coherently. Sumathy quickly piped up with a story – 'Sorry, Guruma. I did not mean to bother all of you. I thought Abi was practising her dance, but she had slipped and fallen into the waterhole. Luckily, a couple of village boys spotted her and rescued her. I ran back to our room and got her a change of clothes – I was in a hurry and so did not tell anyone.' Guruma still looked suspiciously at both of them but softened considerably when she saw Abi shiver again.

She took them to her room and got one of the girls to bring steaming mugs of herbal tea for them. Abi calmed down once she had had a few sips of the hot tea – the warmth spread through her body and she felt more in control. 'Your aunt had to leave suddenly. Her friend had an accident and had to be taken to the big hospital on the outskirts of the town. She left you a hurried note,' said Guruma, handing Abi a folded piece of paper.

Abi read the letter out loud so Sumathy could hear its contents:

Abi – I am so sorry that I have to go away like this. I got a message from Varun through a person in the village. He has been involved in a very big accident – the villager said that he had been taken to the big hospital as the doctors nearby did not have all the equipment required. He's asked for me to pack everything and come away. I will write to you from England. You are doing so well – I am proud of you… with love, your Aunt Jo.

Abi pondered over the letter. Of course there was no accident – Varun had been hurt in the fight, but how could he get a message across to Jo so quickly? Then it struck Abi that this may have been part of Varun's plan to get Jo away from the school. If he had managed to attack and kill Abi in the lake, he did not want her aunt to find out immediately. So he had tricked her away in the hope that by the time she reached the hospital, he'd get there and weave some tall tale. Sumathy looked at Abi with dawning comprehension – maybe Abi was telling her the truth after all about Varun!

Guruma did not keep the girls too long – she seemed mollified by their story. She was concerned about how Abi slipped and fell into the waterhole but seemed to accept that some of the banks were very slippery following the unexpected rain. She warned the girls to stay away from the lake and asked them to go and rest for a while. The girls got back to their room and then pulled the gem out to take a closer look. 'It's like nothing in this world – it sparkles and dazzles so beautifully,' sighed Sumathy. Then she went to her battered aluminium trunk and rummaged through the odds and ends inside it. 'Ah, there it is,' she said, pulling out a little stringed pouch. It was beautiful – the pouch was made out of rich, shimmering brown brocade silk and had little pearls stitched around its mouth. When drawn, the pouch had two long stringed loops that could be used to hang it around the shoulder. 'My grandmother gave this to me – you should put the gem inside this and hang it around your neck and tuck it behind the folds of your sari. That way you can carry it on your person without anyone else knowing about it. You just have to be careful while bathing.'

Abi shook her head. 'I can't take something so lovely – and it's from your grandmother…'

But Sumathy was firm. 'We need to be careful with the gem and this is ideal for it. Besides, it is mine to do with as I please. I want you to have it – it is my little contribution,' said Sumathy shyly. Abi gave her a sudden hug. She felt so grateful that she had friends like Sumathy and Krish.

———⚬❧⚬———

The next few days passed in a flurry. Most of the girls had returned as the new school year was to start soon. Abi was glad to see her friends and classmates return. She had gone back to practising her dance with renewed fervour. She felt battered after her recent adventures and as usual turned to her dance to forget about it. Without fully realising it, she had developed a very soft spot for Varun; even though she knew that he may be a magical creature and that he could be dangerous, her heart had resolutely refused to believe that he would actually want to harm her. The lake incident had shattered that belief, leaving her very hurt and confused.

Sumathy had been of great help. Although she did not understand the extent of emotional trauma that her friend had undergone, she was able to somehow empathise and relate to her and was supporting Abi in a gentle and patient way. Abi also found relief in Krish's company. She often sought him out in the forest and had long conversations with him. His wiser-than-his-age comments made her smile, and at the same time she found his advice very relevant and useful. On one occasion, when she had been more upset than usual, he had given her a knowing smile and said, 'You can't always get what you want, and at times you have to face disappointments in life; but if you treat every disappointment as an opportunity to find or do something new instead of a setback, you will find that something good will be waiting for you round the corner most unexpectedly.'

Taking courage from his words, she had applied herself to her dance with even more energy and focus.

———⚬⚬⚬———

School reopened and all the students gathered in the courtyard to hear Guruma's opening address. Abi watched Guruma's impressive figure towering over all of them and her gentle yet quietly confident voice welcome them to the next school year. 'Another year – many of you have accomplished very good things in the last year. Now is the time for you to apply yourselves even more and turn those good things to great things.' Top awards for the last term were read out, and those students who had their names mentioned had to join Guruma on the stage. Abi felt a strange apprehension in her heart when Guruma started calling out names: 'Anushree Pandit – for top marks in mythology; Vidya Mathur – for getting the highest score in dance theory; Jayalakshmi Iyengar for top scores in Sanskrit...' The list went on for a while.

Abi whispered quietly to Sumathy – 'What is the top prize?'

'It is the best dancer – once in two years, the best dancer will get to go to the Sun Temple Festival in Konark... do you remember I told you about it when you joined? This year, it is a very special treat as legend goes that the sun god appears every twelve years (this year) to grant the winner a wish. Bet it will be Pooja who gets this, though – I wish it were you instead!'

'Shh, girls' – Guru Uma was standing behind them and gave them a glare.

Guruma finished calling out most of the top awards and looked around at the expectant faces with a smile. 'I know you are all waiting with bated breath to hear who is going to represent the school in the Konark Dance Festival this year. Whoever is chosen will not be attending the usual classes. I will be training the chosen one in more difficult aspects of dance. It is a great privilege to be chosen – at the same time, it will be hard work and they will have to try hard to win the dance festival for Gurukul.' Guruma once again surveyed the eager young faces in front of her. 'I am sure you will not be surprised when I announce the name of Pooja for the Sun Dance Festival!' The girls applauded as a triumphant Pooja walked up to the stage. Her face was set in a determined and superior expression. Her long, oily plait swayed below her waist as she climbed on the stage and looked around to find Abi in the crowd and sneer at her.

Guruma continued speaking. 'But this year, there is a special surprise. There is one other student who has been chosen to represent the school. This is unheard of; but this student has been absolutely brilliant and has improved her dancing by leaps and bounds in the last year. I have never seen anyone pick up and become such a good dancer in so short a time. And it's not just dance that she has excelled at – she has been an exemplary student. Abirami, please come and join me on the stage.'

Abi looked at Sumathy in shock – the whole school erupted into loud and cheerful applause, and Sumathy grinned and pushed Abi towards the stage. Abi shyly walked up to the stage and was sure that her face was the same shade of red as her clothes when she stood next to

Guruma. She could just see Pooja's face morph into a black scowl. 'Now I have a couple more surprises. Both Pooja and Abi can choose two other students to join us for the Konark Dance Festival. Pooja and Abi will be performing individual items for the winner's prize. However, there will be one group item that they need to perform, and the two students they choose will join them in that group item. They have to give me the names by the end of today. I am sure they will choose wisely.' From her vantage point on stage, Abi looked around at the girls in front of her. She saw eager and anxious faces – Sudha, Aishwarya, Kalyani – the young ones from her initial batch gave her a "choose-me" smile. This was going to be difficult.

The girls had only a few classes that day, and there was much time to talk to each other and swap summer vacation stories. Many girls came over to congratulate Abi and wish her luck. Even plump Dhanya turned up – 'I always knew you were better at dance than cooking, Abi,' she gushed. Abi smiled mechanically, and her eyes looked around, trying to seek out Sumathy, who seemed to have disappeared.

At lunchtime, Abi started getting positively anxious when there was no Sumathy to be seen anywhere. Abi skipped lunch and walked back to their room to see if her friend was there. She had a moment of relief when she spotted Sumathy sitting on her bed and staring vacantly through the window.

'Where have you been – why aren't you at lunch?' demanded Abi hotly.

Sumathy turned away from Abi and started folding and smoothing her bed sheet, though it looked pretty neat in the first place. 'I was not hungry. Congrats on your going to the Konark Festival. If you win, you can ask the sun god some tips on how to find and climb the magic steps.' Abi looked at her friend in dismay – it looked like Sumathy had been crying. She wondered why. 'Have you selected a partner for the group dance? Kala is good – so is Arundhati. Choose someone who is around the same height as you as otherwise you will look incongruous on stage,' said Sumathy, keeping her eyes carefully averted.

A sudden realisation dawned on Abi – this was why Sumathy was behaving so oddly. 'Sumathy, you chump; do you really think I would choose anyone other than you? I want you to dance with me – will you?'

Sumathy looked at Abi – her wet eyes were uncertain. 'Are you sure? I am not really the best dancer...' she began.

'I am very sure that I want no other. You are part of all the adventures now... unless you don't want to be?'

Sumathy's eyes were now shining. 'Of course I want to be. Nothing would give me greater pleasure.'

Abi grabbed Sumathy's hand and led her to Guruma's room. Guruma was sitting in her usual seat and looked at them expectantly. 'Guruma, I have come to let you know the name of the person that I would like to take with me. It is Sumathy.'

Guruma smiled at both the girls. 'A fine choice. Sumathy – you need to practise hard and watch what you eat. Your grandma's nutrition tips would be more relevant now than ever. More yoga and meditation as well. I will work with Guru Uma to plan your routine.'

Sumathy looked relieved that Guruma did not question Abi's decision.

The two girls were about to leave when Pooja entered the room with another girl. She looked contemptuously at Abi and Sumathy and turned towards Guruma. 'I would like to take Arundhati with me, Guruma. She is a very good dancer – extremely flexible and quick to learn.'

Guruma nodded – 'I do know about all of my students, Pooja. That's fine, if that is your decision.' Guruma smiled at Arundhati. 'Welcome to the group. All four of you have to work together – the group dance is not part of the prize dances, but it means a lot and will have a large audience. If all four of you get along and enjoy learning, it will be a great experience for everyone.' Pooja hastily hid her scowl and nodded sagely. Abi smiled at Arundhati – she knew her slightly and thought of her as a nice, amiable girl. She was very petite and wore a yellow sari, just like Pooja. She had a light delicate complexion, greenish eyes and soft brown hair characteristic of the part of Western India that she hailed from.

As the girls left Guruma's room, Arundhati looked at Sumathy and Abi and said, 'I am glad to join all of you. I am looking forward to it – aren't you, Pooja?'

Pooja drew herself to her full height and looked haughtily at the others. 'Well, Sumathy – you better practise hard. Not sure what Abi was thinking selecting you. But I won't be happy if you let me down.' She turned around and walked off. Arundhati looked apologetically at Sumathy and walked away as well. Abi and Sumathy looked at each other and burst out laughing at the same time. Pooja was such a pompous idiot!

Abi received a letter from her aunt that day. It read:

Abi, I am posting this at Delhi Airport. Varun was badly hurt but made a surprisingly quick recovery. The doctors were most puzzled by the speed of his improvement. He is still limping and is bandaged all over but wants to go home. The two of us have officially split up, but I'll still be friends with him – I thought you'd like to know ;-) Take care of yourself and I'll write again from the UK.

Abi read her aunt's cheeky comment about their split-up and smiled to herself. Little did she know how things had changed since her underwater adventure!

The first day passed quickly and it was soon bedtime. Abi said goodnight to Sumathy and turned away from her to look out of the window. The moon was shining bright and full. Abi thought wistfully of her father and Vy. It had been a strange year – coming away from England, the school, their manic daily routine, her love of dance, her discovery of her celestial heritage and finally the gem. She felt the gem, still hanging around her neck in the silk pouch. She was not sure what the future had in store but knew that her new school term promised to be as exciting as the last one. The training for the dance festival would be arduous but fun, and the festival itself was said to be amazing. But most of all, Abi knew that she would be focussing her mind and efforts to find the seven magic steps. She looked at the inky-blue night sky and whispered softly to herself, 'Mother, I am coming – I will find you in heaven… whatever it takes!'

The quest had begun!

The
Quest

16

PREPARATION

'I cannot dance anymore.' Sumathy sighed and sank to the ground, exhausted. She looked up at her best friend who was continuing their dance routine.

Abi stopped and walked up to her. 'You cannot stop now – we're nearly done. Just one more item… come on, you can do it.' Both the girls had been practising non-stop for three hours, stopping for a few seconds in between dances to take a sip of lemonade. Sumathy looked at her in slightly resentful admiration – Abi had joined the school just a year ago but had picked up dance better than any other student could ever hope to. Some of it was genetic – they had discovered last year that Abi's mother was an *apsara*, a celestial dancer who lived in heaven, but much of her talent was due to sheer hard work and determination. Sumathy got up reluctantly and continued the dance alongside an energetic Abi.

Guru Uma walked into the courtyard, carrying baby Vi on her hip and looked at both the girls appraisingly.

Sumathy looked much the same as she did the year before –slim and beautiful, if you could ignore her protruding teeth. She moved steadily and gracefully on the dance floor. Abi had changed considerably in the year that she had spent in Gurukul. She no longer looked tomboyish, but elegant and attractive – with her dusky complexion, expressive eyes, high cheekbones and well-chiselled features. She had lost a bit of weight and this made her look even taller. Her dance had improved beyond recognition, and there was an incredible preciseness to her movements, a remarkable energy that she poured into every step. The girls moved together in perfect rhythm, and although they were both tired, they gave it their best effort. Guru Uma was amazed at how much Abi had progressed from the time she had arrived very reluctantly at the dance school. She and Vi applauded them as they finished their dance. 'Well done, girls. That was much better than the last time.' Then a frown creased her plump young face. 'Where are the other two? Why are you all not dancing together?' The other two girls, Pooja and Arundhati, were nowhere to be seen. Guru Uma's face was turning pink – something that always happened when she got angry. 'I thought that Guruma made it clear that the four of you need to try and get along properly – otherwise, you'll bring shame upon the school.'

Sumathy piped up, ever eager to please the teachers. 'We are sorry, Guruji, we have been looking for them too but have not seen them at all since morning.'

There was a rustle and giggling behind Guru Uma – she turned to see Pooja and Arundhati enter the courtyard. Pooja's deep brown eyes twinkled with mischief, and haughtiness marred her pretty face. Pooja's pride at her ability to dance followed her to the stage every single time. She clearly thought that she was better than everyone else. She looked at her rival, Abi, scornfully and was just about to say something sarcastic when Arundhati, her dance partner, tugged at her arm. She had noticed Guru Uma glaring at them. Pooja immediately recovered her poise and stammered out an explanation: 'Guruji, we were practising. There's a wide ledge at the edge of the forest and it is an ideal location for practice.' She glanced at Abi with a sneer while saying this, and Abi instantly knew that Pooja had discovered her secret practice spot.

'I don't care if it is at the edge of the forest or the edge of the world. The four of you need to practise together. After lunch, Guruma will take your lessons. If I don't see you here promptly at two, ready with your anklets, there will be punishment all around; and don't blame me if Guruma refuses to let you go to the festival.' Guru Uma stalked off and the four girls looked at each other in silence.

The animosity between Pooja and Abi was rife in the air and you could cut the tension with a knife. Arundhati looked shamefacedly at Sumathy and shrugged her shoulders sheepishly. If it hadn't been for the tension between these two girls, they could have been reasonable friends. The girls walked away in different directions. Sumathy shook her head sadly. This year was proving to be much harder than she had imagined.

They did not have to attend regular classes, but both Guru Uma and Guruma were putting them through a gruelling schedule. They had to learn various aspects of practical dance, music and dance theory. They were expected to understand the meaning of all the songs that they danced to – much of this music was in Sanskrit and the girls had to work hard to pick it up. They had a vigorous yoga and martial arts routine followed by long periods of meditation. They had to learn how to apply their own make-up and create their own costumes, including stitching their dance outfits. They also had to study some parts of their class' academic syllabus. 'This is so that you can make up for your lost year and join your classmates next year,' said Guruma.

Their dance routines were getting more and more complex as time went on. Besides the group item, Pooja and Abi had to perform individual dance items in order to be selected. So they had to practise harder and longer than the other two. All this was having a negative effect on the girls' sense of humour, and tempers were frayed.

Guruma was very grim that afternoon. She still looked very majestic and impressive in her white robes, her silver hair tied back in a loose plait. Her lips, stained red with betel nut juice, were set in a straight line, and her grey eyes looked sharply at the girls. 'I am disappointed to see how you are treating each other. If you cannot be friends, I want you to be classmates and co-dancers. If you cannot make an effort to be even this, then I do not want to teach you anymore.'

The girls looked at their principal in shock – this was the last thing that they expected. Being chosen for the festival was a great honour for the girls, and bringing good artistes to the festival was also an honour for Gurukul. Most of the school was sure that Pooja would win the festival this year, and this would have brought a lot of accolades. Abi and Pooja exchanged apprehensive looks – was Guruma serious? Guruma seemed oblivious to this as she turned and walked away to her room, leaving the girls distressed. Guru Uma came up to them and shook her head in regret. Baby Vi put her arms out to be carried by Abi. Abi picked up the child and considered the situation carefully. Guru Uma seemed to understand what the girls were thinking. 'Don't think she's making empty threats. Guruma is intolerant of rivalries like this. A few years back, she cancelled the tour, even though we were all sure that the student chosen would win.'

Abi stared at the ground – her dislike for Pooja bubbled in her and she knew this feeling was mutual. She closed her eyes and thought of her mother. After all, this festival was much more than just a dance competition for her; it was her gateway to heaven. Abi involuntarily reached to feel the magic sapphire, tucked in a little pouch hidden in the folds of her sari. She could not afford to risk her chances of meeting her mother due to a schoolgirl feud. Baby Vi gurgled at her, as though she was advising her to do the right thing.

She made up her mind and looked up at Pooja. Pooja was still staring dumbly after Guruma. Abi held out her hand. 'We don't have to be the best of friends, but we can try not to be enemies. Are you ok with that?'

Pooja turned and looked at Abi for a long moment. Then she held her own hand out. 'Yes, we can at least try. I am sure Guruma will reconsider once she sees that we are trying our best.' Sumathy and Arundhati looked relieved and shook each other's hands, and then all the girls turned and walked towards the practice stage a bit more genially.

———

Days turned to weeks, weeks to months. Guruma had been difficult to convince but after much pleading had come back to teach the girls. The girls were working harder than they ever had in their lives. In Gurukul, students were expected to pitch in with chores such as cleaning and cooking. The four girls were no exception, despite their training schedule. They were practising dance for over eight hours every day and then using the rest of their waking hours to cram in studies and chores. They found respite only at night and during meditation.

———

One day, Guruma summoned all of them to her room in the afternoon. They were joined by Guru Uma and a number of members of the school's orchestra. 'I am very pleased with the progress the four of you have made so far. I am also satisfied that you're not fighting with each other all the time. So, I think you are nearly ready for the festival. I wanted to introduce you to the orchestra. Arun will be on the mridangam and Shishupal will play the violin. Sundar will provide the vocals. And I will provide the nattuvangam, the cymbals that will give you the dance beat. Guru Uma will join us as general support.' The girls looked happily at the orchestra and at each other. Guruma had chosen the best musicians for the festival.

'For the next two weeks, you will do your entire practice in full costume. You will do your hair, make-up and wear your dance outfits for all rehearsals. This will get you used to your accessories and clothes. And yes, you can bring all the various make-up items you've created using your grandma's ancient recipes!' Guruma smiled at Sumathy. 'In two weeks' time, we set off for Konark. It will be a three-day journey. You will then have one week there to practise before the festival begins. Now, I want to talk to each of you alone about what you need to focus on and improve.'

Abi and Sumathy swapped notes later that night on what Guruma had told each of them. 'She wanted me to focus on my arms and the sharpness of my movements. She asked me to increase my exercise routine and suggested that I get you to observe me,' said Sumathy with a sigh. 'More work!'

Abi smiled at her then said, 'I am not sure what to make of Guruma's words to me. She asked me to increase my meditation time. I nearly started arguing with her on this point – this would take away time from dance practice, I said. But she quelled me with a look and would not say any more. What do you think she meant?'

Sumathy shrugged her shoulders. 'I think you should just do what she says. I'm sure she knows what she's talking about.'

Abi frowned and looked unsure as they turned out the light and went to bed. 'I am not sure I can afford to sacrifice my practice time for meditation. I'll pretend that I've done it but continue practising,' said Abi softly to herself.

17

BEAUTIFUL KONARK

It was a strange group that made its way to the railway station, comprising four very excited schoolgirls, two teachers and a motley crew of men carrying various musical instruments. They had spent most of the day travelling down to the nearest town, and now they were due to take a train to Konark. The adults looked tired but the girls' excitement and curiosity were palpable.

Abi looked around the station, absorbing every bit of the scene around her. There were little stalls selling magazines and multi-coloured packets of crisps and biscuits. A wizened old man was frying some delicious-looking but probably very unhygienic goodies in a large wok in a corner. There were a lot of people milling around, some waiting for their trains, others looking to buy eatables at the stalls. Porters in red uniforms rushed past with suitcases and bags balanced precariously on their heads. Their train pulled into the station just then, and Guruma ushered all of them to their compartment. There was a mad but brief scramble to find their seats.

———⌘———

The train journey was wonderful. Guru Uma got the girls together to play a version of dumb charades using dance moves. The orchestra joined in and it was a marvellous game. A while into the train journey, Guruma started unwrapping packages of food that had been made up for them especially for this leg of the journey. 'Is it me or does everything taste so much better when you're eating it on a train?' remarked Arundhati, chewing on a *kachori*, a fried Indian dumpling with a spiced onion stuffing. There were *kachoris*, batter-fried vegetable *pakoras* of different kinds, a mixture of spiced nuts, cardamom-flavoured Indian sweets and a large variety of fruit.

Ever since Guruma's ultimatum, the girls had made a real effort to get along. Pooja even grudgingly admired Abi's performances during rehearsal, much to Abi's surprise. Arundhati and Sumathy got along well anyway, and Abi had to reluctantly admit that all their dance practices were much more enjoyable than before. The girls helped themselves to some delightful snacks, played games and chattered away in the train until it was night-time and Guru Uma sternly told them to go to sleep. 'Oh, Guruji, I wish you had brought Vi with you. She encourages me so when she's watching me dance,' sighed Abi, who was missing baby Vi's constant company.

Guru Uma made a moue. 'It's hard enough looking after you lot! She will be fine in Gurukul. Guru Usha will have her work cut out,' she added with a wicked grin. 'The journey continues for another day and a half – at this rate, you'll exhaust all topics and tire yourselves out on the first day itself. Come on; go to sleep!'

———⚬≫⚬———

Guru Uma's dire predictions did not come true –the girls had enough to talk about, and by the time they reached Konark, they had taken their dance dumb charades to a new level. Various people from other compartments kept dropping in to talk to Guruma. She did not introduce any of them to the girls as they were quite caught up in their game, but Guru Uma did slip out several times to shake hands or to touch someone's feet. Abi found this latter habit a curious one, since she had never seen anything like it in the UK.

'In India, we touch people's feet to show them respect,' explained Sumathy in response to Abi's quizzical look.

'There are many famous dancers and musicians on the train. They are going to Konark as well,' said Guru Uma to the girls. 'You will meet them when we reach the place.'

Abi kept an eye out to try and assess the other artistes and dancers who came to meet her teachers through the journey. One particular man caught her attention. He was a tall Westerner with a wide smile and greenish-brown eyes that twinkled with mischief. *His accent sounds Irish. I wonder who he is!* thought Abi.

———⚬≫⚬———

They reached Konark early the next morning. The small town was already buzzing with activity and Abi could feel strange electricity in the air. Winter had arrived, and although Konark did not get very cold, there was a pleasant chill in the air. 'There are many sights to see in this ancient town. And there's the sea nearby as well,' said Guruma with a smile.

All the dancers had been provided with accommodation in a little village consisting of small mud huts with basic facilities. The four girls were to share a hut and the orchestra, another. The two teachers had little huts of their own. After a wash and change, the girls eagerly joined the rest of the group for breakfast. 'We will first go and see the glorious Sun Temple. It is sheer poetry carved in stone. You will love it,' said Guruma. 'Sadly, the weather has been getting worse with global warming, as you all know! But they're doing a great job in preserving this ancient building despite all the rain and storms.'

The Sun Temple was indeed poetry in stone! It had been created in the thirteenth century in the shape of a horse-drawn chariot to pay homage to the sun god.

The temple had been carved exquisitely – the girls looked around in awe at the chariot that was pulled by seven stone horses and the various intricately carved figures of animals and men all around. Abi had never seen such an imposing building. Guru Uma pointed out the stage at the entrance to the sun temple. 'This will be decorated in a few days. You will dance there.'

Ahead of the stage was a set of stalls selling miniature sculptures of the temple. The girls browsed through these, and Sumathy and Pooja bought themselves a miniature chariot, while Abi purchased a minutely carved small stone wheel. 'It is very well-maintained. And the surrounding area is so lovely as well,' Abi said admiringly.

'Yes, Abi – it is a World Heritage site now. They work hard to preserve it properly. And the dance festival lends it a real prestige. It is a big tourist attraction, and rightly so,' replied Guruma.

The girls were then taken round to visit a few other temples and attractions nearby and finally made their way to the beach. 'The sea is so calm – I thought it would be much more powerful,' said Sumathy. She had never been to the seaside before and did not quite know what to expect.

Guruma smiled enigmatically. 'Don't be fooled by the calm on the surface. There is more power in there than you can imagine. When the sea rises up and shows its might, it is truly fearsome!' Abi tried to imagine the sea rising, remembering stories of Poseidon from Greek mythology, but the gentle ripples, squelchy sand and the sun shining on a lazy blue surface inspired more joy than fear.

It was past lunchtime when they got back to the dance village. The orchestra had stayed back as they had been to Konark before. The girls met them in the large hall in the centre of the village where tea was being served. The hall was moderately crowded. 'These are the other dancers and troupes. Come, let us introduce you. If Guruma introduces someone as a respected guru or teacher, you must touch his or her feet,' said Guru Uma.

Guruma introduced them to a number of different

artistes. They were all famous and came from various parts of India and specialised in different Indian dances. Abi was struggling to keep up with the names. Guru Samahit Mahapatra, the famous Odissi exponent; Guru Rajalakshmi Santhanam, another Bharatanatyam dancer from the south; Guru Mahaveer Sharma, the famous Kathak teacher; Guru Priyanka Rao who danced Kuchipudi; Guru Niveditha Nair, the Mohiniattam specialist, were just some of the names. Abi had been taught about the different Indian classical dances but soon found her head whirling with information about the dancers and their schools.

Finally, she was introduced to the Irishman who had caught her eye in the train. 'This is Professor John Dreelan. He has been studying Indian classical dance for many years and is an absolute expert on the theory and history behind our dance,' said Guruma, greeting him warmly.

The professor extended his hand in greeting. 'Call me John. I am really looking forward to seeing you dance,' he smiled.

There were many small stages that had been built around the village for the dancers to practise on, and the girls soon found themselves one. Some members of their orchestra joined them for the rehearsal. Shishupal was missing. A frown clouded Guru Uma's features as she noticed him missing. 'Where is he? He has no discipline at all,' she said. Abi knew that wasn't being fair – he was just a young, fun-loving boy and had probably lost track of time.

Sundar and Arun looked shamefacedly at the teacher

and mumbled, 'He has not been well since lunch. He is sleeping; he should be better tomorrow.' Guru Uma's frown did not leave her forehead all through practice.

———∞∞∞———

The girls gathered round the stage early the next morning to start their rehearsals in earnest. Guru Uma was almost foaming at the mouth in anger when she saw only two members of the orchestra present. Even Guruma looked troubled when Sundar informed her that Shishupal was still suffering from a stomach ache. 'We took him to the doctor early in the morning, but it looks like he is going to be out of commission for a while. We may have to send him back home.' The girls cast worried glances at each other – it was absolutely essential to have an instrument like the violin or flute to accompany the drums and vocals. Without this, their orchestra would be incomplete and their dance items lacklustre.

'You seem worried. Can I help?' said a gentle voice behind them. Guru Samahit Mahapatra had wandered up to them to enquire. His troupe was practising on the adjacent stage. A thin, old man with a salt-and-pepper beard that matched his salt-and-pepper hair, he had a calm, beatific expression on his face. Guruma explained their problem to him. 'Is that all? Do not worry. I have an extra member in my orchestra. Dhruva plays the flute excellently and he has worked with Bharatanatyam dancers before. Although he is not South Indian, he is very familiar with South Indian Carnatic music. I can lend him to you if you like.'

This was an instant answer to their prayers. Guruma accepted gratefully, and Guru Samahit called out to Dhruva to introduce him. Dhruva was a clean-shaven young boy with long, oily hair swept back, set against dark skin. He was wearing dark glasses. 'Dhruva cannot see, so his sense of hearing and hence his sense of music are even more enhanced!' Guru Samahit said proudly, as he clapped the boy on his back. Abi had been told that Guru Samahit was a master flutist. He clearly considered Dhruva his protégé.

Guruma welcomed him warmly and introduced him to the girls. Abi stared at Dhruva. There was something vaguely familiar about him, but though she racked her brains, she could just not place him. The rehearsal began and Dhruva easily integrated with the orchestra. Abi had heard the flute being played before thanks to Krish. However, Dhruva's music was much more classical and its melody seemed magical. As Abi danced to the soothing strains of the flute, she closed her eyes and thought of her mother. She was acutely aware of how close she was to her goal of reaching her in heaven. If she danced well enough, she would be so close to the prize! She smiled as she danced… her plan was in full swing!

18

THE FESTIVAL

The festival drew closer and the practice sessions continued with full gusto. A small group always gathered to watch when either Pooja or Abi practised their solo dances. 'You are the best dancer in the festival,' Sumathy whispered in admiration after Abi had put up a particularly good performance. But Abi knew otherwise – she had been paying attention to Pooja's dance and realised how experience counted. The day before, an incident had brought this fact home to her. Abi had been practising for a while and was very pleased that it was going well. She could see that Guruma was satisfied. Suddenly, her earring came off – it had been a bit wobbly that morning when she'd worn it, and a vigorous movement had brought it down on the stage. As the music continued, Abi found it very hard to concentrate on the dance and the rest of her performance fell apart in a distracted mess.

Pooja was on next and Abi sat down to watch her graceful dance. The dance continued elegantly; but near the end, Pooja's anklet shattered. Beads flew across the stage; but Abi watched in awe as Pooja continued her dance as if nothing had happened. Her awe increased when she learnt later that Pooja had cut her feet on the shattered beads and had bled quite badly.

Guru Uma took Abi aside later that day. 'You saw Pooja's focus even when she lost the anklet. You must try developing that. Things can go wrong on stage, but how you react is the most important thing.' Abi knew then that Pooja's stage experience made her a much better dancer; but this event only served to increase Abi's determination to improve her own performance.

———

The village was abuzz with activity the day before the festival. Bright yellow garlands of marigold adorned the stages. There were tiny oil lamps near all the huts, casting a festive look on the whole village. The girls had made another trip to the Konark temple and found that the dance stage there was heavily decorated with flowers and lamps. Seats were arranged neatly for the audience, and a tent had been put up to serve as a temporary green room or make-up room. Abi smiled as she thought of Sumathy's make-up bag. Her friend was almost as excited about getting ready as she was about the dance.

Abi had wandered away from the rest and was admiring the beauty of the main temple when she heard a soft voice behind her. 'Is it magnificent? I have heard so much about it, but I can't begin to imagine what it looks like,' the voice said. Abi turned to see Dhruva standing beside her. She smiled at him. The group had warmed to him very quickly. He was pleasant, friendly and incredibly talented.

Abi often thought wistfully of her little friend Krish's flute-playing when she heard Dhruva practising. 'Yes, it is very imposing. I do admire their craftsmanship, and given it was built centuries ago, they would have done it without the tools and equipment that we have in modern construction nowadays! I really admire the artists who created this… but you're a great artiste yourself, I'm sure you can imagine its glory!'

Dhruva gave her a dazzling smile. 'I know you are a great dancer, too, Abi. I cannot see you but can hear the rhythm in your feet. You have never slipped up once. Do you want to win very badly?'

Abi hesitated – the only person that she had confided in so far was Sumathy. But there was something very magnetic about Dhruva's personality, and she suddenly wanted to tell him everything. She was not quite sure where to begin as it was such a long story. 'Well, you see, my friend Sumathy has convinced me that an ancient myth is true and as per that, this year, the sun god will appear in front of the winner and grant her a wish. I am absolutely desperate for a wish.'

Dhruva laughed. 'Aren't we all? What's your wish?' He paused as she shuffled her feet. 'You don't have to tell me if you don't want to.'

Abi smiled at him – she liked him and decided to trust him in that moment. 'Nothing like that. Not sure you'd believe me, though. I want to go and see my mother in heaven. I have one little thing that would help me, but I think Surya will be able to guide me towards some magic steps that I need to climb to get to her. Without his help, I don't know if I can reach her.' To her consternation, Dhruva became very quiet and thoughtful, and Abi started wondering whether he thought that she was making up tall tales.

'Abi, Dhruva, come, we have to go,' Guruma called out. Abi was surprised to see Guruma at the temple suddenly but then realised that she was probably keeping a closer eye on the girls as the festival drew nearer. She quietly started walking towards Guruma.

Dhruva put his hand on her arm. 'I believe that you have a real reason to win, Abi. I wish you all the very best!' Abi turned and looked at his face. It was very hard to make out any emotion behind the dark glasses that he always wore. But he broke into a dazzling smile and held his hand out to Abi, who grinned happily. She felt as if she had made another good friend. She took his hand and walked back with Guruma to the dance village.

——

The festival was due to last three days. The first day consisted of an opening ceremony – all the dance schools were performing group dances that day. These dances would not be judged for the award; however, they would be watched by the largest audience and the reputations of the schools were at stake. The second day consisted of individual dance items by nearly twenty- five dancers. At the end of the day, just before midnight, results would be announced as to how many dancers had made it to the finals. Traditionally, only four dancers made the cut. The last day consisted of the final dances, and then there was a grand ceremony to award the winner the prize, which consisted of a statue and scholarship money for further dance education.

Abi woke up on the first day of the festival with a swooping feeling in her stomach. The earring incident in the rehearsal had shaken her confidence. She remembered Guruma's advice about meditation and spent the next hour doing yoga and meditation, both of which calmed her down. *Abi, this may be your only chance to dance in such unique surroundings. Do it for the experience and don't worry about the result. Enjoy the ride,* Abi told herself again and again. She repeated Akash's Sanskrit *shloka* to herself several times before joining her classmates and teachers for breakfast. The mantra always made her feel at peace and in control. The girls had their final rehearsal that morning, after which they had to start getting ready for the opening ceremony that afternoon.

The girls started getting ready. Their costumes were beautiful – made of colourful silk with gold brocade borders. They had all been able to choose their favourite colours. Pooja's was orange with a deep blue border. Arundhati wore a bottle green outfit embroidered with gold. Sumathy's costume was very fetching; it was deep red and had a bright yellow contrasting border. Abi had chosen a white outfit with a bright blue border. It was very unusual as nobody else was wearing white, and she stood out in the crowd. They took their time to get their make-up on and plait their hair into the elaborate hairstyle that was traditionally worn by dancers. Sumathy helped Abi with her make-up, and even Abi had to admit that her grandma's make-up formula was first class as she added the finishing touches to Abi's glowing face. Abi wore her jewellery and stared at her painted face in the mirror. A few years back, she would never have guessed that she would one day be dressed like this and dance in front of a large audience. She wished her father and her sister could have been here to see her performance – her life had changed beyond imagination, and she desperately wished she could have shared it with her family. She closed her eyes and prayed to her mother on an impulse. 'I hope I can make you proud today!'

The opening ceremony was very grand and a number of speeches were made. The girls were ready, and although they were hearing the speeches, none of them was paying any attention. Abi smiled absent-mindedly as Professor Dreelan's Irish twang reached her ears. The excitement and apprehension she felt drowned out any speech. The performances began and were well received by the audience, whose applause resonated in the ancient temple and encouraged all the dancers.

Finally, it was time for the girls to perform their group item. Abi noticed the anxious look on Guru Uma's face as they took to the stage. But Guruma had a calm, confident air about her as if she knew her girls would do a great job – and they did! In the past, during all of their rehearsals, something had always gone wrong. Once, Arundhati had lost her beat; and another time, Sumathy had made a big mistake in her steps. Even Pooja and Abi had slipped up a couple of times. But this time, everyone was perfect. They were incredibly well coordinated and knew instinctively that it was their best performance yet. The girls were thrilled to have a standing ovation from the audience. Abi smiled as she looked at Sumathy's shining face. She wanted it to go well particularly for her best friend as this was the only chance Sumathy would have here on stage.

—⚬∞⚬—

The competition began on a fierce note the next day. As Pooja and Abi's performances were scheduled only in the evening, they spent the morning watching some of the other dances. Pooja turned a sombre face towards Abi. 'The competition is very tough this year. I have not seen such complicated and competent performances ever!' Abi nodded in agreement. Some of the girls had clearly taken their choreography to a totally different level. 'I hope my performance matches up,' she said, more to herself than Abi.

'I am sure you will do very well, Pooja; all the very best.' Pooja looked surprised on hearing this for a minute, but then she smiled and wished Abi good luck as well.

After lunch, as the girls began to get ready, Guruma took Abi aside to talk to her. 'Did you practise meditation as I had asked you to, child?'

Abi looked sheepish. 'No, Guruma. I did not initially; but in the last few days, I have started doing more meditation, and I can see that it's helping me. It particularly helped me yesterday.'

Guruma smiled. 'I am not going to chide you for not obeying me from the start, but I am so happy that you have seen the benefits. I think you would have been able to deal with the loss of your earring on stage better had you done this from the start. But it is not too late.' Abi nodded. She was ashamed that she had not believed Guruma's recommendation initially, and as if to compensate for it, spent the next half an hour meditating before putting on her make-up. She changed into a new costume of sunshine yellow – her tribute to the sun god.

⚬⚬⚬

Maybe it was the meditation or the wonderful ancient location or the electric atmosphere on stage that helped Abi that day. She was very calm and collected as she took to the stage. It was as if everyone was willing her to do well – the flute had never been more melodious, the drums so rhythmic and the vocals so pleasing. As was her norm, she closed her eyes just before the dance began and imagined herself to truly become the character she was playing in the dance. She put in all the energy and focus that was humanly possible into her dance and gave a flawless performance. While she whirled around the stage, she did not think about her mother, the sapphire still tucked away in her sari, or the seven magic steps. She got lost in the hypnotic melody of the flute and

174

forgot about the audience and the competition – she only thought about her dance and really felt the emotions that the character was going through in that performance. The sun was setting and the whole stage lit up in its orange glow. When she finished, there was pin-drop silence for a few moments. Guruma's eyes were glistening. The audience exploded in applause.

When Abi got off the stage, she was greeted by Professor Dreelan. 'You were amazing, Abi!' he exclaimed. 'It was picture-perfect. In one of my books, I have written about the perfect dance, the one that Shiva danced in the heavens. You were dancing that perfect dance, too.' Abi was a bit embarrassed by his exuberance and blushed a bright pink. She liked his enthusiasm and his open, direct style. His twinkling eyes put her at ease. He had raised her spirits with his appreciation of her dance.

Pooja and the other dancers followed Abi's performance, but none got the kind of ovation that Abi received. Abi watched Pooja's performance, admiring her grace, and then retired to the green room to remove her make-up; just then, she heard a pathetic sobbing from outside the tent. She walked out to see Pooja sitting under a tree, sobbing her heart out. 'What is it? What happened?' Abi exclaimed.

It was strange and heart-wrenching to see the normally confident Pooja crying copious tears, make-up running down her cheeks. 'I... will... not... be... in the finals...!' Pooja sobbed.

'Why do you say that? The results will be announced only at midnight. I watched you dance. You were wonderful, as usual.'

Pooja wiped her tears away fiercely, controlled her sobs and looked at Abi with a strange ferocity in her eyes. 'I performed a good dance item. But you were absolutely spectacular. They are bound to choose you, and I don't think they'll select two dancers from the same school.'

Abi disagreed. 'I don't believe that for a minute. If we are both good, they have to take us both. Besides, this is not the end of the world, Pooja. You're crying as if disaster of the worst order has struck you!'

Pooja turned her face away, fiercely. 'This is my only dream. All my life I have dreamt of being in the final of the Konark Dance Festival. To be ousted at this stage is no less than a calamity for me. To be in the finals is everything I have ever wanted.' Abi watched helplessly as she broke down again, crying as if her heart would break. Arundhati must have seen the two of them together, for she walked up to them with her face concerned. Abi left her to console Pooja and walked back to the green room, disturbed and upset at seeing a normally confident and cocky Pooja lose all hope.

19

THE FINALISTS

As she walked out of the green room, she heard someone call out her name. 'Abi, there you are! Can you come with me, please?' Abi started and was surprised to see Professor Dreelan standing there. 'I have been searching for you for a while!' There was a mischievous smile on his lips when he asked Abi to follow him to the judges' tent. Heart thumping with excitement, Abi followed him into the tent.

There were a number of people seated behind a long table. She recognised Guru Samahit in the crowd. Guruma was among them, too; but to Abi's consternation, she looked grim. The main judge of the competition was Professor Hari Tagore, a great scholar and dance critic. He was a legendary dancer who had lost his legs in an accident and now concentrated on teaching and ran a famous dance school. The professor was nearly bald with a crescent of grizzled white hair. His deep brown skin, hooked nose and large eyes reminded Abi of a character from a book that she used to read in England. He smiled at Abi.

'Abi, you dance very well. I have yet to see a dancer so wrapped up in her performance. You were almost in a trance. Am I right in saying that you were so lost in your dance that you couldn't even see the audience?' Abi nodded. 'Good, good. That's the mark of a great dancer – one who dances to an ever-pervasive audience. We enjoyed it, too. Young lady, we would like to offer you a place in the finals. It has been much harder this year and we are only selecting four dancers. You are one of them.'

Abi's face brightened up instantly. 'Thank you, sir. That is wonderful!' she exclaimed. Then a sudden realisation hit her. 'What about Pooja? Has she been selected too?'

Professor Tagore glanced at the others before replying. 'I am sorry, Abi. That's not something that we can share with you yet. You will have to wait and see! You shouldn't discuss this with any of your friends; they need to wait for the ceremony. We are only calling the finalists and telling them the result separately before the announcement. In fact, you're one of the last ones to be told.' Abi left with mixed feelings. She was delighted that she had made it to the finals, but she wasn't sure what that meant for Pooja. Pooja's tears meant that she hadn't been called in by the judges. She had known Pooja to be strong, confident and very talented. Although all through last year, she had often wished to beat Pooja in the one competition that would matter most to her, Abi had never actually meant to hurt her. Having seen her outburst earlier, Abi was convinced that Pooja would take the news very badly.

John Dreelan followed her out of the tent. 'Why are you so morose? You should be looking like the cat that's got the cream!' Abi looked at him pensively. Here was a perfect stranger – should she pour out her difficulties to him? Then something told her that his would be the most objective advice she might get. Sumathy was bound to take her side, and Arundhati would take Pooja's side. If she had been at school, she'd have sought out her friend Krish for advice. And before that, she would have always asked her father, who could be totally unbiased and objective. But then, John did not know much about her, and that might be an advantage in this instance. She drew a deep breath and told him about Pooja's breakdown.

'Abi, hand on heart, tell me what kind of a person Pooja is. Is she someone wonderful, gentle and kind?'

Abi shook her head. 'She's a great dancer but she's very spoilt and proud and often not very nice to others.'

John looked into her eyes gravely. 'Pride comes before a fall, they say. The lessons you learn when you're young help you develop into a much better person later on. Some children have always been given whatever they've asked for. They never learn the value of earning something and the lessons that failure teaches you. This is a good opportunity for her to get a valuable lesson in life. I wouldn't worry about it if I were you – this is actually good for her!' He winked and smiled and walked away. Abi looked doubtfully after him.

There was only half an hour left before the results were announced. She missed her father more than anything at this moment. She wished she could speak to him or even to Krish, for just a minute. Her head muddled with conflicting thoughts, Abi walked slowly towards the stage and sought out Sumathy, who was sitting in the audience watching some ad-hoc performances. Abi had no intention of sharing recent incidents with her – she knew she would not understand her feelings. Her loyalty to her best friend would prevent her from empathising with Pooja.

'Where have you been? I have been looking for you everywhere!' Sumathy said, her eyes glued to the stage. Abi made a non-committal remark. 'Hush! The presentation is starting.' Abi looked around and found Pooja and Arundhati in the row behind them. Pooja gave Abi a wan smile before shifting her focus to the stage. The stage was now being cleared to prepare for the presentation ceremony. Abi felt awkward sitting there, so close to Pooja, when she knew full well that it might be bad news for her.

The presentation began soon. Professor Tagore smiled at the audience. 'We have seen some remarkable dancing today. The performances have been absolutely exhilarating. I think all the judges agree with me that the standard of dance this year has been beyond anything we have ever seen.' He paused and looked around.

'He looks like an old vulture with his hooked nose – though he does have a kindly face,' whispered Sumathy.

The professor continued. 'After careful consideration, the judges have unanimously agreed on the names of the finalists. I will now read them out in no particular order and request the dancers and their gurus to join me on stage. Odissi dancer Indu Tripathi and her guru, Samahit Mahapatra; Kuchipudi dancer Mohan Shetty with his guru, Priyanka Rao; Kathak dancer Namita Swarup and her guru, Mahaveer Sharma.'

Abi felt a sinking feeling in her stomach as he paused and looked at the audience. The professor started talking again. 'The sheer brilliance demonstrated by the artistes this year has made this a very special year. And we also agreed that no one deserves a place more than our last finalist. Could I ask Bharatanatyam dancer Abirami Forbes to join us on stage, with Guru Shakuntala Devi, please?'

Abi sat in silence while the audience turned around to look at her and clap her on. 'Go, Abi. They are waiting for you,' Sumathy said, shaking with excitement. Abi slowly walked up to the stage in a daze. She carefully avoided looking at Pooja but was glad to notice that Guruma was smiling proudly at her. John Dreelan was standing with the other judges and gave Abi a smile.

Professor Tagore addressed the audience. 'Well, ladies and gentlemen, this is all for today. Our four finalists will perform several dances tomorrow. They will be judged on their grace, precision, beauty of form, focus and complexity of their choreography. I predict that this will be a final like no other. As this is the Sun Festival, the dances will go on all day, starting at midday, and all night. The winner will be announced after a prayer at sunrise the day after tomorrow.'

Abi walked down from the stage and was greeted by an excited Sumathy. Her eyes sought Pooja but couldn't see her. She absent-mindedly gave Sumathy a hug and walked away to try and think a bit. She was delighted to have a place in the finals but strangely, she was also upset because Pooja's dreams had been shattered. A soft voice shook her out of her reverie. 'Abi, congratulations; and well done!' Dhruva was walking slowly towards her.

'How did you know it was me?' demanded Abi, laughing. She was constantly amazed at how perceptive he was.

'I use my hearing and sense of smell much more than any of you do. And my instinct, too; and my instinct is telling me that all's not well. Is something wrong?' Abi hesitated. Dhruva reminded her so much of Krish that she decided to confide in him. She rattled off the whole story, starting with Pooja's upset, then the events in the judges' tent and John's advice to her. Dhruva listened quietly to everything she had to say and remained thoughtful for a few moments after she had finished her tale.

'So, where are you off to now?'

Abi scuffed her feet uneasily in the sand. 'I was wondering if I should tell Guruma that I want to give my place up for Pooja. That would be the best way out for all,' said Abi, not sounding convinced.

Dhruva chuckled. 'So, you will make the great sacrifice! Do you think that will truly make you feel better? In fact, I think it will frustrate you from inside. Giving up what is rightfully yours is a choice you make,

Abi. But if you make this choice for the wrong reasons, you will never be happy. I agree with the professor – Pooja has much to learn in life. You shouldn't be the person stopping her learning a valuable lesson. Don't pretend to be a saint; you'll only be bitter and angry with Pooja for the rest of your life. You may think you're being Miss Goody Two-Shoes by doing that, but I can bet that it won't help Pooja – she's a proud girl, she needs to feel that she's won it fair and square.' He turned around and started walking slowly towards the dispersing audience. Abi stared at him for a while and then decided to join him. There was a smile playing on Dhruva's lips that Abi had failed to notice.

Abi couldn't sleep that night – she was still racked with guilt and was sure that Pooja was sobbing her heart out somewhere as she hadn't come back to their hut. Finally, she walked out and sat under a tree, staring at the stars in the sky. She felt very lonely and very unhappy. She looked up as a figure walked up to her. 'Congratulations, Abi!' Pooja's voice was subdued and she looked as if she had been crying, but she gave Abi a tired smile and sat down beside her.

'Pooja – I am so sorry,' Abi began, but Pooja cut her short.

'Don't worry about it; you were much better than I was and the best dancer deserves the place.' Abi stared anxiously at Pooja. She couldn't believe that she was taking it so calmly. Pooja seemed to understand Abi's unasked question. 'I was very upset at first, but then Guruma came to talk to me. We spoke for a very long time and she helped me accept the situation. I think I have been too proud, too confident and I did not continually work to improve my performance, unlike you. I am not happy but I understand it better and accept it now.'

Abi looked pensively at her and hesitantly voiced her deepest thoughts. 'Would you be happier if I gave up my place for you?'

Pooja stared at Abi in horror. 'No, of course not!' she said, fiercely. 'Abi, I wanted to get to the finals on the strength of my performance! Not through someone else's charity. I could never be happy – even if you hid the fact that you gave up your place, I would know I just hadn't done well enough.' Then she calmed down and gave Abi a watery smile. 'It is quite sweet of you to even want to do such a thing for me – especially when I've been so mean to you in the past. You are a lovely person and I'd like to be your friend.' She held out her hand and looked at Abi seriously.

'Of course, Pooja – you are my friend!' said Abi, grasping her hand.

Pooja grinned. 'Listen, now that I am out of the competition, it is up to you to make it to the top. You have to get Gurukul's name up there.'

Abi looked at Pooja's earnest face and beamed. 'Thanks, Pooja! I will do my best, for all of us!'

Abi returned to bed, feeling relieved and much happier.

20

THE WINNER IS ANNOUNCED

All of Konark was alive with excitement at the finals. Many in the audience were regular visitors to the dance festival – all of them agreed that this year had surpassed all previous years. Everyone sat entranced through the performances. The four finalists alternated with each other and danced specially selected items that showcased their skills. Some items focussed on facial expressions, others were devoted to beauty of form, and yet others were a mixture of all the attributes of a great dancer. Each item was well appreciated and applauded by the audience. The sun shone brightly in a cloudless sky throughout the course of the day – it was as if Surya himself had no intention of missing any of the dances.

Lamps were lit as the sun set in the evening, and the dancers continued, their energy undiminished. There were gaps provided in the programme for lunch and dinner. It was a tribute to all the dancers that the audience sat and watched the whole programme, taking hardly any breaks. Abi enjoyed performing her items as much as the audience enjoyed watching her. Her guilt had vanished and had been replaced by a sense of relief after talking to Pooja the previous night. She felt an incredible buzz when she danced on stage. She danced like she had never danced before. She completely lost herself in her art – she imagined that she was dancing on that rocky stage in the forest, in the presence of the mountains, the sun, the wind and all her animal friends. Some of her dance moves were more complicated than anything anyone else attempted, but she was able to deliver a flawless performance each time. The audience marvelled at her delightful expressions and remarked how she brought the meanings of the songs truly alive. The orchestra was superlative – Dhruva's flute and the perfect drum beats seemed to contribute to her incredible energy levels that night. The notes reverberated on the ancient sun temple walls that added a depth and echo to it.

At the end of her last dance, Abi smiled and bowed to the audience's uproarious ovation. She thought of her family at that moment – she missed her father and Vy more than ever. *I wish they were here to cheer me. That would have been so magical.*

The final dance had now been completed. The inky-blue sky was turning brighter and the sun was about to rise. Once in twelve years, a special tribute was paid to the sun god, and a big prayer and meditation session was held at sunrise. The priests had arrived with their paraphernalia and they now occupied the stage. Professor

Tagore took to the stage and explained the process to the audience. 'As is the practice, once in twelve years, we perform the Maha Surya Namaskar ceremony at sunrise. The priests will chant Sanskrit *shlokas* and my student Kamakshi will take to the stage and demonstrate the physical steps of the Surya Namaskar. I would request everyone in the audience to please stand and follow her. After it is complete, everyone should sit down cross-legged and close their eyes in meditation. The whole sequence will take half an hour and we will indicate the end by ringing a bell. We will then announce the winner of the dance festival.'

Abi and the other girls stood in the last row, at some distance from everyone else. Kamakshi, a tall and graceful girl in a red sari, started demonstrating the Surya Namaskar – a salute to the sun. As Abi followed the steps, she felt a powerful energy in the atmosphere – it was as if warm air was flowing through her body. At the end of the salute, everyone sat down to meditate. When Abi closed her eyes, she could see an intense brightness all around her. It was as if a bright light was glowing in the distance. In her mind's eye, Abi saw herself walking towards this light. The light got brighter and brighter until it almost started hurting her eyes. She opened her eyes with a start and looked in amazement at the wonderful sight in front of her.

There was a very tall, handsome man sitting on a golden chariot drawn by seven white horses. He was dressed in shimmering yellow silks and wore a golden crown. He smiled brightly at her. His whole body glowed as if it were made with burnished gold. There was a delicious warmth in the air around her, and Abi gasped in the realisation that she was in the presence of Surya. While she had started to believe in the myth, it still amazed her that the story was true. She folded her hands in the classical Indian "Namaste" position in deference to the sun god. His voice was gentle, yet it penetrated her very being. 'Well done, Abi. You have danced incredibly well. You do your mother proud. As the best dancer, I would like to offer you a wish. Please ask me what your heart desires!'

Abi felt very small when she stood in front of Him in all his magnificence, and shyly asked for her dearest wish. 'I want to go to heaven to meet my mother.' When she saw him frown, she hastened to add, 'I believe that there are seven magic steps that I need to climb to reach heaven. I already have the magic sapphire in my possession to aid me. Could you please tell me where I can find these steps? I want to get there through my efforts and not just through a wish.'

Laughter echoed around her like gently pealing bells. 'Abi, I am pleased that you want to make the effort; but it is not "where", it is the "how" that you need. You have learnt that space and time are dimensions. There is another that man does not know much about – thought. Thought is another dimension that takes you places. And deeds are enablers of thoughts. The seven steps are Courage, Patience, Sacrifice, Focus, Trust, Contentment and Goodness. And you have already climbed one of the steps. Do you know which one?'

Abi looked blankly at Surya. 'Focus, of course. You focussed all your energies on improving your dance and learning all the things that were being thrown your way. It was a difficult journey for you and you started off not knowing anything about dance; and look where you have reached. Your determination and focus are commendable. Now all you need to do is to climb the other steps – and there are no clues. I have told you what the steps are. You have to find a way to do the deeds that will enable you to climb these steps spontaneously. If you try too hard and it is contrived, you will not succeed.'

Abi thanked him for explaining the path to heaven and Surya smiled once again. 'That was not much to ask for. You are a very special person. I want to give you a proper gift. In your quest, you will come across much darkness and it is easy to lose your way in the absence of light. I give you the ability to see in the darkest of places as if the sun were shining brightly. I give you the gift of special sight!'

Abi opened her eyes and found that she was still sitting in the audience with the others. A bell was tinkling away on stage and everyone was slowly coming out of meditation. Professor Tagore was back on stage. 'Ladies and gentlemen, the judges have made their decision. Each finalist should take immense pride in being selected to dance in the finals. It is no mean feat and all of them performed brilliantly. But in such a competition, only one person is crowned and invited to receive the award.' He looked around the audience. When his eyes rested on Abi, he gasped in astonishment. 'And it looks like Surya agrees with us. Abirami Forbes, please join us on stage to collect your award. You are the winner of the Sun Temple Dance Festival this year.'

There was a standing ovation from the audience as Abi walked up to the stage. When she climbed up, she realised that everyone in the audience was staring at her. There was a murmur of voices – people were whispering excitedly to each other. Abi wondered what it was all about. Even Professor Tagore seemed to be looking at her strangely. 'Abi, we can see that you've been in the presence of Surya,' said the professor.

'How could you know that?' Abi blurted out before she could help herself.

The professor chuckled. 'Firstly, it is because I believe in the tale that once every twelve years, the sun god appears to the winner. Secondly, you have to see yourself in the mirror! Have a look at the colour of your hair.' Abi pulled her plait forward and to her amazement, it was full of scintillating golden flecks. She looked at her hands to see that her brown colour had turned to a shiny bronze – the presence of Surya had left its impact on her.

Abi gave the still clapping audience a dazzling smile as she collected her award. It was an exquisitely crafted bronze statue of the sun temple with the date of the festival carved on it. 'In addition to this, Abi will receive a scholarship to further her dance education, and this will be paid directly to the school,' Professor Tagore told the audience. 'With this, I declare the festival formally closed. Thank you all for your presence and appreciation. We hope to see many, if not all of you, next year once again. Our best wishes and thanks to all the artistes and their teachers who have participated in this year's festival.'

Abi was joined by a jubilant Sumathy and Dhruva when she got off the stage. Arundhati and Pooja also joined them shortly and clapped her on her back. 'You did it, Abi – you did it for our school!' Abi was glad to see Pooja trying to look pleased, although she knew that she must be hurting inside. Spontaneously, Abi walked up to her and gave her a hug. Pooja was taken aback but seemed much happier after that.

The rest of the orchestra joined them and finally the gurus came over. Abi noticed Guruma quietly patting Pooja on the back. 'I think all of you have done brilliantly,' said Guruma, looking around her. 'I am proud of each and every one of you. We will be going back to Gurukul with our heads held high.'

21

PATIENCE

Life in school seemed tougher than ever when the girls returned from the festival. They had to work doubly hard to catch up with the studies that they had missed due to the competition. There were only a couple of months left for the school year to end, and Guruma had been very firm about the girls taking the exams just like the rest of the students. 'She did warn you that it is going to be difficult. You just have to work harder,' Guru Uma said when the girls complained about the pressure.

Of all the girls, Sumathy seemed to be taking all of it particularly badly. Even her grandmother's recipes were not interesting her any more. 'We don't even have the time to work out what to do about the seven steps,' she wailed to Abi at regular intervals.

Abi tried not to think about this fact and concentrated on trying to make sense of the copious amounts of lessons that they had to catch up on. 'Sumathy, we knew it would be tough. If we can't change it, we might as well go with the flow and do our best. Come on, you can do it,' Abi encouraged her best friend every time she panicked. Abi was coping much better with the workload, and she secretly attributed this to the fact that she was now meditating every day.

The four girls had become good friends after the experience at Konark. Pooja and Arundhati often joined Abi and Sumathy, and they became a foursome. They had also become very friendly with the orchestra. Dhruva had requested to join their troupe. 'I would like to learn more about Bharatanatyam. Please allow me to join your orchestra and learn for a year,' he had pleaded with Guruma. Abi felt that Guruma had seemed very uncomfortable and almost a bit uncharitable about it, but after much pressure from Guru Samahit and increasingly desperate pleas from Dhruva, she gave in.

Abi was delighted that he was joining them. Dhruva was friendly, pleasant and incredibly talented. She liked spending time with him, but the impending exams did not allow her to. He often asked her to take him to the ledge where she practised. She had taken great pains to describe the ledge and surroundings to him when they were in Konark, and he had seemed fascinated. 'One day, after the exams are over!' she promised. Abi was happy that at least one of the new friends she had made in Konark had been able to join her. She missed her other friend John's smiling face – she had been sad to say goodbye to him but had exchanged contact details and had promised that she would stay in touch.

Time flew and the girls soon had to sit for their exams. Abi found them more difficult than the previous year's but thought that she had done reasonably well. Pooja and Arundhati also seemed satisfied with their performance, but Sumathy was sure that she had done very badly and needed much consoling. The girls did very well in their dance practical exams. All the rehearsals for the dance festival had paid off.

A wave of relief swept over Abi. For the first time since their trip to Konark, she thought about family and friends. She had written a very short letter to her Aunt Jo just a few days ago, after receiving several letters from her enquiring about Abi's performance at the festival. Akash had also written, asking about her studies and dance, but she had not had the chance to respond to him yet. She decided to write long letters to both Jo and Akash right away and got busy with these. She thought about Jo's friend Varun and his green eyes, while writing to her aunt. In spite of suspecting that Varun was a shapeshifter who had nearly killed her to get the magic sapphire, Abi still found it hard to dislike him and often wondered wistfully where and how he was.

'How was it, Abi? How was your practical exam? Are they all over now?' Abi raised her head from the letter she was writing to see Dhruva standing outside her window.

'How did you know I was here?' she demanded curiously. She was forever amazed at Dhruva's ability to know where everyone was without the gift of sight.

'I met Sumathy who said you'd gone back to your room, and I could hear you scribbling as I walked past the window. You must be relieved that the exams are over. Now will you take me to the stage?'

Abi smiled at his earnest face. 'Of course. Come on; let's go now.'

She put the letters away, took Dhruva's hand and led him through the forest towards her secret stage. Abi faithfully described all the flora and fauna around them as they walked through the trees. 'It seems quieter and more sombre than usual in the forest today,' she said, 'but that could be because I haven't been here for a while and I may be imagining it.' They were approaching the heart of the forest when they heard the delicate strains of the flute. 'That must be Krish!' Abi exclaimed, her eyes gleaming in delight. 'He's my little friend from the village. I'd love to introduce you to him. He also plays the flute. I haven't seen him in ages!'

Abi was so thrilled at the prospect of meeting her young friend that she did not notice Dhruva's discomfort and hesitation. She was walking fast, taking long strides towards the sound of the flute when she realised that Dhruva was no longer with her. She turned around. He was hanging back, looking unhappy.

'Are you all right? What's wrong?'

Dhruva slowly shook his head. 'I am not sure your friend will like me. Maybe you should go on your own.'

'Nonsense!' said Abi. 'Why should he not like you? Come on; you have to come with me. I insist.' Abi took his hand and ushered him forward.

'Abi, is that you?' Krish's sweet voice came from behind the trees.

Abi rushed towards Krish and gave him a big hug. 'Yes, it's me. It has been so long. I won the competition,

Krish! We all did well. I wanted to tell you, but we had to work terribly hard for the exams. How are you?' Abi said, noticing her friend's slightly sad expression.

'I am ok. I am missing my father a bit as he and the other villagers have gone to town to the market. Bal has also gone with them. I wanted to go with him, but he said I was too young and it was too dangerous nowadays!' Krish scowled then laughed as he looked at Abi's concerned face. 'I'm just being childish. I am so happy for you. I knew you'd do well. You look like you've been close to Surya – you're baked golden brown!' he exclaimed. 'Who is your friend?' he asked, noticing Dhruva for the first time.

Abi introduced the boys. 'Dhruva plays the flute, too. He was brilliant at the festival. The two of you must play together one day.' In her excitement at meeting Krish, Abi had not noticed that neither Krish nor Dhruva looked happy at the thought of playing together, or even pleased to meet each other. Dhruva pulled at Abi's hand. 'Abi, I think we should go back. I think it may rain.'

Abi was about to pooh-pooh his suggestion when Krish piped up. 'Yes, Abi, you must go back. It's been raining quite a lot lately and there can be landslides in the mountains.'

Abi looked doubtfully at the sky, but all she could see were green leaves against a clear sky, but it certainly was getting dark. As both Krish and Dhruva seemed insistent, she reluctantly took Dhruva's hand and walked back to the school. Sumathy was waiting for her when they arrived. 'There you are! I was wondering where you'd gone. I want to talk to you, let's go,' she said, absent-mindedly nodding at Dhruva.

Abi said goodbye to him and walked with Sumathy. 'What's up? Where's the fire?' she asked her best friend.

Sumathy looked at Abi in surprise. 'Don't you want to start working out what to do about the steps? I thought you wanted to go to heaven and meet your mother more than anything in the world. Yet, you haven't even mentioned it to me in the last few weeks!'

Abi smiled. 'The sun god told me that I should climb the steps spontaneously. If I contrive or plan too much, it won't work. Of course, I want to meet Mother more than anything in the world! But I don't know if I can do it in a hurry. One of the virtues Surya mentioned was patience. I am trying to cultivate mine through meditation. Maybe that will help.'

Sumathy looked unconvinced. 'I can't be patient when our goal is so close. You have the sapphire, and the sun god has declared you the winner. Don't you want to just find the steps and climb them?' Abi looked at her friend thoughtfully. In the beginning, she had found it hard to be patient as well. But every morning, without fail, Abi took time out and meditated. She tried to keep any stray thoughts out of her head and focussed on praying to the sun god with great sincerity and a pure heart. This helped her stem her impatience.

'Every time I feel worked up or impatient, I think about the calm yet dazzling face of Surya and remind myself that I have to prepare well to climb the steps. Surya explained that these are not physical steps that I need to climb. There are deeds that I have to do – and the chance to do these can appear to me anytime. If I am not calm and patient, I may miss these opportunities and not be able to climb up to heaven.' She went on, 'Sumathy, trust me, I am doing all I can. Guruma asked me to meditate to develop my abilities. That is what I am doing. After all, I climbed one step already without realising that I was climbing it. Maybe you should try and meditate with me – that'll help you. I find it very calming and am really enjoying my morning routine.'

Sumathy looked at Abi, exasperated but also slightly in awe. 'I don't know how you do it,' she said grudgingly. 'Yes, I will try and meditate with you and see if it helps me as well.' Abi smiled. It had been a tough year, and now it was hard to know when and how she would realise her dream of going to heaven. But she was determined to enjoy the journey as much as reaching the goal.

22

A Friend in Need

Abi had a very restless night. She tossed and turned and just could not sleep. Krish's face kept appearing in her dreams. When the first light of dawn lit the sky, she gave up all pretence of sleeping and went out for a walk. The morning air was crisp and she could smell the sweet dew on the leaves around her. She turned as she heard a rustle and was surprised to see Dhruva, who seemed to be walking towards the stream. 'Good morning, Dhruva. What are you doing here?'

He looked startled for a second but smiled as he recognised her voice. 'Abi, you're up early. I try and take a walk in the mornings. It helps me recognise the smells and sounds around me. How are you?'

Abi walked up to him and held his elbow lightly, leading him towards the main path. They walked in silence for a short while. 'Abi, you never told me if Surya granted you the wish and told you the secret of the magic steps.'

Abi looked at Dhruva, frowning slightly. She had forgotten that she had told him about her quest. The events in Konark came back to her and she smiled as she remembered them. 'Yes, Dhruva – the seven magic steps are very strange; they are not real steps. They are deeds that I need to do to show my goodness, sacrifice, patience, courage and so on. Sumathy thinks I am not doing enough to find the steps, but unless I get the opportunity to demonstrate some of these virtues, I am not sure how to progress.' She looked at Dhruva and sighed. 'Any suggestions?'

He shook his head. 'No, but I think you should just keep your eyes and ears open. You never know when the opportunity may present itself.'

They walked for a while and Abi described the beauty of the nature around them. She felt sad that her friend couldn't see it, and so made an extra effort to describe things in great detail. When they turned towards the stream, Abi realised that all the other girls had already freshened up. They must have walked for longer than she'd realised. She left Dhruva to get back to the courtyard and got ready in a rush.

Abi spent the rest of the day with her classmates, enjoying the relief that always accompanied the completion of examinations. Later, she looked around for Dhruva, but he was nowhere to be seen.

'He must be practising somewhere,' said one of the other musicians. Abi went back to the girls and they spent a delightful afternoon talking and telling each other stories.

'So, what shall we do tomorrow?' asked Sumathy as dusk fell.

'I'd love to go and give Krish a surprise visit!' said Abi, sitting up. 'I want to go to his village and see where he lives. The problem is that I don't know the way.'

Pooja piped up, 'Abi, are you looking for the village that's just beneath the school? I have been there several times. I can take you.'

The next morning, Sumathy and Arundhati had to stay back to help Guru Uma rearrange and redecorate the make-up room. Pooja and Abi were just about to set off after breakfast when Dhruva joined them. He insisted on accompanying them, despite Pooja snubbing him. She finally gave in when he stubbornly refused to stay behind. 'I am not too happy about it as it's not the safest of roads to take... er... someone like you through.'

Dhruva smiled enigmatically. 'I can see better than people with sight can. Don't worry about me, Pooja.'

Pooja knew a shortcut to the village. 'This is the path that the goatherds use. It runs a bit up and down and it's slippery, so please be careful,' she cautioned. She was clearly nervous about Dhruva managing to navigate the unknown terrain. They carefully made their way down the path. Abi was pleasantly surprised at how sure-footed Dhruva seemed. He actually helped the girls a couple of times, although he couldn't see. He just seemed to sense his way around. After about twenty minutes or so, they could see the tops of the first few village huts below them. A little more walking took them to a wider path. They had reached the village.

Abi looked around her in wonder. She had never seen Krish's village except from a distance. 'It looks deserted. Why is no one around?'

Pooja pointed at some of the huts. 'They all look burnt down and pillaged!' she gasped. The thatch covering some of the huts was burnt. The doors of the huts were broken, and bricks and wood lay scattered on the ground. As they walked further, Abi was stunned to see the extent of the damage. There were small patches of vegetables, but even these seemed to have been plundered. There was still no one in sight.

'It is very odd,' Pooja agreed. 'Normally, there are little kids, goats, dogs and people all around the village. Where is everyone? What has happened here?'

'Who are you? What do you want?' a feeble voice called out. An old man was sitting outside a burnt hut. A pair of crutches lay on the ground next to him. Abi noticed that he only had one leg. The other one was amputated below the knee. He looked very thin and weak.

'Baba, what happened here? We are looking for little Krish. Do you know him?' Abi spoke gently to the old man.

To their dismay, he started sobbing. 'Once a year, all the able men in the village go to the town in the valley to sell their goods at the crafts fair. All our men went away last week. They were expected back at the village last night. Before they arrived, we were attacked. There were many men; they were dressed in black. They came and plundered the village and took everything. They razed all our homes to the ground and burnt our vegetable plots and fields. Our men came back in the midst of this mayhem and they were captured by these dacoits. They even carried away our goats and animals. Now there are only women, old people and little children left in the village. We have lost everything.' The old man began to wail.

'Abi, what are you doing here?' Krish had appeared from behind a broken hut.

'I came to see you. I am so sorry to see all this, Krish,' Abi said in a hushed tone.

Krish nodded and gave the girls a watery smile. 'Don't worry. We are ok. You'd better go – I am helping my mother and brother to rebuild our hut.'

Abi looked at him in concern. 'We would like to help. Please let me help you.'

'You cannot help us. You should go. Please leave us alone,' said a clear voice. Abi turned to see a woman standing behind them. She wore old, tattered robes. Her hands and feet were chapped and bruised. Her skin was withered, but her face was of a woman not more than forty years old. Despite her impoverished appearance, her face radiated beauty. There was something mesmerising about her.

'Mother, this is my friend Abi, from Gurukul. She is trying to help us,' said Krish, tugging at his mother's sari.

But his mother did not want them around. 'Please go! Come, Krish; we have work to do.' With these words, they turned and left Abi and Pooja staring after them.

Abi was very upset on their way back. 'We must help them somehow!' she kept repeating.

Pooja shrugged her shoulders. 'Yes, but how? I think they were attacked by the mountain dacoits. They are very dangerous people. I hear that they leave us alone only in deference to Guruma.' Abi silently remembered the figure in black that she saw lurking in the bushes when she'd run away from school. Had that been a mountain dacoit?

Dhruva had been very silent throughout the journey, but when they reached the school, he turned and spoke to both of them. 'The villagers need our help! We must do something for them. Abi, let us talk to Guruma and see if the school can help in any way.' Abi was overjoyed with his suggestion.

Pooja ran behind them. 'Abi, what are you going to do? Guruma will be upset if she hears that we went to the village without permission.' But Abi had made up her mind. She felt confident in Dhruva's presence. They entered Guruma's room after knocking at the open door.

'Yes, how can I help you?' Guruma smiled at them. Abi recounted their experience at the village; and when she finished, she had tears threatening to spill from her eyes. Guruma listened gravely to the whole story and to her relief, stood up and congratulated them. 'Thank you for coming and telling me about this. I don't want you to take any rash steps. I will arrange for someone to go to town and inform the police. Leave this to me.'

Pooja turned to go but Abi and Dhruva hesitated in the room. Guruma gave them an enquiring look. 'Guruma, I think we should start looking for the captured villagers now. They may be in trouble. The town police are not known to be very effective. Even if they do come immediately, I am not sure if they'll succeed,' said Dhruva fiercely. Abi was very impressed by his determination and nodded vehemently in agreement. She would normally not dream of standing up to Guruma like this, but Dhruva was giving her confidence. And she was genuinely worried about Krish's father.

Guruma looked at them sternly. 'Absolutely not! There is no way that we are risking our lives, and I certainly will not risk yours. The dacoits aren't playing games, you know. You have told me about it – now you must trust me to do the right thing!' Abi recognised the dismissal and led Dhruva out of the room. She could still see Krish's face, tired and hungry as he helped his mother build their hut.

She suddenly turned back and went into the room. 'Guruma, is it all right if some of us go and help the villagers? After all, the exams are over. If we lend a hand, at least they can start rebuilding the village.'

Guruma looked surprised but smiled slightly. 'Abi, I am going to need the teachers to do other things. I am happy that you want to help the villagers, but will you be able to organise the students? Firstly, see how many volunteer to come and help you. You can't force them!'

Abi looked at Guruma, her face full of doubt. She was hoping that Guruma would ask the students to come and help, and if she did, they would all obey without a word. Why would they listen to Abi? She was nervous. Guruma's eyes seemed to challenge her silently.

'I will try to convince the students, Guruma,' she said. She really wanted to help the villagers and was willing to give anything a go.

'Good – but I don't want you to just try; I want you to do. Now leave the rest to me,' Guruma said.

──⊶⊷──

'What are you planning to do to persuade the others?' Pooja asked again. Abi knew that Pooja was sceptical about the whole thing.

'I am not sure. Maybe gather everyone in the courtyard and talk to them.' Abi needed time to prepare, time to think. But there wasn't enough time. She could not bear the thought of the young children in the village spending more nights out in the open, amidst their broken and burnt belongings. She made her way quickly to the make-up room where Sumathy and Arundhati were adding finishing touches to a much neater and cleaner room.

'Look at the way this room looks now…' began Sumathy excitedly, but stopped when she looked at Abi's grim face.

Abi hurriedly explained the situation to her and asked for her support to gather the rest of the students in the courtyard. As always, her best friend proved her worth. Within fifteen minutes, the courtyard was filled with students and members of the orchestra. The teachers had already gone to Guruma's room to be briefed by her. Abi suddenly felt the weight of the world on her shoulders. She had never made a speech to such a large audience. Her stomach started churning and she felt her heart pound loudly. Her knees trembled. Dhruva laid a friendly hand on her shoulder and gave her a smile. Abi smiled back and closed her eyes. She imagined how she would prepare herself to dance – all she needed to do was get into character. And now, her character had to be that of a friend, a friend who would do everything in her power to help Krish. She thought of the young seven-year- old boy's courage as he helped his mother and brother rebuild their home without complaint. He had probably not eaten anything while he worked. She could also see his mother's gaunt face, proud and determined. Their fortitude in the face of adversity and Dhruva's reassuring presence gave Abi the courage she needed to step up to the stage.

She addressed the school: 'Friends, our neighbours in the village are in trouble. They have been attacked by dacoits and their homes have been destroyed. At the moment, there are only women, old people and children left in the village. They need help rebuilding their homes so that they can shelter from the elements. You know that it's been raining badly recently and that will expose them to other dangers. It is our duty and privilege to be able to help them. Will you join us in lending them a hand?' Abi looked at her schoolmates earnestly. Some of the girls looked doubtfully at each other. Others smiled and nodded.

'Are we not putting ourselves in danger? What if the dacoits are still around?' asked one girl. Abi looked uncertainly at them, wondering how to dispel their fears.

Suddenly Dhurva's clear voice rang out. 'What if the boot was on the other foot and we had been attacked? Would you not want the villagers to help us? There are little children and old people trying to lift bricks and wood to help the brave women in the village rebuild their homes. They have no shelter, very little food and no support. Gurukul is the centre of knowledge – we are all here as we seek this knowledge. Of what use is knowledge if we cannot use it to help others? We are all lucky that we have a roof over our heads, warm food on our plates and clean clothes to wear. The world is now giving us the opportunity to repay this luck and give something back to the world. If we do not act now, we will regret it forever.' Dhruva stopped and turned towards Abi.

She gave him a smile that he couldn't see and turned towards the others. 'I am going to help the villagers and so is Dhruva. Those who feel the same way as we do, please join us now. Thank you.' She walked down the stage and took Dhruva's arm. She was so lucky to have someone like him with her. She stopped short as Guruma came out of her room. Abi found Guruma's voice deeply reassuring as she spoke.

'Child, all the teachers are with you. We need to organise ourselves first and carry the necessary supplies to the village. I will be sending a few people to town to get help. Guru Usha will join you and take you to the village,' said Guruma, patting Abi kindly on her back.

Sumathy tapped Abi's shoulder. 'We are all behind you, Abi; look at the number of volunteers!' Abi was amazed to see that all the girls had rallied round to join them. Her eyes swimming in tears of happiness, Abi walked up to Dhruva and suggested that he stay behind.

'We need someone to coordinate at the school. Someone who can organise supplies if required. You will be best placed here.'

But Dhruva would have none of that. 'No, Abi; my place is with you. I want to come with you – surely you can see that I mean to?'

Abi looked at Guruma, who nodded. Guruma then addressed the audience. 'The teachers are organising the supplies. Could some of you please stay behind to help carry these? Everyone else can start off; we have much work to do!'

23

THE REBUILD MISSION

Guru Usha walked alongside Dhruva and Abi, leading the way to the village – they took the longer route this time to avoid the rocky goatherd's path. They were met at the entrance by a group of women who were trying to erect the roof on a recently rebuilt hut. They stopped their work and looked at the crowd in surprise. 'What's going on? Why are you here?' demanded one of the women. She was a large elderly lady and seemed to be clearly in charge.

Guru Usha came forward. 'We are from Gurukul. We discovered your misfortune and would like to help. Please allow us to be of help to you.'

The village women looked at each other – their hostile expressions gave way to relieved smiles. 'That's great; we could do with some help. Thank you.' Some of the girls and two boys from the orchestra joined forces with the women and erected their roof in no time.

Guru Usha took the elderly lady aside to speak to her. 'Our teachers are coming down with supplies. We think that we should send someone down to the valley to report to the police. In the meantime, we should probably start planning the best way to rebuild the village.'

The old lady nodded. 'Call me Granthi. I am the chieftain's wife. I will invite Yashoda to join us. She is good with plans. She made us rebuild that hut first as it could hold many people.'

Granthi disappeared for a few minutes and reappeared with Krish and his mother in tow. 'This is Yashoda,' said Granthi, introducing her.

Yashoda looked grim and suspicious. 'Why do you want to help us? What is in it for you?'

Abi smiled at Krish and turned towards his mother. Guru Usha looked calm and in control. 'You are our neighbours. I hope you would do the same for us.'

When Yashoda still looked disbelieving, Abi piped up. 'Plus, Krish here is a dear friend. He saved my life once. This is my chance to help him out.'

Yashoda looked doubtfully at Krish. 'Mother, they are good people to want to help us. We should accept. Abi – thank you so much.' Krish's enthusiasm seemed to melt his mother, and she gave Abi and the rest a slight smile and invited them in to rebuild the hut.

'I am sorry; I see evil everywhere after that attack,' she said apologetically to the girls.

Guru Usha and Yashoda started planning the best way to rebuild the village. Abi worked with Pooja, Sumathy and Arundhati to assign different tasks to the volunteers. By the time Guruma and the rest of the teachers arrived with tools, food and other supplies, the girls were well into their building activities. Some of the girls took up ration duty and started distributing food and water to the villagers. Guruma selected two singers from the orchestra and sent them to the valley with a note to the chief of police. The volunteers worked through the evening and nearly until midnight. A big village hall had been rebuilt and this, combined with a few other huts, had enough capacity to house all the people left in the village. The schoolgirls stayed back in the hall to rest for the night. Luckily for them, the weather held and there was no rain.

The next morning, the volunteers started early and worked with the women and children to finish the rest of the huts. Guru Uma came down with baby Vi, and the child cheered up the village women while Guru Uma helped them organise their meals. Some girls began work on the fields and vegetable plots. By lunchtime, the village was looking much like its old self. Guruma sought out Abi in the crowd. 'The work seems to be going very well. But you must encourage the volunteers, Abi. Speak to them – you are their leader.'

Abi dutifully followed Guruma's suggestion and walked around, meeting and talking to all the volunteers. She offered them words of encouragement and praise, listened to any problems or suggestions that they had and noted if they needed any more supplies. Abi was just waving goodbye to the two girls who were going back to school to bring the additional supplies when she saw Krish standing behind her.

'Abi, do you want to come and help me sort out some of the fields behind the huts?' Abi nodded and walked with Krish, avoiding broken bricks and heaps of burnt wood to find herself in the middle of an open field. The field was in a total mess. It looked as though someone had been on a rampage in it: half the crop was burnt and the rest uprooted or broken; it looked like a large someone or something had been stamping on it.

Abi drew a deep breath and looked at Krish. 'This is hardly something that you and I can clear out without help. Does anyone have a tractor around here?'

Krish gave her an amused smile. 'Tractor? All our farming is done using traditional methods. But don't worry; I have friends who can help.'

Abi was puzzled. She couldn't see anyone around. Krish was wearing a peacock feather strung on a chain around his neck. He fingered it thoughtfully and walked up to a group of trees on one edge of the field. There was a horde of monkeys playing around on the trees. Abi couldn't hear Krish from where she stood, but it seemed like he was talking to them. She started walking towards him, worried that he may have lost his mind with all his recent troubles.

To her shock, the monkeys seemed to be talking back to Krish. 'What's happening?' asked Abi in amazement, as all the monkeys swarmed into the field. They quickly got to work and started pulling out the destroyed crops from the ground.

Krish smiled. 'If you talk nicely to any creature, they are happy to help, aren't they?' Abi couldn't believe her eyes – the field was being cleared in no time – there were hundreds of monkeys at work. It looked as though the ones on the trees had summoned their friends to join in.

'Krish! How did you do it?'

'Magic!' Krish winked. 'Come on, they can only do so much. You have to guide them. Show them how to dig up the field with a plough and they will follow suit.' Abi stopped wondering about her friend's strange hold over the animals and got to work. Minutes rolled into hours and soon the fields were cleared and freshly ploughed.

Abi and Krish stopped after a long time and inspected their handiwork. The monkeys were chattering among themselves, looking very pleased with what they'd achieved. Krish thanked them and waved them goodbye. 'Aren't you going to tell me how you talk to the monkeys?' asked Abi, watching them retreat back to where they came from.

'Maybe one day...' said Krish, 'but for now, I want to thank you. All the work that you have started is going very well. Yesterday, we were distraught; we did not know where to start. Thanks to you, our lives are getting back in order,' said Krish, squeezing Abi's hand.

'You saved my life. What I am doing is very small compared to that,' said Abi.

Krish disagreed. 'Saving your life was a matter of luck. This is a well-thought-out plan. It must have been difficult for you to convince your friends. Yet you did. You are a good person, Abi. I am sure good things will happen to you.'

By the end of the day, they had rebuilt most of the village and cleared the vegetable plots. 'Let's take a break and go back to school tonight. Tomorrow, we can help plant fresh seeds in their plots and fields. And hopefully we will hear from the two men who have gone to the valley. Well done, everyone,' said Guru Usha.

The volunteers got back to school that night. Sumathy walked alongside Abi. 'That was wonderful. Such a feeling of achievement! Abi – it was a great idea, and I'm so glad we had the opportunity to do something like this!'

Pooja walked behind them. 'Abi, I was very sceptical about this, but now I agree with Sumathy. I am so glad I came along. It is very satisfying to help other people.' Abi smiled at her friends – she was tremendously happy that they were able to help Krish and the others. She was proud of her schoolmates who had rallied around her.

That night, Abi and Sumathy retired early to bed so that they could get some rest before another hard day's work in the village. They were just about to turn out the light in their room when there was a knock on the door. Sumathy opened the door and was surprised to see Dhruva. 'What happened? Is anything wrong?' asked Abi.

'Shh, quick, follow me. The men are back from the town and are just speaking to Guruma. Don't you want to find out what happened?'

Abi hurried behind him and Sumathy followed hesitantly. They tiptoed across the courtyard. Guruma's room was lit up and they could see the shadows of many teachers inside. Abi took the lead and quietly hid behind the doorway to listen to what was being said. She avoided looking at Sumathy's panicked face as they all crouched low in the darkness. The men had been waiting for the rest of the teachers to join in and had just begun their update.

'We couldn't meet the Chief of Police. Apparently there's a big political rally going on in town and most of the force has been sent to guard the VIPs. However, they've promised to help as soon as they can. I'm afraid we don't think that will happen for two or three days.'

Guruma sounded worried. 'That is no good. I am not sure the village men will be safe with the dacoits for that period of time.'

There were some worried murmurs in the room and another voice rang out. 'Guruma, it's even worse. There are stories in town about the dacoits engaging in slave trade in this day and age. They may have taken the men for that. I fear that the men will be sold off very soon.'

Abi frowned at Sumathy, who had just audibly gasped. Luckily, there was too much noise inside Guruma's room and no one heard them. 'We better get out of here. The teachers may start coming out soon,' whispered Dhruva. The three of them tiptoed back to the girls' room.

Abi looked really worried. 'This is dreadful news. If the police are not going to be here for another two or three days, it will be too late!'

Sumathy tried to console her. 'You don't know that for sure. Also, Guruma will do something.'

But Dhruva seemed to agree with Abi. 'What will she do? She will never risk anyone's lives – whether it's the teachers or the students. She'll just ask us to spend our time rebuilding the village and wait for the police. We must do something.'

Abi looked at him in surprise, hearing the urgency in his voice. Sumathy stared at him as if he'd lost his mind. 'What are you talking about? What can the three of us do? Don't be silly.'

Dhruva sounded very determined. 'I am sure Abi doesn't want to let her friend Krish down, do you? Abi, I told you I walk in the forest every morning to familiarise myself with the sights and sounds. I am sure I know the way to the dacoits' hideout.' Abi and Sumathy stared at each other in stunned silence for a few moments. 'I have heard rustling noises downstream in a particular spot. I think the dacoits think that I can't see a thing as I am blind; but of course, I can hear them. If I lead the way, will you come with me, and maybe we can think up a way to outsmart them together?'

Sumathy protested. 'Why didn't you report this earlier if you knew about the dacoits?'

Dhruva shook his head. 'I didn't put two and two together until I found out about the dacoits; but now that I have, I think that's where they must be!'

Abi was sold on the idea. Dhruva's confidence helped her make up her mind. 'Sumathy, I am going with him.

You don't have to come. I have to try my best to help Krish's father.'

Sumathy looked very unhappy. 'Dhruva is being ridiculous – I can't understand why you're even listening to him. What is your plan? How will you save these men? You are being silly.' But no amount of pleading would change Abi's mind.

Abi picked up some ropes and a torch and followed Dhruva out of the door. Sumathy was desperate and nearly in tears, but this didn't move Abi at all as her mind was firmly made up. Dhruva set off, leading the way through the forest, walking confidently although the night was pitch black. Abi realised that this was how it must be for Dhruva even in broad daylight. They had just started their journey when they heard running steps behind them. Abi's heart was pounding when she turned – she was visibly relieved to see Sumathy's form come into sight. 'I couldn't let you go on your own,' she panted. 'I will join you.' Abi squeezed her hand warmly and they continued on their way.

In a short while, the trees became denser and they could hear the stream gurgling away in the distance. Dhruva stopped and drew them close. 'Hush, girls; be very quiet. I am sure they'll have a guard posted somewhere nearby.' The girls exchanged scared glances and moved slowly forward. Sumathy jumped as an owl hooted in the distance. 'Shh,' chided Dhruva and carried on inching forward, listening intently for any noise. Although Abi had a torch with her, she was frightened that the dacoits would see the light if she switched it on. Thanks to Surya's gift, she was able to see clearly and made sure that she kept Sumathy close by.

Something must have alerted Dhruva as he indicated that they should stop all of a sudden. Abi held her breath – she was scared to even turn her head. She was listening with all her might for any sound when something hit her on the head, and she collapsed into unconsciousness on the damp and leafy forest floor.

24

ABI'S FOOLISH MISTAKE

When she regained consciousness, the first light of dawn was already appearing in the sky. She saw Dhruva's body crumpled on the ground in front of her. Her head ached as if she'd been hit with something hard and heavy. She got up groggily and held on to a tree to try and stand up. The world was moving in dizzy circles. After a while, when the dizziness abated, she moved forward and touched Dhruva's shoulders gingerly. She could see blood on his head – it was dark and crusted, so he must have been hit a while back. He moved slightly as she gently shook his shoulders and slowly gained consciousness. Abi remembered Sumathy and looked around her. To her horror, her friend was nowhere to be seen!

'How could I be so foolish!' sobbed Abi as tears streamed down her face. She was limping back towards Gurukul, with Dhruva leaning heavily on her for support. He had been hit harder than her and must have lost a lot of blood. Abi felt very stupid that she'd decided to embark on that foolhardy venture with him last night. *Sumathy kept warning me and I didn't listen to her! Now look where that has left us. I can be so pig-headed. The dacoits must have captured her. Oh, my poor friend!* thought Abi, frightened at the thought of her friend being caught by the dacoits and imprisoned in some dark and dingy place.

She tried to hurry up but stopped when Dhruva moaned slightly. 'Dhruva, you're badly hurt. We need to get back and get some medication for you.' Dhruva sank to the ground. Abi looked at him in panic. 'Dhruva, wake up. We have to get back to school,' she said, half shouting.

'Abi, is that you?' A familiar voice reached her ears. Abi looked up in relief to see the friendly face of her martial arts teacher, Guru Rama, in the distance. Guru Rama was slim, muscular and very boyish, even though she was dressed in a sari. She ran up to them and gasped when she saw the blood on Dhruva's head and clothes. 'What happened?' she asked, trying to raise him by one shoulder while Abi took the other.

Abi was shame-faced as she recounted the goings-on from last night. She was glad that they were walking side by side and she couldn't see the expression on her guru's face. 'That was not clever, Abi. Do you not trust us? You should have come to one of us. How can you be so foolish?'

Abi nodded at all the criticism. 'You're right – I should have come to you straight away, but I thought it was a great adventure and I stupidly went out into the night. Poor Sumathy – she tried to stop me and now she's been captured, thanks to my foolishness.' Abi was again overcome by tears and couldn't stop sobbing. Guru

Rama gruffly asked her to stop crying; and the three of them walked as fast as they could, with Dhruva supported between the two of them.

⁓

They were met by Guru Uma and Guru Mahesh outside the courtyard. Luckily, it was still very early in the morning and none of the students were around. The teachers took Dhruva to the medical room where he was tended to by Guru Mahesh. Guru Usha checked Abi for injuries. Luckily, besides a sore head, there were no other visible marks on her. After the check-up, Guru Rama grimly took her hand and led her towards Guruma's room. Abi's heart was pounding as she stepped in through the doorway. Guruma's face was expressionless as she heard the story, shortened and recited concisely by Guru Rama. Abi looked contritely at her feet when Guruma spoke to her.

'Do you have anything to say, child?'

Abi looked up into her principal's intense grey eyes. 'I am sorry, Guruma. It was very foolish. I don't know what I was thinking.'

Guruma stopped her. 'Were you? Thinking, I mean. Did you actually think about what you wanted to do when you got to the dacoits' camp?'

Abi shook her head. 'No, I wasn't thinking at all.'

Guruma nodded. 'Just as I thought! Abi, it is easy for us to get carried away by passion. If you're clear about your purpose, I think passion is a very good thing; but to jump into something just because someone asks you to, without thinking, is dangerous – not just for you, but also for others around you. But – treat it as a lesson for the future.'

Abi nodded and wiped her tears. By now, they had been joined by some of her teachers. Gurus Uma, Mahesh, Rama and Usha were standing behind her, dressed in camouflage clothes and backpacks, as if they were about to go on a trekking expedition. Guruma looked at the group with a satisfied smile. 'That looks good. Are we all prepared?'

Abi looked puzzled and opened her mouth to ask a question but held back when Guruma turned towards her. 'Child, you didn't think we were going to leave the villagers to suffer and be sold off by the dacoits? We have also been planning. I have often suspected that the dacoits live in the cavern below the riverbed. There's a rocky ledge above the school from where you can make your precarious way down to the cavern, but I am sure that is the way the dacoits use and it will be guarded. I think there is another lesser-known route.

'There is a cave inside the forest near a giant tree. The roots of the tree have spread into a hole in the ground. This hole is large enough for us to crawl through, and I think it extends down to the cavern; but it will be very difficult for us to go down that path without any lights. And if we use lights, the dacoits will be forewarned. So we planned to wait for dawn in the hope that it might help us at least part of the way, though I am not sure sunlight would reach the depths of the cavern. However, we have to rethink our plans now that Sumathy has been captured. The dacoits are bound to be alert and we shouldn't take a risk. We'll have to try and go at dusk.'

Abi jumped up as a brilliant idea occurred to her. 'Guruma, I have the ability to see in the dark. The sun god gave me that as a gift. I can help you!'

'Quite out of the question, Abi. I cannot risk your life or the life of any other young student. Sorry, can't be done,' said Guruma firmly. Abi appealed to Guru Rama. Guru Rama was very adventurous, and it was known that she almost resented being a woman and had applied all her energy to developing her martial arts skills. She was considered one of the best in the country and took pride in regularly beating men in competitions.

Abi knew all this about her and decided to use this knowledge to her advantage. 'I have been foolish, I admit. But now I have an opportunity to make amends. I am good at martial arts – and you've always said that to me. This is a good chance to put that and Surya's gift to good use.'

Guru Rama gave Abi a smile – Abi was one of her favourite students and had excelled in martial arts from the beginning. 'Worthy words, Abi; but there's a lot of danger, and we can't subject a young schoolgirl to it.'

Abi knew she was going to get into trouble with her teachers, but she was not going to give up that easily. She pleaded and appealed to all the different teachers in the room but got the same response. Finally, she pretended to give up and was sent to rest in her room. Within five minutes of being sent to the room, Abi tiptoed back to the courtyard and hid outside Guruma's room to listen to the conversation inside. Guru Mahesh was speaking in his usual monotonous drone. 'Guruma, I know we can't risk her life, but it would be handy to have someone like Abi to guide us. After all, if it's too dark and we trip over something or fall in the river, we will alert the dacoits.' There were other murmurs from people in the room.

Guru Rama pitched in with her characteristic cough. 'Ahem, yes, I agree with him. She's a good martial arts student, and I can keep an eye out for her.'

Abi stood outside, hoping that her teachers would change their minds. However, Guruma sounded very firm. 'You know we can never risk a student's life in such a way. It's bad enough that poor Sumathy is in danger – there's no way that we can add Abi to this. I promised her parents that I would look after her – how can I take her and break my promise? By the way, Usha – you should go and see if she's really sleeping –she's very keen to do something, and I hope she doesn't do anything foolish again.'

Abi heard Guru Usha get up from a chair. 'You're right, at night we should lock her door before we leave in case she decides to sneak after us. I will just look in on her now. If she's sleeping, I'll go back and see her at dusk.' Abi urgently made her way back to her room and pretended to be asleep when Guru Usha came to check up on her. Inadvertently, Guru Usha had given her an idea. She knew that they'd lock her in with the lock that was hanging outside the door – she had a duplicate key to this lock and if she gave that to Pooja and coaxed her to release her, she could follow the teachers in the evening. She knew she'd get into awful trouble later; but having heard the teachers' conversation secretly, she hoped that they'd accept her if she turned up at the right time. Abi turned her face away from the pillow – it was flushed and her heart was beating rapidly. Once again, she had the familiar feeling of diving headfirst into adventure!

25

JOURNEY TO THE CAVERN

Later that afternoon, Abi woke up and sneaked outside. She ran up to Pooja's room and was delighted to see her in. Pooja was totally absorbed in a storybook and didn't hear Abi until she was right next to her. 'Abi! You gave me a shock. Is everything all right?' Abi was breathless with excitement and gave Pooja a very short account of what had happened and her plan.

Pooja looked aghast. 'That's silly – you're doing exactly what they're worried you'll do. How will you help them? If you catch up with them before they go down the cavern, they're bound to send you back.'

Abi's face was very grave. 'I know it's a risk but she's my best friend. I have to help her. I hope that they won't send me back as it will cause too much trouble. I have to try. Please, Pooja – can you do this for me? I would have asked Dhruva but he's so badly hurt.'

Pooja rolled her eyes in exasperation. 'You're a troublemaker. Anyway, how can Dhruva help you? He can't see. Don't worry, I'll let you out.'

At dusk, Guru Usha came over to the room with a plate of food for Abi. She was dressed in black and had black make-up on her face. 'This is to blend in with the surroundings. Guru Uma, Mahesh, Rama are all dressed and ready to go. We're just waiting for Dev and Milind from the orchestra to join us.' Abi nodded – she'd heard of Dev. He played the drums but it was well known that he was an excellent wrestler in his spare time. She remembered that he had a chubby, pleasant face and an innocent smile that belied his wrestling prowess. Abi did not know much about Milind and asked Guru Usha about him. 'Milind sings in the orchestra, but he is also an ace swimmer. We need someone who can help others if anyone falls into the river,' she said ominously.

'How is Dhruva?' asked Abi, feeling guilty that she had not gone to see him.

'He's hurt but that didn't stop him from wanting to come with us. I've had to get the doctor to sedate him so that he sleeps instead of trying to follow us.' Abi nodded at her as she said goodbye. She heard her bolt the door and lock it from outside.

No more than five minutes after she'd left, Abi heard the sound of keys rattling at her door. Pooja burst in, looking red in the face. 'I'll get into awful trouble if anyone finds out. Good luck, Abi.'

Abi had not eaten much – she put the plate that Guru Usha had brought her aside and got ready quickly. She changed into black clothes and found some black make-up in her things to rub on her face. Pooja watched her anxiously as she locked the empty room and tucked the key into her clothes. 'Be careful, Abi – hope it works out. Please be careful, won't you?'

Abi hid behind a bush and waited for the gurus to start their journey. She could see them in the distance and stayed hidden until they'd crossed the path that led to the girls' rooms and beyond, towards the river. Soon, they were walking alongside the river and she could hear the gentle sound of water sloshing down the mountain. Abi followed them silently – her ability to see in the dark helped her, and all she had to do was to make sure she didn't make any noise. The path was now quite steep and climbing upwards. Abi wondered what Guruma's plan could be once they reached the cavern. They went deeper and deeper into the forest. Abi had never been anywhere close to this area.

'We must be close to the cave, quiet now,' said Guruma, leading the way.

Ahead of them stood an enormous tree with a gigantic trunk. *It must be centuries old*, thought Abi. The tree trunk was twisted and surrounded by big boulders.

'The cave is just behind the tree,' whispered Guruma. Abi could barely hear her from her hiding place. She was not sure if this was the right moment to reveal herself. She crept a bit closer to try and hear what Guruma was saying to the team.

Abi was about to make a move when a strong hand covered her mouth and another held her hands so she couldn't move. 'I have caught someone!'

It was a male voice that Abi did not recognise. For a moment, she was terrified that the dacoits had caught her but then realised that the teachers were moving towards her. Guru Usha looked very annoyed and also a bit shamefaced that Abi had escaped and followed them. Guruma came up to her. 'So, you couldn't stay away! You're a bit of a nuisance, Abi.' Guruma looked gravely at the rest of the teachers – there was an unspoken conversation that took place between them. Then she turned back towards Abi with a frown. 'It pains me to say this. We can't send you back now as that would mean we have to send someone with you, and we don't have the time or anyone to spare. I'll have to speak to you about this incident, but for now, we need to focus on our task ahead.'

Abi struggled to say something but the hands held her tightly. Guruma nodded at her captor and he released her suddenly. Abi turned back to see a young man with dark eyes and wavy black hair grinning behind her. 'Hi, Abi – my name is Milind. I don't think we've met properly.' He chuckled as she rubbed her wrists – he had held her too tightly. She looked towards Guruma for further instructions. The expression on Guruma's face was a mix of exasperation and urgency. Abi had guessed right – they were now forced to let her join their team!

'The plan is simple. We will go down to the cave where the river goes underground. Around the mouth of the cave, there is a rocky ledge. I think this ledge carries on through to the cavern. Unfortunately, we cannot see underground and it is too dangerous to carry lights. We'll have to be extra vigilant. So, we are at your mercy. If you cannot see in the dark properly, then we may have to call the plan off if it gets too difficult and think of something else. You must not lie to us; is that understood?' said Guruma, looking searchingly into Abi's face.

Abi nodded and asked, 'What happens if we do manage to reach the cavern?'

'Mahesh and Rama will lead us. We will have to try and overpower the dacoits and release the men.'

Abi looked doubtful – it seemed too simple a plan. 'What if we get caught?'

Guruma looked seriously at her. 'Well, we have to try and avoid that, don't we? Let's go.'

They had to crouch to enter the cave. 'Watch out for the roots,' said Abi. There were giant roots from the tree snaking their way on the ground. The group gingerly made its way into the cave. It was dark in there, but there was some light from the entrance of the cave. Abi spotted the large hole in the ground immediately.

A large portion of the tree's roots blocked the hole. Milind crouched down to check it out. 'It's very dark and I cannot make it out.' Guruma looked at him for a few minutes before making up her mind and turning towards her.

Guruma took hold of Abi's shoulders and spoke to her in a quiet voice. 'Abi, we are going to attach you to Dev with a rope so that if you fall, we can get you. I want you to enter the hole and see if there's enough space in there for all of us to make our way down. I don't think you should go too deep. If you have a problem, tug on the rope and we will pull you up.' Abi silently wondered what they would have done had she not come along.

Dev had a sturdy piece of rope with him. He tied one end around his own waist and the other end around Abi. 'There's plenty of rope so you'll have plenty of leeway. Don't worry, I have tied the knots firmly,' said Dev, flashing a boyish smile.

Abi took a deep breath and got down on her knees to crawl into the hole. She could see a sloping path leading down into the ground. She hoped that Guruma was right in thinking that this path would lead all the way to the cavern. If not, they would have to turn and make their way back, which would be difficult and not very pleasant. 'I hope no one is claustrophobic,' said Abi, returning to the mouth of the hole. 'I think there's space for all of us to crawl through but it is very narrow in places.'

Tied to each other with a single rope, they made very slow progress. The tunnel in the ground was very narrow, damp and rocky. Abi could see very clearly, but she knew that the others behind her couldn't. She imagined that she was leading Dhruva and was very careful to point out any obstacles on the path to the people behind.

It was hard work crawling on one's hands and feet. Abi was sure that her knees were bruised and bloody. At one stage, the path got very narrow as the roots had spread. Abi was able to crawl through, but Dev's broad shoulders gave him a lot of trouble. After a great deal of pushing and pulling, he made it through. His robes were torn and his face was scratched and bleeding.

Abi waited at a distance while the others made their way through the narrow spot that Dev had just widened for them. She quietly admired Guruma for engaging in such athletics without a complaint. She wondered how old Guruma actually was – she seemed so fit.

Up ahead in the distance, Abi could see a bronze glow. *We must be reaching the end of the tunnel and must be quite close to the cavern,* she said to herself. Slowly, without a sound, Abi crawled up towards the light. In a while, she reached the end of the tunnel. The mouth was closed with small boulders and there was water dripping from the ceiling, making it totally wet and muddy. There was a small hole between the boulders where the light was shining through. Abi looked through the hole but could not see any movement. She turned around and looked quizzically past Dev at Guruma.

'Try moving the stones very carefully in order to make room for us to get out,' Guruma said. Abi and Dev worked on the mouth of the tunnel and took a long time shifting the small rocks and boulders that closed them in. Soon there was a hole large enough for Abi to crawl through. 'Abi, please be very careful. Go out and see where we have reached if you can,' Guruma whispered.

Abi was sure that the dacoits would hear the thudding of her loudly beating heart. She crawled out quietly. She was on top of a rocky roof, inside an enormous cavern, and the tunnel had led them to a very wide roof-like ledge that extended in front of them. The light was coming from somewhere below.

Taking great care not to make any noise, Abi moved closer to the edge of the roof. Below her, she saw a dacoit sitting on guard with a lantern that was emitting the light she had seen earlier. He seemed half-asleep, his chin resting on his chest. Abi looked around her. It seemed that there was a cave or maybe more under the roof-like ledge she was standing on. She could hear faint sounds of activity below.

Abi moved back into the shadows when she saw another dacoit appear. He shook the guard awake, speaking in a rough guttural local dialect that Abi could just about understand. 'Wake up. Fine way to guard the entrance! We have to feed the captives. We have to move them to the buyer by the morning and we need them to look a bit better than they do at the moment. Come, help me get the food organised.'

Abi had to hold her breath to stop from gasping aloud. They had very little time to make a move! She crept back to the tunnel quickly but quietly, and helped Dev remove more stones so that he and the others could come out onto the roof. Very quietly, she whispered what she had heard the man in the cave say. Guru Rama and Mahesh glanced at each other, stony-faced. It was clear that they had a lot of work to do to help the prisoners escape!

26

THE RESCUE

Silently but surely, Guru Mahesh took charge. He divided the group into two – one group comprising Guruma, Guru Mahesh and Milind, and the other had the rest of them. 'Dev, Rama, it is your mission to safeguard Abi,' said Guruma, looking worried. Abi gave her a quick, confident smile. She was happy to be with Dev and Guru Rama– she was sure they'd do their best to protect her. The first group was led by Guru Mahesh and the second by Guru Rama. It became clear to Abi that they had already planned their moves, as they had not talked at all on the way to the cave; and even now, they were going about their tasks without a hasty conference. She tried not to show it, but she felt slightly miffed that they had not shared the plans in any detail with her.

'Come, Abi; we are the first to go down. We'll descend from the left,' Dev whispered, leading her forward. Abi noted that the other group was climbing up instead of down. They all soon disappeared behind the rocks. Abi's group carefully made its way down to the mouth of the cave in the meantime. The guard had disappeared –probably to help the other dacoit organise food for the prisoners. He had left the lantern behind and so the cavern was still well lit. Abi wondered how the other group was faring in the dim, flickering light that created several dancing shadows on the rocks. Rama placed a hand on Abi and quietly guided her to a safe point behind a rock. Dev and Guru Usha had disappeared by now. From her hiding place, Abi could see four dacoits approach the guard's empty seat from the path opposite the cave. *That must be the path the dacoits use to enter the cavern,* Abi thought.

All the dacoits were big, burly men; but one of them was particularly striking. He was large with a bushy beard generously peppered with grey hair. He wore black robes and a red turban. His dark eyes were lined with kohl and were quite menacing. Abi could barely discern his slit of a mouth under his generous moustache. He had a cruel look about him and it was clear that he was in command. 'Why is there no guard here?' he asked loudly.

A pair of scurrying feet from inside the cave produced a guard a moment later. 'Sorry, Chief; I was sorting out food for the prisoners.'

The chief gave him a dirty look. 'I don't care if the prisoners go hungry – but I do not want the entrance left unguarded. Is that understood? You will be punished next time!' The guard nodded meekly and took his position at the entrance.

The chief and the other dacoits disappeared inside the cave. The guard had his back turned towards the mouth of the cave and sat down facing the path leading out of the cavern. Guru Rama moved so fast that Abi did not have time to even blink. She silently glided behind the guard, held a cloth in front of his mouth and pressed on a nerve by his neck to overpower him. She held him as he crumpled and slowly let him lie down on the floor. Guru Usha appeared from behind a rock and tied his hands and feet up. 'Better put a gag in his mouth, too,' whispered Guru Rama. The unconscious guard was then dragged behind a rock out of sight. 'Come, Dev will stay here to handle any problems while you, me and Usha go in,' Guru Rama whispered.

The cave was dark, but Abi could see quite clearly once inside it. When they had walked for a while, Abi realised that this particular cave led to three more caves. 'There's nothing here. Should we go into one of the others?' Abi asked Guru Rama. Rama silently pointed to the one on the left. The entrance to this cave was very small and they would have to enter on their hands and knees. *I wonder why she has chosen this instead of the other two*, Abi pondered, but she asked no questions. They made their way slowly through the narrow entrance, Abi praying silently that none of the dacoits would choose this exact moment to come out of the cave.

Luckily, they managed to enter without meeting anyone head-on. The cave opened up a little after its narrow opening, and the roof was now high enough for them to stand up without bumping their heads. It was dimly lit and several moments passed before their eyes could take in their new surroundings, but Abi could see some movement in a corner. Her heart beat faster as an image of the evil-looking chieftain arose in her mind.

Guru Rama led the way quietly towards the corner. Abi breathed a silent sigh of relief when she saw the prisoners. Her face fell when she saw the dejected slump of their shoulders, but her eyes were looking only for Sumathy at this moment. To her dismay, Sumathy wasn't with this group of captives. They had taken a few more steps forward when the dacoits ambushed them.

Abi fought bravely – she tried to remember her martial arts lessons and was able to take down two fully grown men, to her surprise. Guru Rama was like a whirlwind – she subdued four men. Unfortunately, Guru Usha was no warrior. A dacoit held a knife to her neck and Abi and Rama stopped fighting and looked at the captured teacher in dismay. 'They fight like wildcats. Tie them up with ropes and let us take them to the chief,' said one of the remaining three dacoits. They were tied up and led into the main cavern.

Abi let out a yelp of pain as a dacoit pushed her roughly forward. Guru Rama snarled at her captors and looked more angry than afraid. Abi wondered what fate awaited them now. Would they be made prisoners, too? Or would something worse happen to them, now that it was obvious that they had come to rescue the others?

This cave was very well lit with flaming torches standing in crude brackets cut in the rocky wall. It looked more lived-in than the other cave and had clothes, food and weapons piled up along its sides. Abi looked around and found rocky recesses along the wall on one side. These recesses had little mattresses made out of rough cloth – the dacoits probably slept in these. She scanned the recesses frantically for Sumathy. Abi was still taking in her surroundings when they came to an abrupt halt. In front of them, reclining on two large flat rocks, arranged like a chair, was the dacoit chieftain.

He leered at them for a moment before asking one of his men, 'Are they from the school? I knew one day that school would be a liability. The only reason we haven't attacked it so far is because my father, the previous chieftain, forbade us from doing so,' he said, looking at one of his men.

The other dacoit was an older, kinder-looking man. He was perched on top on one of the stone recesses with his legs dangling into the cave. 'Your father was a wise man, Chief. If he said it was not to be attacked, he would have had a good reason.'

The dacoits who had captured Abi and the others agreed. 'Chief, these two girls fought like wildcats. If we had not captured the fat one, they would have beaten us. Why, these two overpowered six of us before we got to the third one.'

The chief looked even more menacing as he stroked his grey beard thoughtfully. 'Why are you here?' he demanded, looking at Guru Rama.

She threw her head back defiantly. 'We want you to release the prisoners. The villagers have a hard enough life. Why did you kidnap the men?'

The chief gave a rumbling laugh. 'Because they will fetch us good money! There's a fine market for men who can toil and work hard. We will get a good price for them. As a matter of fact, maybe we can throw you in for a few extra rupees.' There was a roar of laughter from the remaining dacoits.

'You have also got one of our schoolgirls – I demand that you release her immediately,' Guru Rama continued bravely. The chief looked angry.

'She was prying – you are all a bunch of troublemakers and will be dealt with appropriately!'

Abi suddenly spoke. 'Please release her. She never meant you any harm!'

The chief looked at Abi and his face broke into the most evil grin she had ever seen. 'The buyer is going to give me loads of money for her. If you want, you can buy her – I only want to be rich – I don't care where it comes from.' Abi gritted her teeth and bit back an angry retort.

The chief gruffly asked his men to take them to the rest of the prisoners, but before they left, he rambled on for a while, making dire predictions about their fates. Abi did not pay much attention; something he said about money was giving her ideas.

Finally, the men pushed the women out of the cave. Abi was still thinking furiously – the dacoits did not know that she had something very precious hidden in her clothes. It would be a wrench to part with the sapphire; but as they walked, Abi thought about Sumathy's kind face and her toothy smile. She was her best friend and she would do anything for her; but giving up the sapphire meant that she was also throwing away the one chance she had of seeing her mother. And yet, Sumathy's life was in danger. Could she really risk that?

Making up her mind, she asked the dacoit by her side to take her back to the chief. 'I have something to tell him. You must take me to him.'

Guru Rama turned around sharply. 'Abi, wait!' she called out, but Abi was already being led back into the cave.

The chief looked at her in some surprise. Abi pulled herself up to her full height and looked at him without a trace of fear. 'I have heard that you men have a code of honour and you won't go back on your word. I have something that can buy all the prisoners. But before I tell you about it, you must promise me that you will let them go if you think it's worth the price.'

The chieftain guffawed with laughter but stopped after a few minutes when he saw Abi's expression. He believed the girl was speaking the truth. He nodded, gruffly promising to keep his word. Abi's voice was hoarse. 'It's worth more than you can imagine. Will you take this and release the prisoners?' She fished the magic sapphire out of her sari and held it up in the torchlight. The chief and the dacoit near him stared in astonishment. Their jaws dropped as the sapphire gleamed and twinkled in the light.

'Where did you find something like that?' asked the chief in a hushed voice, totally mesmerised by the stone. He grabbed the gem and was still staring at it in wonder when the dacoits leading Guru Rama and Guru Usha came running back into the cave, dragging the two ladies with them.

'Chief, they have escaped. There are no prisoners in the next cave… only our six men who were overpowered and are still lying unconscious on the floor!'

The chief pocketed the gem, gave a roar of frustration and sent his men in different directions to search for the escaped prisoners. He walked up to Guru Rama and twisted her arm roughly behind her back. 'Where are they?' he yelled. Abi was incensed at the way he was treating her teacher. She noticed that most of the dacoits had left in search of the prisoners and only the chief and his old sidekick had remained in the cave. The chief was a big man and she knew that she did not have the strength to attack him. She was still wondering what to do when she noticed a blue light enveloping the chief's legs. He started staggering as if he was drunk.

'The sapphire! It must be paralysing him,' she thought, noticing how the light spread from the gem in his pocket to below his knees. In a flash, she knew what to do. She kicked him behind his right knee and he buckled as if his legs could not hold him up any longer. Abi put her hand in his pocket and pulled the gem out quickly; hoping nobody had noticed what she had done. The old sidekick jumped down from his position with greater agility than Abi gave him credit for, and moved menacingly towards her.

Guru Rama swung into action and was tackling the chief who was trying to get up. To Abi's enormous surprise, the old dacoit was attacked by Guru Usha, who sent him flying with a couple of well-aimed, martial-arts-textbook-perfect kicks. As he crumpled to the ground, Guru Usha gave Abi a quick wink and turned around to help her colleague.

It was then that Abi understood the extent of Guruma's plans. Their capture had been very much part of the plan. While the dacoits were distracted by Rama's group, Guru Mahesh's group had freed the prisoners and they had all escaped. Abi looked at her teachers with new respect in her eyes. She always knew they were good, but she had underestimated just how good they were!

27

VILLAGE FOLKLORE

Abi was still admiring the slickness of the operation in her own mind as they reached the entrance of the cavern. Five dacoits were lying unconscious on the floor, and Dev was methodically trussing them up with ropes. 'I got these five and there's one more behind the rocks. Unfortunately, two got away! I think they went after the prisoners. Hopefully, Milind will manage,' said Dev, giving Abi a big grin.

'How did the others escape with the prisoners? Is there another way out of the caverns? Did you plan all this? Is Sumathy safe?' Abi kept rattling off questions at a rapid pace.

'Not now, Abi. She's safe but only for the moment. We have to get back to the school. This was part of the plan, but until we tie up all the dacoits and get the villagers back home, it is not over,' Guru Rama said grimly.

They left Dev to complete his task and made their way inside, towards the third cave. Abi followed her teachers, wondering what fresh horrors the third cave would contain. It was smaller than the one the dacoits were using as their living quarters. There was one oil torch throwing some light on the rocky interior. Abi could make out large sacks and boxes piled neatly in a corner. Guru Usha went up to the nearest box and threw it open. Abi's eyes widened in amazement as the box opened to reveal gold coins and stacks of banknotes. 'This is their stash of loot!' Guru Rama said.

Abi could not resist asking: 'How did you know that the first cave would contain the prisoners and not this one?'

Guru Rama smiled at her. 'Abi, the first cave was the narrowest and was very damp. They would not want to use a wet cave like that for themselves or their treasure – but I thought it would have probably given them a sadistic pleasure to leave the prisoners in such surroundings.'

Having secured all the unconscious dacoits, Dev and the ladies made their way back outside the cavern using the mountainous path. It was a narrow path but much easier than the tunnel that they had to use to get into the cavern. The path led them to the edge of the forest, not far away from the ledge that Abi used as her secret stage.

How lucky that I never came to practise at night – the dacoits may have seen me, Abi thought.

They met Milind smiling at them from the top of a rock. There were two dacoits tied up at his feet. They looked bruised. 'They tried to attack me with a rock,' explained Milind. 'Unfortunately for them, it backfired and they knocked themselves out.'

Dev snorted: 'Don't try and be modest. Doesn't suit you!'

Abi looked at her companions in silent awe. She was still amazed at the professional way that they had managed to overpower a dangerous gang of robbers. She gratefully felt the sapphire, now tucked away safely in the little pouch hidden in her sari folds. She knew that its magic had helped them, but no one else, except Sumathy, would need to know about that.

Milind had been waiting for them and took them to the village as per Guruma's instructions. Guruma was standing outside the village, and when she saw them arrive, she gestured to Abi to walk with her, away from the rest. Guru Rama and Usha followed behind her.

Guruma looked stern. 'Abi – running away after you were explicitly told not to come with us is not impressive. I don't want you to feel that now that we've achieved success, it was absolutely fine for you to disregard our instructions. Your actions do not show respect for the teachers; this is not how I expect my students to behave.' Abi stared shamefacedly at her feet.

Guru Usha joined in the conversation. 'How did you escape anyway? I was so worried that I hadn't locked you in properly, and I have been blaming myself ever since. If some harm had befallen you, can you imagine how I'd have felt?'

By now, Abi had tears in her eyes. Guru Rama tried to come to her aid. 'I know she made a mistake, Guruma; but without her, we may not have had success.'

Guruma quelled her with a look. Abi knew she'd have to face up to this. She looked at Guru Usha's reddening face and apologised profusely. 'I never meant all of you to feel bad about it. I know that you had my best interest in mind, but I was desperate to do something for Sumathy. It was my fault that she'd been captured, and I could not sit and wait in my room while all of you risked your lives for her.'

Guruma sighed and patted Abi on her head. 'You are still grappling with impatience, child. You won't realise it now, impatience causes you to go back a step. What you gain through goodness, you lose through impatience.' Abi stared after Guruma as she walked away uttering these mysterious words. What could she mean by that? Did she know about Abi's magic steps to heaven?

Guru Usha gave her a teasing smile. 'I can't be angry with you for very long, but I am going to give you some extra chores when you get back – and not very nice ones at that.'

They had a wonderful welcome when they walked into the village. The villagers were delighted that their men had returned safe and sound, and were very grateful to Guruma and the others. Krish came running out and gave Abi a tight hug. 'You have been wonderful. Without you, my father and the others would have never escaped.' Abi smiled but her eyes were searching for Sumathy. Krish seemed to understand. 'Come with me, I'll take you to Sumathy.'

Abi ran along with him towards his hut and stopped short when she saw a pale but smiling Sumathy sitting on a plastic chair. 'Sumathy, are you ok? I am so sorry about what happened,' Abi began, but she was hardly able to get the words out, she was so overcome with emotion. She dropped down on her knees and hugged her friend gingerly.

Sumathy had a bandage around her head but otherwise looked unhurt. She returned Abi's gentle embrace, smiling wanly. 'Don't be silly – it's not your fault. We were ambushed when we went into the forest at night. I think there were two men. They hit you hard but I think they hit me and Dhruva lightly. I pretended to fall over but got up and followed them. I didn't realise that there was a third man who must have seen me, and I was taken prisoner. When I woke up, I found myself with the rest of the prisoners.'

Abi smiled through her tears. 'I'm so glad you're not harmed. You must be mistaken about Dhruva – he was actually hurt quite badly – they've had to sedate him.'

Sumathy's voice was a whisper that only Abi could hear. 'I don't think I was mistaken – I hadn't been hit hard and I saw him fall down. He was hardly hurt. Do you think he was pretending?'

Abi pursed her lips. 'Sumathy, he was badly hurt. He could barely walk back. Why should he pretend anyway? He was the one who wanted us to save the men – he was so insistent on trying to help the villagers, too. Why do you think badly of him?'

Sumathy looked unconvinced, but they were distracted when Krish's mother Yashoda came out and gave them a beaming smile. 'Well done, Abi – I believe you were instrumental in saving our men and this young lady.'

Abi blushed. 'I didn't do anything. It was the others who planned it all and executed it well.'

She felt a warm hand on her shoulder. 'Don't underestimate yourself, Abi. Without you, I don't think we could have made our way through the tunnel. Also, without your persuasion, we may have never even come to the village to help everyone out. Well done. You should be proud of yourself. I am,' said Guru Rama with a kind smile.

After the initial excitement, Abi began to feel really tired and wanted to go back to her bed. Guruma organised a few things – Milind and Dev were to go down to the valley and inform the police about the dacoits. The villagers were asked to build a secure fence around the village, and after promising to return the next day to join their celebrations, Guruma took the other teachers and Abi and Sumathy back to Gurukul.

Pooja and Arundhati came running to meet them and were dying to ask them all about it. 'Not now, girls. They need to sleep and so do we. You can talk all you want tomorrow and join us in the village for the celebrations,' said Guruma with a gentle smile.

Pooja hesitated and looked red in the face. Then she burst out, 'Guruma, don't blame Abi for everything. I helped her escape and unlocked the room. I am really sorry but I felt bad for her and knew how worried she was about Sumathy.'

Guruma's face was impassive but she nodded at Pooja. 'I am so glad that you've owned up to it. I am not happy with Abi, but I know both of you had good intentions.

However, you will join her in doing the extra chores that Guru Usha will mete out to you.'

Pooja and Abi looked at each other, then nodded. This was the least that they expected. Abi thanked Pooja and gave her a quick hug. Sumathy was touched by their concern for her and burst into tears. Guruma broke them up at that point. 'Off you go – you need rest!' The girls dutifully obeyed her and sank into a deep sleep for several hours.

When they finally woke up, it was nearly midday. There was a lot of excitement at school. The students who had stayed behind after the exams were invited to the village. The villagers were already celebrating the return of their men as well as a tribal hill festival. 'There will be a lot of singing and dancing,' said Sumathy, rubbing her hands in glee.

'You better not be thinking of exerting yourself,' said Abi, pretending to be stern.

A little while later, when they got a moment alone, Abi told Sumathy about the powers of the sapphire. 'The gem is yours now – it probably sensed that the chief was evil and paralysed him. Abi, how exciting!' said Sumathy when she heard the story.

'What are you talking about?' Dhruva asked, appearing suddenly.

Gosh, you startled me!' Abi exclaimed. Sumathy looked uncomfortable, but Abi trusted Dhruva even more after their adventures. 'You know I mentioned that I have a little something that would lead me to my mother? It turns out that it protects me – it paralysed the chief in the cave and that helped us escape. But of course, even without its help, I am sure the teachers would have got us out!' said Abi loyally.

Dhruva clapped her on her shoulders and said, 'In that case, Abi, I am extremely grateful for whatever it is!'

⁓

A bit later, all the girls dressed up in their best saris and adorned their hair before walking to the village. Abi helped Sumathy get ready as she was still a bit pale from her ordeal. Dhruva joined them as they left Gurukul; he had made the effort to dress up, too, and was wearing his best silk *kurta*. His head was still covered in plasters, but he must have been feeling much better. He looked a bit sheepish when he spoke to Sumathy, but Abi was just so delighted that all of them were together again that she barely noticed. They were given a hero's welcome by the villagers who greeted them with flowers, rosewater and vermillion. This was the traditional way of receiving warriors who came back victorious.

The village was festooned with flowers and paper buntings. Yashoda was looking radiant, standing with her happy, smiling husband. Even old Granthi looked nice as she garlanded Guruma. She was accompanied by her husband, the chieftain of the village. He was an old man with silver hair and deep, penetrating eyes. He led all the visitors to the centre of the village where seats had been set up for them. Once they were all seated, he climbed up on a makeshift dais and made a little speech. He thanked all of them with a great deal of sincerity. Abi was touched and had to blink away a tear or two at the end of his speech. She looked around embarrassed and was gratified to see that others were wiping their eyes as well.

The celebrations started in full earnest. There was much singing and dancing and many of the schoolgirls joined in alongside the villagers. There were little stalls serving unusual delicacies. 'These rhododendron *pakoras* are yummy,' said Pooja, looking at a stall where an old lady was frying flowers dipped in batter. The girls and Dhruva went around all the stalls and sampled all the goodies. Krish and his brother Bal joined them and they had a great time talking and laughing all evening. Even the coolness between Dhruva and Sumathy disappeared.

As the sunlight faded, the village was lit up by a series of little terracotta oil lamps. Dev and Milind came back from the valley and informed everyone that the dacoits were now in police custody. The police were delighted with the capture and the chief inspector had promised to organise the return of the villagers' property as soon as possible. The village would also get a monetary reward. The general mood improved even more at the news. Abi felt really content looking at all the happy faces around her.

'Come, old Baba is going to tell us a story. His stories are fascinating,' said Krish, dragging Abi away. Abi held on to Dhruva's hand to lead him there and some of the other girls followed. Everyone sat around a charpoy, a kind of bed made with wood and ropes, on which sat an old man. He was toothless and bald but had an enormous grin on his face and was clearly enjoying the attention that he was getting. Baba told the group many stories. Some were fairy tales with a prince or princess and always had a happy ending. Others were folklore – some of these had a moral and others were scary.

Abi was fascinated by one such tale about a hidden temple in the mountains. 'Anyone who enters the temple on his own will benefit from it for the rest of his life. But it is only the bravest of braves who can get to the temple. There are many obstacles in its path... darkness beyond the darkest night, eerie noises that can scare even courageous men, slithering snakes that hiss into your ears, wild animals that can attack you silently, scary ghosts and even man-eating demons,' said the old man melodramatically, looking keenly at his audience. He paused and stared pointedly at Abi. 'If you manage to enter the temple, even the gods will acknowledge you for being very courageous.'

Abi gave a start as she felt someone pinch her hand. She looked around to see Sumathy staring at her with suppressed excitement. Abi waited until Baba took a break to drink some tea before turning back to Sumathy. 'What is it?' she whispered.

Sumathy's eyes were gleaming. 'Abi, don't you realise? Baba has just told you the way to climb a magic step! One of the steps is courage. And if you manage to get to the temple, even the gods will have to acknowledge that you're courageous,' said Sumathy quietly, so that none of their companions could hear her.

Abi started feeling a rush of excitement, but she still had a few doubts. 'Do you think he's telling the truth?'

Sumathy had another of her usual good ideas. She turned to Krish who was sitting in front of them and asked him: 'Are these tales true, Krish? Is there a hidden temple or is it in Baba's imagination only?'

Krish turned to Sumathy. 'Of course it's true. Baba never lies. But it is very dangerous. So don't you go around trying it!' he warned. But the girls had already stopped listening and were staring at each other in delight. The path for their next adventure had been lit up by Baba's stories. Abi's joy faded a little when she thought of the wild animals, snakes, ghosts and man-eating demons that she'd have to face, but she flicked them away for the moment.

I'll worry about those later. Let me enjoy the idea of climbing another step closer to my mother, Abi thought, glowing with anticipation and eagerness.

28

THE NEXT STEP

Abi and Sumathy were in a state of dizzying excitement that night. They were now certain that they had the clue to the next magic step. 'You must prepare carefully before you embark on the mission,' said Sumathy seriously. Abi agreed. Although she was still feeling the buzz of finding the next step, Baba's warnings about the dangers in the forest sobered her. She was just a young girl – how could she enter this dark realm that even brave men feared entering?

'It is study time,' Abi said, turning to her comfort zone. 'I need to learn as much as I can about snakes, wild animals, demons and ghosts. Then maybe I have a chance of facing them.' The girls started hatching their plans together. Abi would have to read up a lot of the mythology lessons.

'Abi, don't worry about the animals. You will charm them automatically.'

Abi looked doubtful – charming deer, rabbits and peacocks was easy. She was not so sure her magic would work on panthers and bears.

The excitement had been better than medicine for Sumathy, and she looked more alive than ever. As per their plan, Sumathy was going to go back to the village to try and wheedle more information out of Baba about the whereabouts of the temple. She had another brainwave the next day, soon after breakfast. 'Abi, I have been thinking for a while. There's a book that Guru Mahesh often refers to – it has a list of mythical creatures and how to deal with them. Maybe you could ask to borrow it and go through it while I tackle Baba?'

As soon as Sumathy left for the village, Abi went up to Guru Mahesh and borrowed his book. To her surprise, she found the book fascinating. It was extensively illustrated and had very good descriptions of the various mythical creatures that Guru Mahesh had taught about in class. *Baba probably meant rakshasa when he talked about man-eating demons and pisacha or bhuta when he referred to ghosts*, thought Abi to herself. She made copious notes about all three creatures and studied their likes, dislikes and characteristics in detail. 'Rakshasas* are frightening and like to eat human beings, but they can also be a bit stupid and easy to outwit. Of course, this is a bit of a generalisation and there can be some very intelligent ones, too. Let's hope ours is not too intelligent. *Pisachas* and *bhutas* are more difficult to deal with, but there are complex Sanskrit mantras that will send them away. I am trying to learn these by heart,' said Abi to Sumathy when she returned.

Sumathy's trip to the village had also been successful. She had used all her charm on Baba, who was only too happy to tell her all he knew about the hidden temple.

The girls were happily exchanging notes when there was a knock on the door. Abi got up to open the door and was surprised to find a pensive Krish standing outside.

'What is it, Krish? Is everything all right?' Abi asked, thinking the worst.

Krish nodded and asked if he could come in. He entered and sat down next to Sumathy and looked at both of the girls seriously. 'I know I am very young and you probably will not listen to what I say; however, you are my friends and it is my duty to tell you what I think.' His next few words caught her by surprise. 'I know you are going to attempt reaching the hidden temple!'

Sumathy and Abi exchanged shocked glances. Krish continued: 'It is very dangerous and I am very worried about you. Can I persuade you to please reconsider?' Abi was quiet for a few moments. There was something very heart warming about this young child's friendly and caring demeanour. She decided to tell him the truth. Very briefly, she explained their adventures from last year – how they had discovered that her mother was an *apsara* and about her mission to climb the seven magic steps to go to heaven and meet her mother.

Krish listened to the entire story without interrupting. At the end, he sighed deeply and looked at Abi gravely. 'Abi, I do understand your eagerness to go see your mother. The way to the hidden temple is very dangerous. I can see that you're preparing yourself, but there would be dangers that you're not even aware of. Do you have to choose this way to prove your courage?' Krish beseeched her, but Abi's mind was made up.

'If I cannot make my way to heaven to see her, I will lose all my purpose in life. Please understand, Krish. I have to do this.'

Krish nodded resignedly and fumbled in the folds of his robes to pull out a little peacock feather set in a chain. 'Then please take this. It is a little charm that may save you in your hour of need.'

Abi looked at it in wonder. 'What is it?'

Krish continued to be sombre. 'Abi, all you need to know is that it will help you when you need it most.' Abi gave him a big hug and put the chain around her neck. Before leaving them, Krish gave Abi a few more tips on how to survive in the forest en route to the temple. 'There will be little *thalis* or plates with a lamp, rice, fruit, money and other offerings placed by the foot of some trees. You must avoid looking at these as the trees are likely to contain the *pisachas* or *bhutas*. The tribals in the area make these offerings to the spirits so that they do not harm them. Also, if you encounter any dangerous wild animals, touch the peacock feather – it will bring you help.'

When Krish left, Sumathy turned to Abi and said something that upset Abi greatly. 'Abi, I know you've often confided in Dhruva about things, but I feel you shouldn't tell him about this plan. I don't trust him – I have had too many doubts in my mind since the dacoits' incident.'

This raised Abi's hackles at once. 'Sumathy, why are you so prejudiced against him? What could he possibly want by getting you captured by the dacoits?'

Her friend shook her head. 'I have no idea – I have been racking my brains trying to think about it. Maybe he was going to get something from them in return. I don't know.'

Abi now started feeling angry. 'Not guilty until he's proven so. Please stop suspecting him – it really bothers me.'

The argument got more heated and the two girls glared at each other until Sumathy gave up with a sigh. 'You're right, let us not fight over something that neither of us is sure about. It's time for bed.'

—⁂—

That night, Abi could not sleep at all. She kept thinking of Krish's warnings and worked herself up about all the dangers in the forest. Finally, giving up, she opened her eyes and sat up on her bed. Sumathy was fast asleep. It was still very dark outside. Abi absent-mindedly walked up to the window in their room and looked outside. To her shock, she could see Dhruva standing behind a tree, staring straight at her. Abi rubbed her eyes and looked away for a minute, trying to digest this information.

Could Dhruva see? He had convinced everyone that he was blind. Dhruva was standing in the shadows, behind a tree. There was no light around him and he probably thought no one could see him in the darkness. However, Surya's gift came to Abi's aid once more. She pretended to glance around aimlessly but in the process, observed Dhruva a bit more. He had removed his usual dark glasses. His green eyes glimmered in the darkness. The shock of seeing those green eyes was too much for Abi. She turned away from the window and ran back to her bed, her heart thumping agonisingly in her chest. She knew those green eyes. Dhruva was none other than Varun!

Abi spent the whole night thinking about what she had seen out of the window. She remembered how Varun had changed into a great fish and had attacked Abi when she tried to take the magic sapphire from its hiding place. She shuddered even now as she thought of her narrow escape. Now he seemed to have changed himself into Dhruva, who did not resemble Varun in any way, except for his eyes. Abi had grown very fond of Dhruva as a friend over the last few months and trusted him – but his green eyes were so unique, so familiar. So Sumathy's suspicions were well founded after all! Abi was inexplicably infatuated by Varun, but it was clear that he was not a well-meaning friend. *What could he want? Does he want to kill me? Why? Or does he want the sapphire and to reach heaven himself? Why can I not hate him?* She kept repeating these questions in her mind but could not arrive at any conclusions.

When Sumathy woke up that morning, Abi looked a wreck. 'Have you not slept at all? You look terrible,' Sumathy commented on seeing her friend. Abi mumbled something about not feeling well. She did not want to worry Sumathy further by telling her about Dhruva.

Abi spent most of the day in bed. Sumathy had informed the teachers that Abi was not feeling well. Guru Usha had come to visit and had decided that Abi simply needed to rest. Pooja and Arundhati also visited Abi later that day. When they were alone, Abi asked Sumathy to start thinking of an excuse they could use to slip away from school and go to the temple. But Sumathy was one step ahead and had already done some thinking.

'We should tell Guru Usha one day next week that Krish and his family have invited us to the village the day after. Then that night, the two of us can climb up to the mountain where the forest of the hidden temple is. I will wait outside the forest as you need to reach the temple alone, and you can go and come back.'

Abi was amused at the matter-of-fact tone that Sumathy had adopted about her trip to the forest. 'What if I don't come back?'

Sumathy shivered. 'Don't even say that! You have the peacock feather, you are working on the mantras and hopefully would have learnt it all by next week. I think you'll be safe. But if you are not back by the morning, I will enter the forest in search of you.'

Abi stared at her best friend, horrified. She did not want her risking her life to come in search of Abi. But no amount of persuasion would change Sumathy's mind. 'Don't worry, Abi. I am also studying up on black magic and how to escape demons and ghosts. Between the two of us, we can manage.'

⁘

The week passed by in a flash. Both the girls spent every spare moment studying books and learning more about *rakshasas*, *pisachas* and *bhutas*. They discussed various means and techniques with Guru Mahesh, who was pleasantly surprised at their sudden interest in mythology. Abi also worked on her Sanskrit mantras – they were complex but her pronunciation had to be perfect in order for them to work. The girls also worked hard on their martial arts exercises to improve their physical stamina in case they had to run away from any danger.

All through the week, Abi avoided Dhruva. She was worried that he would sense the fact that she knew about him if she spent time with him. She used excuses about extra work, visiting Krish and a pretend illness to avoid being with him. Luckily for her, Sumathy did not notice as she herself was preoccupied with their tasks. Abi tried hard to work out what she would do if she was attacked by Dhruva – but somehow no ideas came to her. Despite her fears, she still felt a mix of love and friendship towards the man she knew as both Dhruva and Varun.

Finally, the day of reckoning arrived. Sumathy told Guru Usha their story about going to the village early next morning and got permission to be away before breakfast. So the girls knew no one would miss them the next day. That evening, after everyone had gone to bed, both the girls crept out of their rooms and embarked on their adventure.

The journey to the mountain was not very long, although it was very convoluted. The girls were used to climbing up through narrow paths, and Abi could see perfectly despite the darkness. They carried a small torch for Sumathy in case they were ever separated. After a couple of hours of steady climbing, they reached the edge of the forest where the hidden temple was. 'I am so glad Baba told you the way. It would have been very tricky to find the temple without his directions,' Abi panted.

The girls stood at the edge of the dark forest with palpitating hearts. 'This forest looks nothing like the one that we have down by the school. The trees are so twisted and gnarled, and there seems to be no gap at all between them!' exclaimed Sumathy. Abi silently agreed. The forest looked more frightening than anything she had imagined. There was a spookiness about it; everything was pitch black, and yet Abi had the awful feeling that someone inside was watching them.

For a minute, Abi's heart dragged her heels. *Don't go in there! You'll never come back.* Fearful thoughts raced around in her head.

The terrified expression on Sumathy's face did nothing to dispel her own dread. She took a deep breath and tried to fight the paralysis in her limbs by talking sense to herself. *Abi, this is your one sure chance of getting closer to your mother. For your mother's sake, don't give up now!* Without further ado, she decided to take the plunge. She squeezed Sumathy's hand in a goodbye gesture and stepped into the forest without looking back!

29.

WHAT LIES WITHIN

Abi stepped gingerly on the forest floor, afraid of disturbing the creatures living there. The darkness totally enveloped her – even Surya's gift enabled her to only see up to a short distance. She walked slowly, trying to keep track of the direction in which she was going. Periodically, she stopped and tried to mark her position by piling a mound of stones or twigs in a corner. She had learnt this boy-scout trick from the storybooks that she had read in the UK. She also carried an old compass that she had in her school bag in an attempt to find the temple without getting lost.

She could just not shake off the feeling of being watched. She turned back several times to see if there was anyone around, but there was nobody. The forest was full of eerie noises, just as Baba had predicted. There was a sound of scurrying feet in front of Abi, as if rats or other animals were moving around on the ground. Abi jumped as she heard a loud hoot next to her and then calmed down as she saw a great big owl take flight. She could hear the hum of insects around her. Cicadas or crickets were rubbing their feet together to produce a sharp trill that added to the atmosphere.

The trees were gnarled and thorny. Abi had never seen such a dense forest in her life. There were prickly bushes that often tangled in her hair and sari. Abi chided herself on being slow, but it seemed impossible to move any faster. Her heart started beating painfully once again when she saw an orange glow ahead. She made her way cautiously forward and found a *thali* under a tree, just like Krish had mentioned. She averted her eyes immediately to avoid any encounters with a ghost and looked for the best way to get past the tree without any mishaps. As she walked past it, she heard a fierce hiss. Shocked, she turned around to find a snake dangling on a thorny branch of the tree. It was a cobra and it had its hood raised in self-defence.

Abi was at a safe enough distance; she tried walking past the tree quietly when she realised that the snake was stuck on a large thorn. Abi felt a stab of pity mixed with a shudder of revulsion; she loved all animals and empathised greatly with them; but she did not like reptiles or anything that crept or crawled! Then she remembered how her twin Vy was really fond of them. To see a beautiful snake pinioned to the tree by a thorn would have been unbearable to Vy. She couldn't walk away and leave the creature in pain. 'How did you manage to get stuck like that?' It was almost as if someone had thrown the snake on the thorny branch.

Abi was now in a quandary. In order to free the snake, she would have to go close to the *thali* that Krish had asked her to avoid at all costs; but there was no way that Abi was going to walk away from a creature in need, especially after her sister's memory was urging her on in her head. She walked up to the *thali* and without touching it, reached across to try and free the snake. The snake squirmed on the branch. Abi was very careful as it was possible that the snake would attack her in fear. She distracted the snake with one hand and while it moved its head away, quickly freed its tail from the thorn to release it. The snake fell on the ground with a hiss and disappeared into the undergrowth. Abi wiped the sweat off her brow and turned around to move away from the tree. She recoiled in horror as she saw a wispy white creature with bloodshot eyes standing behind her.

'Who are you?' Abi nearly screamed. The creature was terrible to look at – it had a semi-transparent body that Abi could almost see through. Its face was sinister and evil, its eyes round and bulbous. It had a great mass of wispy white hair on its head. The spirit stared at Abi for a while, then opened its mouth wide to show a set of sharp, yellowish fangs. *Oh my God, this must* be *a bhuta or pisacha. What am I supposed to do?* Abi wondered frantically.

In her panic, she could not remember the spells that would combat the creature, or what she must do to protect herself. It hissed and walked around her as if inspecting her. Abi was paralysed with horror and unable to move. The spirit brought its face close to Abi. Terrified, Abi closed her eyes; and this saved her. As soon as she shut her eyes, she saw Vy in her head, smiling at her, encouraging her. This vision transported Abi out of her zone of fear. She was able to think more clearly and started breathing deeply, trying to remember all she had learnt. She tried to relax her mind and the Sanskrit mantras flooded back into her memory in a moment. Keeping her eyes closed, she started chanting the mantras in a clear voice. The hissing stopped. Slowly, she opened her eyes, to find that the apparition had disappeared. Abi heaved a sigh of relief, secretly congratulating herself on working so hard to learn the mantras and thanking her twin sister for coming to her aid even if she wasn't physically with her anymore.

———

Abi continued to trudge through the jungle. After a while, a sixth sense warning her of more danger started prickling again. She was sure that she was being followed. Without breaking a step, Abi felt through the folds of her sari. Earlier that evening, just for such eventualities, she had hidden a small mirror in her sari and now she pulled it out and held it in front of her. The mirror would let her see her pursuer without alerting him. The night was still dark, but Abi's boon from Surya once again came to her rescue. At a good distance behind her, she could see the slim figure of Dhruva. He had removed his glasses and his green eyes shone through the darkness of the forest. *So, he's following me. I wonder what he wants. Will he attack me?* she wondered, her heart pounding.

She kept bracing herself for the attack from behind, but it never came. *Maybe he has started thinking of me as his friend and will not hurt me*, she hoped desperately, still watching Dhruva in her hand mirror. By now, Abi had made considerable progress in the forest. She continued to hear all sorts of noises that she couldn't identify, but she was less afraid now than before. With a strange irony, she was actually glad that Dhruva was following her. She almost felt secure in his company, although she knew that there was a chance that he would attack her. *It's probably because he is the devil I know rather than all the ones I don't know*, thought Abi, smirking to herself in the darkness.

———✦———

More time passed. Abi felt sure that she was nearing her destination. The trees were even more gnarled and twisted in this part of the forest. Suddenly she heard a snarl. The sound seemed to come from all around her. An eerie whistle abruptly stopped Abi in her tracks. Then she saw several gleaming eyes in the darkness. She was surrounded by wild dogs!

Abi's fear battled her common sense. She was not afraid of wild animals, because she loved them. However, wild dogs could be dangerous. They were known to attack elephants, wild boar and even tigers. Some of the dogs drew closer, their mouths open in a toothy snarl. She breathed deeply and stood her ground, trying not to let fear numb her brain. The dogs stood around her for a while but did not attack. One of them gave a low yelp and turned around to walk away from Abi. The other dogs followed their leader for a short distance, then all of them turned and looked at Abi. She stared back in surprise. Could it be that they were trying to help her?

If they were domesticated dogs, she would have thought that they were trying to lead her somewhere.

She made up her mind. Firmly pushing her fear away, Abi followed the dogs, taking the path they were taking. They twisted and turned through several paths in the forest, finally stopping in front of a large cave. Abi stepped forward quickly to see where they had brought her. The entrance to the cave seemed to be blocked by rocks. The lead dog started howling loudly. Abi could then hear a lot of excited whimpers from behind the rock. She understood – the entrance had caved in and had trapped the pups inside.

Abi looked at the rocks – they were large boulders. She would have to work carefully to try and ensure they did not cave in on each other and hurt the pups. It would be slow, painstaking work. If she chose to do this, there was a chance that she may not find the temple that night. She looked at the sad faces of the dogs around her and made up her mind. Her father would have approved of her decision. 'I will try my best,' she promised them, and slowly started moving the rocks around. She had to be extremely careful. Once or twice she touched something that caused the rocks inside to rumble, but luckily they didn't collapse. All the exercises that she had done to build her muscles through martial arts came to Abi's aid. With some difficulty, she shifted enough rocks to be able to see inside.

There were at least twenty pups gathered expectantly around the mouth of the cave. If she moved any more rocks, she could cause another avalanche and crush some of the pups. The best thing to do would be to squeeze her upper body inside the cave and bring them out two at a time. It was slow work and she had to be very gentle with the little ones, but she got them all out eventually. After she had squeezed herself in for the final time to check that she had got them all out, she grinned at the joyous reunion of the dogs and their young.

Leaving them to celebrate, Abi quietly sneaked away to get back to her mission. However, all those twists and turns on the way had confused her thoroughly. She brought out her compass to get a sense of where she was, but after crossing a broken stump three times, Abi sat down in frustration. She was totally lost. She pulled out the mirror to look around her but could not even see Dhruva in the distance. *I must have lost him when the dogs took me to the cave*, Abi thought, somewhat sadly. Her thoughts then wandered to her mother. Her longing for her mother, her desperation to see her and the tiredness combined into a powerful wave of emotion in her head. Putting her head on her knees, she began to sob. Will I never get to the temple? Will I never get to see my mother?

30

THE TEMPLE OF COURAGE

Abi raised her head with a start when she heard a whimper near her. She was surprised to see that she was once again surrounded by the dogs. They were all sitting down in a circle around her. Busy in her own misery, she had not noticed their arrival. She wiped her tears. 'Are you all here to see what's bothering me? I wonder if you understand me... I want to reach the hidden temple. Can you take me there?' The dogs cocked their heads, but they didn't move. Abi sighed in disappointment. She hadn't really expected them to understand. Then she remembered Krish and his peacock feather.

She was not sure what the feather would do, but she pulled the chain out from around her neck and fingered the feather thoughtfully. 'I wish the dogs would understand me,' she said aloud.

A voice rang out in the darkness: 'Thank you very much for helping our pups. What can we do for you?' Abi jumped in surprise. The gruff voice belonged to one of the wild dogs.

Abi stared at the dogs, then at the peacock feather. 'Am I dreaming? This actually seems to work!' she said, amazed.

The leader of the pack replied. 'Your feather is a magic translator. It will help you talk to and understand any wild animal. Now, tell us where you want to go and we can help you.'

Abi explained how she wanted to get to the hidden temple. The leader growled thoughtfully. 'There are two ways of getting there. One way is to go via the most dangerous part of the forest where a *rakshasa* lives. There is another way that is known only to us. We can take you along our shortcut path – there's a chasm that you will have to cross. Once you have reached the temple, we will have to leave you. Will you find your way back? After we take you there, we will have to take our pups and find another safe place for them.'

Abi nodded excitedly. 'I was always aware of the dangers of the forest. Please take me via your path and I'll find my way back,' she said, getting up and brushing the leaves off her clothes.

Some dogs stayed back with the pups and others got up to lead Abi to the temple. They took a rough path that was winding its way up a hill. The path was crowded by a dense growth of brambles, and Abi had to fight her way through the thorns. After a multitude of scratches and tears on her skin and clothes, Abi reached an open cliff. The dogs were gathered around the edge. 'Abi, you have to jump off this cliff so that you can land on the rock face on the opposite hill. Can you do that?'

Abi looked down the edge of the cliff fearfully. The hill opposite was at the same level and relatively close by, but there was a chasm between the two hills. If she took a running jump, she could land on the other cliff; but if she hesitated or took a smaller step, it could be dangerous. She watched some of the dogs make their way. They lightly and elegantly jumped across as if they were crossing a small ditch on the ground. Abi felt queasy as she saw the depth of chasm between the hills. Fear rose like poison in her head.

'There is a reason I asked you to meditate regularly, child,' Guruma's voice whispered in Abi's head. Yes, meditation was the answer. She stilled the noises in her head, breathed deeply and told herself that if there was no chasm involved, she could do that jump without any trouble at all. Putting aside thoughts of falling into the chasm, she said a little prayer and took a running jump.

Abi fell with a hard thud on the grass on the other hill. She felt bruised and battered, but when she got up gingerly, she knew she had not damaged anything except her dignity. The dogs were waiting patiently for her to get up. Giving them a sheepish grin, she followed them through the rough terrain of the second hill. 'Although it seems like another hill altogether, the forest actually curves around through the other path and both the hills are linked,' said the leader. They had reached a deeper, darker part of the forest and there was a narrow path snaking into the distance. 'When you come back to this fork, just follow the path we've taken from the cliff and then you can jump across and get to where we started from. Avoid the other path as the *rakshasa* is around there somewhere.' Abi took a good look at her return route and made a mental note to avoid straying into the *rakshasa*'s path.

As they walked further, the path got narrower and darker. The trees grew closer together and there was hardly any light coming through. The dogs took Abi towards a clump of trees and stopped there. Even with Surya's gift, Abi had to strain her eyes to look through this clump. She could see pieces of grey rock between the trees. 'Abi, we have to leave you here. If you walk around the trees, you will find an opening, and this will take you inside. Good luck on the way back. Remember that you have a magic translator – there will be other animals that can help you.'

Abi thanked the dogs for their kindness, and with a heavy heart, watched them disappear into the forest. They had been great company and now Abi felt all alone once more. She walked around the clump of trees and found a dark opening between two of them, as the dogs had predicted. She stepped inside the opening, and to her surprise, immediately there was plenty of light illuminating the temple. She wondered about the source of the mysterious light and walked towards the inner sanctum of the beautifully-carved temple.

There was a deity chiselled into the rock, decorated with fresh flowers. Abi was puzzled. Who had been decorating the temple and the deity in such an inaccessible place? Once inside the sanctum, Abi experienced a stillness and peace that she had never felt before. She sat down cross-legged, closed her eyes and started meditating. There was a flash of light that she could feel even with her eyes closed. Abi blinked, and to her amazement, she saw a charming lady beside her. There was a light emanating from her face that lit up the whole sanctum. Abi realised with awe that she was in the presence of the deity and bowed her head in deference and greeting.

'Welcome to the temple. You are a brave girl, Abi. You have done well in coming this far. The rewards for your courage will be sweet.' Abi rubbed her eyes in disbelief when the lady vanished as suddenly as she had appeared. Had she been dreaming or had the temple deity actually spoken to her? She sat there for a while, trying to ponder this development.

After a while, when no further visions appeared, Abi rose quietly and left the temple. She still had no clue about who was looking after the temple, but she knew that they would make themselves known to her if they wished. She had achieved what she set out to, and hopefully it would be enough for her to climb one magic step. Abi was not sure what to do about the rest of the steps but chided herself that patience was one of them and started retracing her way back through the forest.

Abi reached the fork in the forest path where she had to choose the right one to lead her to the cliff. The hairs on the back of her neck stood up; once again, she felt that she was being watched. Her breathing became shallow out of fear. She looked around her but could see nothing; but the sense that somebody was watching her was intense. In a sudden move, Abi looked up at the trees behind her. Sure enough, the "someone" she had been expecting to see was a panther sitting on a branch. It had large green eyes and a glorious black coat. It stared at Abi for a short while, before jumping down lightly in front of her. Abi touched the peacock translator around her neck and looked at the panther.

'You are not lost, are you?' said the panther in a low growl.

Abi smiled in relief – Krish's magic translator had worked again. 'No, I am just on my way back to my friend at the edge of the forest.'

The panther walked around Abi, its tail swishing. It stretched itself on the ground and purred lazily. 'Who are you talking about? Not the young man who has been captured by the snake-people? I know he was following you.'

Abi started, surprised. Her eyes darkened with worry. 'No, but what do you mean? I know Dhruva was following me – has anything happened to him? Please tell me about it – I must find him,' pleaded Abi.

'This boy has been taken by the snake-people. In order to find him, you will have to take the other path, away from the cliff. You probably know that path takes you through the area where the *rakshasa* lives. If you get away from him, the snake-people are not easy to find or to plead with either. I think you should forget about him and go back.'

Abi looked at the panther in disgust. 'You think I should just abandon my friend and save my skin?' she demanded, her hands on her hips.

The panther was unperturbed. 'Friend? I think you use the term loosely, don't you? He isn't your friend, is he? He was out to attack you. Why should you bother about such a person?' Abi pursed her lips. She still was not sure why she felt this way about Dhruva. She could only think of him as a friend even if she suspected he was the same shapeshifter as Varun! She knew that she could not live with herself if she did not try to rescue him.

'What about your other friend? She is probably looking for you inside the forest now. So you don't care about her, then?' said the panther, his tone mocking. Abi stared at the cat and frowned, angry with herself. How could she have forgotten that Sumathy would enter the forest looking for her, if she did not return by the morning! She had no idea what time it was; in the darkness of the deep forest, day and night seemed alike.

She looked at the panther and begged for a favour. 'Please help me. You must find my friend Sumathy and bring her to me. If she wanders around alone, she will be in danger. Please take this translator – I don't need it but with this, you can talk to her. And then she can come with you. I will wait for you.'

The panther swished its tail lazily. 'Why should I help you? You haven't done anything for me.'

'Because there must be some goodness in you... because I am desperate... because you never know when I can and will help you!' said Abi fiercely. 'I cannot believe that you could ignore my pleas and go to sleep somewhere!' The panther did not seem particularly bothered by Abi's outburst. Abi's eyes were now swimming with tears, and her thoughts were with Sumathy, who was probably wandering helplessly in the forest. She remembered how her best friend had been in grave danger with the dacoits, and her dismay grew.

The panther watched her for a while and then finally gave a low growl: 'Stop whimpering. I'll do it – but only because you may be of help one day! Give me the translator and wait here; I should be back soon.' Abi smiled in relief as she watched the panther vanish into the forest with the peacock chain in its mouth. She hoped that it would not be too difficult for the panther to find and bring Sumathy to her. Once together, they could go to rescue poor Dhruva from the snake-people. In the meantime, she sat down to try and remember her notes about *rakshasas* and racked her brain for ideas on how to outsmart one.

31

THE RAKSHASA'S LAIR

The panther was back with Sumathy crouched low on its back in no time at all. Sumathy met Abi with a relieved hug, looking happy about getting off the panther's back. 'I was worried that you were hurt or you were in trouble when I saw the panther with the peacock feather in its mouth,' she said breathlessly.

The panther growled contemptuously and then turned to Abi. 'I have done this in return for a favour that you will owe me. I will claim it one day. Goodbye – until we meet again.' Abi thanked the panther and waved it goodbye, watching as the dark forest swallowed it. Abi then quickly filled Sumathy in on the goings-on in the forest.

She was careful not to mention that Dhruva was indeed Varun or that he was following her to harm her. 'I think Dhruva was following me to protect me – though I don't know how. But now he has been captured by the snake-people and we have to save him!' lied Abi, not meeting Sumathy's eyes. Sumathy looked uncertain; but being the kind-hearted girl that she was, she was soon persuaded to help rescue Dhruva. The girls discussed Abi's plans on how to cope if they encountered the *rakshasa*, and then they began their journey into the dangerous part of the forest, their hearts beating wildly.

'Even the trees look more frightening here,' Sumathy whispered, looking fearfully around her. Abi agreed. The trees were more sinister in this stretch of the forest; much larger, more twisted and much darker. The girls walked slowly, stopping every time they heard something rustle or move. However, it was almost always a false alarm and they covered a fair distance without meeting the dreaded *rakshasa*.

After a while, they heard a strange noise that shook the ground and the trees around them. 'Is it an earthquake?' Abi wondered aloud, clutching at Sumathy with sweaty fingers. The girls crept forward cautiously but stopped in shock as they saw a giant lying on the ground, fast asleep. He was enormous – more than four times the size of a normal human being. His head was resting against a rock; and every time he snored, there was a loud rumbling noise and everything around him vibrated as if in fear. The girls stood staring at him in pure terror.

Sumathy finally shook Abi's arm and said in a faint voice, 'Maybe we can tiptoe around him and he won't notice us.' The giant stopped snoring at that precise moment, petrifying the girls. But he did not open his eyes. Wordlessly, Abi gestured to Sumathy that the two should split up and approach him from different directions. Sumathy seemed to understand her plan, but she looked even more horrified. Abi tiptoed slowly in one direction, while Sumathy disappeared in the opposite. Taking one step at a time, making sure that she was not stepping on anything that creaked or crunched beneath her feet, Abi was just a few feet away from the giant's head when he woke up with a frightening roar. 'Who goes there... aha, caught you!' he bellowed, putting out a giant hand to stop Abi.

He looked even more terrifying awake. His head was covered with bushy, matted hair. His light brown moustache nearly covered his entire mouth. Abi shuddered when she saw the glint of two large fangs poking out from under the moustache. Luckily, the *rakshasa* had not noticed Sumathy ducking behind a tree. Abi quietly thanked their good fortune that they had had the sense to split up. She now tried to think about her next course of action.

The *rakshasa* laughed so loudly that birds flew away from the trees nearby. 'You silly girl, you thought you could escape me! I may have been asleep but I have a great sense of smell. I could smell a human being at fifty paces! You will make a fine meal!' he said, smacking his lips. Sickened, Abi willed herself to be calm. However bad the situation was, she could panic and make it worse. She needed to rack her brains for what she'd learnt about these beings instead. *Rakshasas are greedy – they cannot help themselves – it is greed for food or power that is often their downfall!* she remembered from her studies.

Putting on her most flattering tone of voice, she said, 'You are such a big, powerful *rakshasa*. You must be the most powerful being in this forest!'

The *rakshasa* looked pleased with this flattery. 'Yes, I am powerful. I am told that there are others in the world even bigger than me. But here, I am the biggest!' he said, expanding his chest to its full capacity.

'Oh, but you can be the most powerful one in the whole world! There is a temple in this forest that can grant that wish of yours,' Abi said, smiling sweetly.

The giant looked interested but also suspicious. 'You are trying to distract me so that you can escape – well, don't count on it!'

Abi shrugged her shoulders. 'I can't see how I can escape from such a powerful *rakshasa*. I was going to give you valuable information before I died. But if you don't want it, that's fine by me. How would it help me whether you are the most powerful in this jungle or in the world? You're going to eat me anyway.' She shrugged, watching his reaction from the corner of her eye.

The *rakshasa* was hooked. To his feeble mind, this made perfect sense. 'Tell me more!' he said, his eyes sparkling.

Abi glanced fleetingly towards the tree where Sumathy was hiding, hoping that she would be listening carefully and understand Abi's plan. 'Well, I can take you to the secret temple in this forest. You need to pray to the deity with full focus and attention. The deity can grant you the wish of becoming the most powerful *rakshasa* in this world.' The *rakshasa* nodded and asked Abi to lead him. They slowly made their way towards the hidden temple. She kept turning back surreptitiously to see if Sumathy was following, but she could not see anyone.

As they neared the temple, the *rakshasa* had a sudden unsettling thought. 'Wait,' he roared. 'I know what you're trying to do. I will close my eyes to pray and you will disappear!'

Abi would have giggled if she wasn't in such a predicament. 'You are clever. But don't worry – just tie me to a tree outside the temple and I can't run away.'

The *rakshasa* was still unconvinced. 'No, I will hold you in my hand. That way, I will know if you try to escape.'

They reached the hidden temple. The *rakshasa* was too big to enter the opening between the trees, so Abi suggested that he kneel on the ground and pray to the deity. 'How will I know if the deity is happy with me?' asked the *rakshasa*.

Abi glanced behind her in the hope that Sumathy was somewhere nearby and said loudly: 'The deity will speak to you and grant your wish!'

The *rakshasa* was now very excited. 'Ok, but you can't trick me and speak like the deity as I will know where the sound is coming from!'

He knelt down on the ground near the opening of the temple. He held Abi tightly in his hands in front of him and closed his eyes to pray to the deity. Abi squirmed uncomfortably in his grasp. She was dangling several feet above the ground, hoping desperately that he wouldn't drop her by mistake. She could still not see Sumathy anywhere. Several minutes passed and nothing happened. Abi was just resigning herself to being eaten, when a loud, familiar voice came from inside the temple.

'Open your eyes, O *rakshasa*. İ am pleased with your prayers. Ask me for a boon!'

The *rakshasa* opened his eyes in delight. 'Thank you, deity. I want to be the most powerful *rakshasa* in the world.'

There was a moment's pause. Then the deity's voice resounded again from the temple: 'That is a difficult boon, my son. There are many other powerful *rakshasas* in the world.' Abi looked at the *rakshasa* – his face fell in disappointment. 'However,' continued the voice, 'I can do this for you, but you will have to observe a few rules. It will be tough; can you do it?'

The *rakshasa* perked up and nodded vigorously. 'Oh, yes. Anything – I can do anything for you.'

The deity's voice was cool and measured. 'Very well. You will have to become a strict vegetarian for one month. You cannot harm any other living creature. You should pray daily and be kind and good to every being around you. If you do this religiously for a month, I can grant you your wish!' Abi was amazed at her friend's quick thinking. This was a brilliant idea; however, she could see suspicion rear up once again in the giant's eyes.

To stop him from guessing what was going on, Abi decided to distract him. 'That can never happen,' she giggled loudly. 'Imagine the *rakshasa* becoming a vegetarian! He doesn't have the willpower to do that!' she said, slyly provoking the giant.

Her plot worked. 'Of course I can. Don't listen to this silly human being. I will become vegetarian from this moment onwards. I will not harm any living creature. Deity, I will come here in a month's time and pray to you once again.' He turned towards Abi. 'I am grateful that you brought me here. As a reward, I am going to let you go.'

Abi was jubilant but managed to remain impassive. 'If you're sure, that's fine. Thank you. Goodbye, O great and powerful *rakshasa*. You will be even more terrifying in a month's time. Good luck,' said Abi, as he put her down.

She turned around and walked away quickly, before he had a chance to change his mind. She hoped that Sumathy would see the direction in which she was going and follow her back to where they had met the *rakshasa*. After half an hour, the two girls were united once again. They hugged and giggled uncontrollably, congratulating each other about outwitting the demon. 'Come, we better hurry and get away from here before he spots the two of us together. Dim as he is, even he may figure out the trick we pulled on him if he sees you with me,' said Abi.

The girls made their way through the jungle in search of Dhruva and the snake-people. Abi was getting more and more agitated and worried, although she did not let Sumathy see her distress. They had prepared a lot for this trip and had magical help before coming into the forest, and this had served them well in outwitting the *rakshasa,* escaping the *bhuta* and dealing with the wild animals; but they had not studied the snake-people. Abi was not sure how they would deal with them and whether they could actually negotiate Dhruva's release. 'I have to find a way,' she urged herself fiercely. Dhruva had been with her ever since the Konark Dance Festival – they had gone through a lot together. She could not desert him now – that wasn't the kind of person she was!

32

THE SNAKE PIT

The girls followed the meandering path through the forest for ages. They were tired and hungry. They managed to find some edible fruit on their way and had eaten this with gusto, but even that was hours ago. Abi felt light-headed and dizzy from hunger. They had spent much more time inside the forest than they had originally envisaged. 'The school has probably discovered that we are not in Krish's village by now and are all worried and looking for us!' said Sumathy, sighing deeply.

The thought of school only reminded Abi of the wonderful food that was cooked and served by the students. She had visions of mounds of steaming rice, spicy dal and various fragrant vegetables. She closed her eyes in agony, wondering when their ordeal would end. They had travelled for hours and had seen no trace of Dhruva or even a snake. They had now reached a part of the jungle where there was no wild animal in sight for miles. Sumathy sat down by a tree, exhausted. 'Abi, are you sure we are on the right path? We haven't seen any creature for a long time. How do we know if we are going the right way?'

Abi sat down next to her. 'I have no idea. I am not sure what we can do. Maybe we are lost!' she said dully, dreading her own words.

The girls studied each other's tired faces. Their hair was all dishevelled, their clothes torn, their skin scratched and bleeding, and their hunger and exhaustion was making them ill. 'I can't go on any longer. My legs won't move!' Sumathy cried suddenly. Both the girls closed their eyes and rested for a while. They must have fallen asleep for a few hours. When they woke up, Abi felt slightly better, although her stomach was still protesting about the lack of food. She looked around her and saw a narrow path; it didn't look much different from the rest of the forest yet some sixth sense told her that they were on the right track. She gently helped Sumathy to her feet without a word, and both the girls set off once again.

This part of the forest was a bit more open, and the forest floor was littered with dried leaves and twigs from the trees. The leaves rustled a lot as the girls made their way through them. In the middle of the path, ahead of them, there was a large ditch. The girls walked up to the edge of the ditch and looked inside. Abi recoiled and jumped back a few steps in horror. The ditch was large and deep. The bottom was covered with leaves and one side had caved into a dark tunnel. The leaves were rustling because the ditch was crawling with snakes! Cobras, vipers and a number of other kinds of snakes that the girls did not even recognise! Abi tried to overcome her revulsion and moved in closer for a better look – maybe this was their destination. She shivered involuntarily.

'Is Dhruva being held in the tunnel? How do we get down there without hurting ourselves?' she wondered aloud, absent-mindedly walking on, trying to get rid of the creepy feeling. Suddenly the earth gave way under her. She had wandered too close to the edge of the ditch. She fell headlong inside, her scream shattering the calm of the forest. She could hear Sumathy's screams mingle with hers, and then the world blacked out for Abi.

—∞∞∞—

Abi woke up and found herself in completely unfamiliar surroundings. She was lying on a golden four-poster bed. The room around her seemed to be made out of gold. There were golden chairs, pillars, and delicate silk and gossamer curtains hanging around her. She wondered where she was as she sat up on her bed and looked around with apprehension. The door to her room opened and a man came in. Abi looked at him, fascinated. He was tall and lithe and had a fluid grace about him. He wore silk robes and a golden crown that had a snake's hood carved on it. Abi had reached the snake-people! She was thrilled with this discovery and really glad he was looking anything but creepy, but she was tongue-tied and couldn't say a word.

The man was carrying a plate of fruit and a bowl that contained some white liquid, probably milk. He smiled and sat down on the chair next to her bed. 'Abi, I have brought you some food. You need nourishment. Please eat.'

Abi accepted the plate gratefully and started eating. The milk was delicious and she started feeling stronger again. 'Who are you?' she asked through a mouthful of fruit.

'Do you not recognise me? I am the snake that you rescued from the thorn at the start of your journey.'

Abi stared at him, dumbfounded. She had forgotten all about that incident – so much had happened since then. There were innumerable questions bothering her, but she started with what mattered the most to her. 'Where are my friends? What happened to Sumathy? And why have you captured Dhruva?'

The snake-man smiled once again. 'All in good time! Please eat your fill. Sumathy is fine – she fainted when you fell in and we brought her down here along with you. When she wakes up, we will feed and look after her.'

Abi's eyes were flashing in anger. 'What about Dhruva? Don't avoid talking about him. You had no right to kidnap him!' said Abi.

Her host looked a bit sad. 'Abi, he is not a friend of yours. He is out to harm you. I wish you would not trust him so much. We are Nagas – the snake-people. We do not harm anyone maliciously. Come, I will take you to the King of Nagas. He can explain more to you.' As the snake-man turned, Abi held her breath in surprise. The back of his head and back were covered with marks that were exactly like the marks on the back of a cobra. Abi glanced at his feet and realised that he didn't have any – his legs were actually like the lower part of a snake's body and he slithered upright on it.

He turned back and smiled at her and gestured for her to follow him. As Abi walked out of her room, she realised that she was inside a palace of sorts. There were other snake-people who wandered about – some men and some women. Some wore crowns on their heads and others did not. But all of them slithered upright, and Abi could see the markings on their backs as they went about their business. Abi and her Naga companion stopped in front of a large elaborately carved gold door. The Naga hissed loudly at the door and it opened automatically, admitting both of them.

Abi realised that they were entering a grand hall – there were Nagas standing at either end of the room. Right in front of them, there was a gold throne on which sat their king. He was resplendent in gold and silk. He wore a large crown that had five snakeheads made of gold on it. He smiled at Abi and welcomed her. Abi greeted him with a 'Namaste' – she once again felt tongue-tied in his presence.

'Welcome, Abi. It is a pleasure to greet you in my court. You have been a friend of the Nagas. You saved this Naga from the thorn – he was cruelly imprisoned like that by an evil *asura*. We are very grateful to you. What can we do for you?'

His smile and kind words put Abi at ease, and she was able to think clearly once more. 'Thank you. It was my duty to protect him, but I would like a favour from you. I hear that you have two of my friends in your custody – Sumathy and Dhruva. Please release both of them and let all of us go.'

There was a hissing noise from all around Abi in the court. Her words seemed to have angered some of the snakes. Abi looked around in fear, but the King was still smiling. He addressed her again. 'Abi, we would certainly release Sumathy after feeding her and would let both of you go back. However, we do not wish to release Dhruva. I want you to know that he is evil and means to harm you. He had actually pinned my Naga to the thorn – he knew you were kind enough to want to release him and hoped that the *bhuta* would get you. He is our prisoner. Why do you want him back?'

Abi fought back her tears – some part of her knew that Dhruva was out to harm her, but she didn't want to believe it and it hurt her to hear these words from someone else. 'I don't care. He is my friend, we have been friends for a long time and it is my duty to protect him,' she said fiercely. When the King did not look convinced, Abi continued: 'I know he wishes to harm me – but he has been a friend of mine for ages. I can look after myself and would like to take him back to our school and ask him why. Once I rescue him from you, I am sure he will not want to harm me at all. I saved your Naga; surely you can do this much for me?' she pleaded.

The King was quiet for a few moments. He then asked the Naga to take Abi to Sumathy's chamber. 'Abi, you are a wonderful, loving person. Please give me a little while so that I can consult my advisors. I will summon you when ready.'

The Naga led Abi away from the court. As they walked back, Abi turned around and made one last plea: 'O Nagas, I understand that you are great people. It is not right that you should have to imprison or harm another creature. I am sure Dhruva will not harm me once he finds out that I have rescued him. Please make the right decision.'

Abi was then taken to another chamber in the palace where she found Sumathy awake and picking at a plate of food. She was delighted to see her, and the two girls spent some time talking to each other. Abi filled her in on what had happened in the court. She omitted mentioning what the King had said about Dhruva being an evil *asura* out to harm Abi. A little while later, both the girls were taken back into the court.

The King looked pensive but welcomed the girls with a smile. 'Welcome. You have been very brave and kind girls. Without your knowledge, your activities in the jungle were watched by our people. We believe that you deserve what you ask for. So, we will release your friend.' The girls looked at each other in delight.

The King then addressed Abi. 'Abi, please remember what I told you and be careful. You are a kind person – but everyone in the world is not kind and gentle like you,' he warned. He looked at Sumathy: 'Sumathy, it is your role now to protect your friend. We know that you will do your best.' Sumathy was surprised but looked pleased with his comments.

The Nagas then brought out Dhruva. He looked thin and dishevelled but unharmed. He was not wearing his dark glasses, and his green eyes looked straight at Abi. Abi returned his gaze steadily. She wanted him to understand that she knew all about him, yet she wanted to rescue him. Sumathy was surprised to see his eyes uncovered, but luckily for Abi, she did not seem to connect him with Varun. The three of them turned to the Nagas and bowed in thanks.

The King addressed Dhruva: 'These girls have risked their lives to save yours. Remember that and ensure you repay them properly. We will be watching.' Abi's Naga friend led the three of them out of the underground palace through a tunnel, and they were soon back in the forest. He showed them which path to follow and said his goodbyes and vanished. Sumathy was full of questions on how Dhruva's sight was now restored, but he was very quiet. Abi signalled to tell her to stop pestering him, and all of them began their journey back to the school.

33

JOURNEY'S END

The trio walked quietly through the jungle for nearly an hour. The path twisted and turned and was very convoluted. Abi kept shooting glances at Dhruva, but he was studiously staring at the ground and avoiding her gaze. Sumathy seemed to be lost in her own thoughts. After a while, Abi realised that they had wandered off into a part of the forest that they had not seen before.

'Does anyone know where we are and how we get back?' said Abi, breaking the silence. She felt a stab of panic when both Sumathy and Dhruva stared at her wordlessly.

'This area is not familiar. What do we do now?' Sumathy was clearly panicking even more than her. Dhruva looked mutinous and he still had not said a word.

Abi would have to be the one to act. She looked around to see if there were any animals that could guide her. It took a while but finally she spotted some monkeys in the trees. Turning the peacock feather in her hand, she looked up at the monkeys and asked in a clear voice: 'We think we are lost. Could you please guide us to the path that takes us out of the forest? We need to go back to Gurukul.'

The monkeys seemed to be chattering to themselves. One or two of them moved down closer, but none of them said anything that Abi could understand. Abi was wondering if Krish's magic feather wasn't effective on these monkeys when she heard an old monkey speak. 'You have wandered a bit off the path. Continue along this way for a few hundred yards and turn right. The path will wind itself around the forest and take you up to a river. It is a dangerous river – you will have to be very careful – think before you act. Good luck.'

Abi thanked the monkey and they continued their journey on the path suggested. Her mind drifted over the monkey's words about the danger in the river, but she dismissed it as something they would have to deal with later. She noticed that Dhruva was now looking even more thoughtful than before. After a while, they could hear the sound of running water and knew that they were close. The path was winding and narrow, but it soon opened up and all three of them were standing in front of a wide, fast-flowing river.

Abi stopped in shock when she saw the water. A gasp from Sumathy told Abi that her friend had also just seen what she had. It was unlike any river that Abi had ever seen – the water was black with a strange viscosity to it. It almost looked like flowing black tar, but it was flowing faster than white water rapids. Abi walked closer to the riverbank and looked in – although black and tar-like, she could see that it housed some strange creatures. She was sure that she caught the glint of fangs and glimpsed a moving tentacle or two in the water. She turned around and looked at her friends – what were they meant to do now?

Dhruva was gazing into the distance. Abi turned around and followed his gaze to find a sturdily built steel bridge a few yards away. She was amazed that they hadn't caught sight of the bridge immediately and smiled in relief. 'Thank God there's a bridge. It looks so welcoming. Come, let us walk that way,' said Abi.

To her surprise, Sumathy held her back. 'No, Abi. Something is not right. I don't like it. I have read about such rivers… let me think.'

Dhruva had started wandering towards the bridge. Abi took Sumathy's hand and started following him with a reluctant Sumathy lagging behind her. Dhruva reached the bridge and inspected it for a short time. 'It looks fine to me. Come, this is the only way of getting out of here.' Abi was pleased to hear him speak, but her pleasure was short-lived as she caught Sumathy's eye.

Sumathy was looking at Dhruva with narrowed eyes filled with dislike. 'Abi, don't do anything rash yet. Let me think and I will tell you the best way forward,' said Sumathy, in a tone that bordered on pleading.

Dhruva started walking up the bridge. He took a few steps and then came back towards Abi. He looked straight into her eyes and took her hands in his. 'Abi, please listen to me. You saved me from the Nagas – I could have never escaped them without you. I want to see you safely back at school. Come with me – the bridge seemed sound when I just walked on it.' Abi felt a swooping feeling in her stomach. This was Varun – and she had never really stopped being infatuated with him. When he held her hands, she felt like someone had shot a bolt of electric current through her. She looked into his eyes and almost felt hypnotised by them. Dhruva started walking towards the bridge, gently leading Abi along.

Sumathy rushed up in front of them and blocked their way. 'Abi, NO! Don't do it. That bridge is dangerous. Please trust me!'

Her panic brought Abi out of her romantic reverie. 'Why do you say that, Sumathy? You just saw Dhruva walking on it.'

But Sumathy was adamant and Abi could see the stark fear in her friend's eyes. 'Abi, this is black magic. I have read about it. The river confuses you, but what looks safe is in fact the biggest danger. Please listen to me. I did read up about it. Trust me. Dhruva, why are you doing this to Abi?'

Abi looked helplessly at her friends. Dhruva (or Varun, as he really was) was her romantic crush, and this was her chance to build on this relationship, and she desperately wanted to take his side. She was sure that he would not want to harm her, now that she had saved him from the Nagas, but she could not leave Sumathy behind – she was her best friend and had been with Abi through good and bad times.

Dhruva snorted and dropped Abi's hands in a huff. 'It is up to you. Would you rather trust that silly girl or come with me?' He looked into her eyes once again and his voice became gentle and persuasive. 'Abi, I want to look after you. Come with me. Let's forget the past and build a future.' Abi almost sighed with pleasure. There was nothing that she wanted more than to hold Dhruva's hand and walk into the future with him. She looked at Sumathy to try and convince her friend to join them.

Sumathy looked very seriously at Abi and said: 'I know you want to go with him. I would not stop you unless I thought it was important. You are my closest friend and I will not let any harm come to you. I will not abandon you – please don't leave me. Do you trust me?'

Abi was torn. She fancied Dhruva, but she was not the kind of girl who would abandon her best friend for a boy. She nodded without looking at Dhruva. Sumathy gave her a quick smile. 'You are not going to like this, but the only way to escape this river is to jump right into it.'

Abi looked at her friend in horror. Surely she had misheard her! She could hear Dhruva protesting at her comments: 'Abi, don't listen to her. She's going to have you killed. What is she talking about? You can't jump into that river! Come with me, let us take the bridge.'

Sumathy was looking searchingly at Abi. All her life, Sumathy had wanted to be a leader but had never managed it. There was still underlying doubt in her eyes about whether Abi would follow her, but there was also a quiet confidence in her demeanour that showed that she knew what she was talking about. Abi made up her mind. 'I trust you, Sumathy. Lead on!' she said, taking Sumathy's hand.

The girls walked up to the riverbank. Abi looked into the deep, murky water and briefly closed her eyes in despair. The creatures in the water seemed to be getting even clearer. Abi was sure she could see great big fish, snakes and all manner of creatures inside. They all looked menacing and frightening. 'Trust me, Abi. I will not let you down. Close your eyes and jump in!'

Abi opened her eyes and looked behind at Dhruva. 'Dhruva, are you coming?' she asked, although she knew the answer. There was a strange light in his eyes when he shook his head.

Abi closed her eyes and tried to ignore the screaming in her mind. 'I trust you, Sumathy!' she yelled and jumped into the water. For a few moments, Abi felt the shock of icy cold water hit her skin and she could not breathe. Her feet were not touching the riverbed – the river was clearly very deep. Slowly, her body got used to the cold and she relaxed. She opened her eyes, expecting to see strange creatures swirling around her, but to her astonishment, all she could see were some weeds. Her feet were now on the sandy riverbed. She raised her head out of the water and found that she was now on the other side of the river. She could see Sumathy's head bob up next to her.

'We've made it,' she screamed in delight. The girls got out of the river and clambered onto the bank. Dhruva was still standing alone watching them from the other side. 'Jump into the water and follow us,' shouted Abi.

Suddenly everything became foggy and Abi heard a soft whisper in her ears: 'Abi, will you forgive me? I know you like me and I don't deserve it. I have always tried to harm you so that I can get my hands on the magic sapphire to take me back home. I was cursed to be on Earth due to my greed and thought that I could steal your gem and use you to make my way back. Even now, I created this bridge out of magic to try and capture you – you are very close to your goal – and I wanted to control your mind so that you could take me with you to heaven, but you rightly trusted your friend and escaped. I wish I could be your friend, but my innate nature is something that stands in the way. Please forgive me and try to forget me.'

Abi tried to look through the mist, and in a little while, she saw Dhruva walk up onto the bridge. As he reached the middle of the bridge, he stopped and smiled at her. She watched transfixed as the mist, bridge and Dhruva vanished into thin air!

34

PIECES OF THE JIGSAW

Abi cried silently all the way back to the school. Sumathy was sympathetic and tactful and thankfully did not say much. Abi was almost expecting her to say "I told you so!" but her friend was more sensitive than that. She held Abi's arm all through the journey and patted her back occasionally.

When the girls reached Gurukul, Abi stopped and composed herself. 'We are in big trouble at school now, aren't we?' said Abi in a sorry voice. 'The teachers will have found out by now that we lied to them about going to Krish's house for the day, and they will have probably mounted search parties. I hope they don't expel us.'

Abi knew that Sumathy had more to lose if they were thrown out of school. She hoped that she could convince Guruma that it was all her fault and ensure that Sumathy escaped being punished. 'Come, let us not think about what could happen. Let's just get it over and done with,' Sumathy said. Both girls resumed their walk. Everyone was busy doing the usual things at school. As it was still vacation time, there were no structured classes. No one stopped the girls as they walked through the courtyard, much to their surprise. Abi decisively led Sumathy towards Guruma's room.

'We need to let her know that we are back. We also need to tell her about Dhruva,' said Abi, hesitating slightly as she said his name.

Guruma was sitting at her table and looked up as the girls entered. She gave them a warm smile. 'Welcome, girls. How was your adventure?' Abi was amazed that Guruma did not look angry. The girls looked penitent and stared at the floor for a while.

Abi then said softly: 'Guruma, it is all my fault. Sumathy should not be blamed in any way. I wanted to go into the forest.'

Guruma nodded sagely. 'Child, I know all about it. I knew that you were planning to go there one day. I saw your face when Baba was telling you the story of the temple in the village. I also knew that I would have to let you face the challenges on your own, or otherwise you would not have achieved what you set out to do.' She smiled and then looked more serious. 'It was very difficult for me as I knew you could get into trouble in the forest and I could not protect you. However, I did my best by teaching Sumathy what I could about coping with the dangers. Sumathy, did you get a chance to use any of your newly acquired skills?'

Abi stared at her best friend in surprise. Sumathy looked sheepish as she turned towards Abi. 'Sorry I could not tell you. But it was Guruma who pointed me in the right direction about what we needed to learn. She asked me to borrow the book from Guru Mahesh and get you to learn all about the creatures in the forest. She taught me special skills for how to deal with black magic and also taught me a lot about *asuras*.' Sumathy looked gratefully at Guruma and asked her whether she knew that Dhruva was an *asura*.

Guruma turned away from them for a second. 'Yes, I am afraid I knew about Dhruva. I was always wary of him. Even in Konark, I kept a close watch. I was very reluctant to let him into the school. However, I also knew that he could not harm you in my presence. And I was tempted to keep him here so that I could keep an eye on him. I had actually tried to lock him away when I found out that you girls were setting off into the forest. But he has some formidable magic skills. He managed to trick me and escape. Where is he now?' asked Guruma, looking into Abi's eyes.

Abi turned away, hoping that Guruma could not see the feelings that she had for Dhruva in her eyes. 'He disappeared by the river,' said Sumathy, looking sideways at Abi to see her reaction.

Abi was in a daze – there was a lot of information here for her to digest. She saw the concerned expression on Sumathy's face and smiled. 'Sumathy, I want to talk to Guruma alone. Would you mind leaving us for a short while?' Sumathy nodded and disappeared. Abi returned Guruma's steady gaze – talking about Dhruva was painful but she needed to know the truth! 'You know that Dhruva and Varun are the same person, don't you?' asked Abi. Guruma nodded and looked solemnly away into the distance. 'Who is he? Why is he out to kill me? What have I ever done to him? And why do I still think of him as a friend?' The questions came pouring out of Abi's mouth.

Guruma was very thoughtful. 'Abi, I didn't want to tell you about it yet, but maybe it is time. Do you know the contents of your parents' will?'

Abi shook her head in surprise. 'Not really. I know that it was very clear about sending me here but I don't know why.'

'Child, you and your sister have been in mortal danger ever since you were babies and your mother left Earth. Her magic meant that no one could harm you while your father was around. However, once he died, you had to be sent to me as this is the only safe place for you in this world! No evil force can touch you in my presence.'

Abi stared at Guruma in shock. 'Danger! From what?'

Guruma's voice was a whisper: 'From an *asura* who has appeared in front of you as Varun and later as Dhruva!'

Abi's head reeled – she could just not comprehend why any *asura* would want to harm her. Guruma continued. 'When an *apsara* leaves Earth, she leaves behind a magic gem for a loved one to find their way to her. This gem opens the gateway to heaven if a very special person acquires it. When your mother left, she hid the gem in a secret location, but your father knew about it. He would never have attempted the trip to heaven as he wanted to look after you and your sister; but your father also knew of a dangerous *asura*, whom you know as Varun – he had been banished from heaven. He would have stopped at nothing to get his hands on the gem.'

Abi was still puzzled. 'But why? If he had been banished...'

Guruma gave her a smile. 'He had been banished, but with his intelligence, knowledge of the scriptures and resourcefulness, he knew that he would be able to make his way back with the gem. Varun wanted to get you in his power so that you could lead him to the gem! If you had stayed in the UK, he would have found you, hypnotised you into obeying him and finding the sapphire for him. You see, an *apsara*'s sapphire can be picked up from its hiding place only by someone who truly loves her!'

It slowly started making sense to Abi. 'Why do I still care for him?' she chided herself, embarrassed.

Guruma laid a kindly hand on her shoulder. 'Do not scold yourself, child. As you know, *asuras* can be as clever, skilled and charming as the gods themselves, if they want to be. And Varun is extremely accomplished. He wanted to charm you and he succeeded. If only he were less greedy and self-centred, he would be revered by many!'

Abi's head was muddled with all the information that she was receiving. She remembered something. 'But if all he wanted was the gem, why didn't he try and take it from me earlier? Maybe in Konark, even?'

Guruma's grey eyes stared into the distance. 'I cannot tell you for sure, but I guess he realised that there was more to you than he imagined. He must have originally appeared in Konark and engineered his way into our orchestra to steal the gem from you. Did you tell him about the seven magic steps?' Abi nodded and Guruma continued: 'If he took the gem, he would have had to work hard to climb the seven steps. I don't think he realised what the steps were until you told him. When he found out, he probably wanted you to do all the hard work so that he could just benefit from it in the end.'

Abi shook her head in stunned disbelief. 'He was so nice – he wanted to help the villagers when the dacoits struck! How can I believe that he's an evil *asura*?'

Guruma laid a kind hand on her shoulder. 'Child, things are often not what they seem! He was not actually trying to help the villagers. When you told him about the steps, he thought he had to give you the opportunity to prove yourself, to do the deeds required. He needed you to succeed. I think he planned the dacoit attack – it's quite easy for a creature of his calibre to hypnotise and get others to act on his behalf. The dacoits have been around these parts for ages, but they never harmed people, and they certainly didn't capture people to sell them as slaves. Do you remember how he persuaded you to follow him and seek the dacoits out? I think he knew that Sumathy would never let you go alone and hoped that her capture would make you want to barter the gem for her life!'

Abi thought about the night in the dacoits' cave. 'Yes, you're right. I did offer the gem to the chief. But I thought you said that he didn't want the sapphire itself – he wanted me to climb the steps.' Abi was more confused than ever.

Guruma smiled patiently. 'He is very intelligent – he did want you to climb the steps, and at the same time, I think he suspected that the gem would harm the person who tried to take it away from you. I think he was just testing that out with the dacoits.'

Abi looked dejected and rubbed away her last tears slowly. 'I have been a complete fool! I don't even know whether I've achieved anything, and yet I feel as if I have lost everything.'

Guruma disagreed. 'No, Abi; I think you've achieved a great deal. And it's not just about your brave adventures of last night. You have proved time and again that you're a true friend and a good person. Dhruva knew that you are more capable of climbing the steps than he is. His goal was to control your mind and maybe even your body so that he could travel with you to heaven. I don't think you should beat yourself up about trusting someone who betrayed you. I hope you will realise one day that your ability to trust people is a gift that is most precious. Go, my child; you need to rest.'

Abi thanked her and made her way back to her room, feeling more confused in spite of being more aware of the facts. The pieces of the jigsaw were falling together, but the picture that had formed was not a pretty sight!

35

CONTENTMENT

Over the next few days, Abi spent a lot of time on her own, often thinking deeply about events of the recent past. Sumathy tried to amuse her or engage her in some inane activity or other, but Abi was hardly interested. One day, she reluctantly agreed to go for a walk into the forest with Sumathy. They walked towards the lake where Abi first found the magic sapphire. It was a fantastic day and the waterhole looked serene. The sun's rays sparkled in the water and a gentle breeze tugged at Abi's clothes. Abi perked up as the sweet strains of the flute reached her ears.

'Krish! I haven't seen him for a long time. And I haven't even thanked him for his peacock feather. We wouldn't have come back alive without his help.'

She saw her young friend playing the flute under a tree and gave him a wave. He looked up and smiled happily at her. 'Abi, Sumathy – how nice to see you after such a long time! How are you?' Both the girls sat down on either side of Krish. Abi was in no mood to relate their adventures and somehow Krish seemed to understand. She thanked him for the peacock feather and gave it back to him. 'Oh no, it's for you! You never know when you'll need it – you seem to get into all sorts of adventures,' said Krish, with a cheeky grin.

They sat and talked about other things. Abi was relieved as Krish seemed more interested in telling her the latest stories from Bollywood than asking her questions about Dhruva. After several delightful hours, the girls headed back to school. Sumathy stopped just outside their room and looked at Abi intently. 'Abi, are you ok? I am sure you've climbed some of the steps over the last few days. I know it doesn't seem like much, but you did manage to make it to the temple. Just a few more days and a bit more work and I think you can make it through all the steps.' Sumathy stopped talking as baby Vi came crawling towards Abi, asking to be held in her arms.

Abi squeezed her friend's hands gratefully before picking the child up with a laugh. 'You know what, Sumathy – I don't really care that much anymore. The last few days have taught me that friendship is the most precious thing in the world, and I am lucky that I have you and Krish and this wonderful little baby who greets me like I am the best thing that happened to her.' Baby Vi cooed her approval. Abi laughed again. 'I would dearly love to see my mother, but I don't have any complaints about my life. I thought a lot about Dhruva and all the things that happened in the past. I am actually grateful that we are here, safe and sound and back at Gurukul. I am content and have no right to be anything but happy. I have a lot to be grateful for and I certainly am grateful. I will look up at the sky and hope that Mother is watching me.'

───⊗───

Abi spent the next few days applying herself to her regular school routine. She started practising her dance again and enjoyed her sessions on the rocky mountain ledge, with the wind, sun and mountains as her audience. She managed to spend a good deal of time with Pooja, Arundhati and Sumathy and felt truly happy that she had such nice friends. Krish's periodic visits and wise words kept her amused. Baby Vi was growing up fast but didn't seem to be able to say any intelligible words yet. Abi wondered if the child couldn't talk as she was sure babies started saying at least a few words at a younger age, but she was healthy enough and Guru Uma seemed happy to see her thriving in Abi's company. Abi missed her aunt but always looked forward to receiving her letters and learning more about what was going on in her life in the UK. There was much laughter and joy when she spent time with her friends, and there were moments of sadness or gravity when she thought of her family and the friends she was separated from. Abi learnt to enjoy her life as it was and savour all the bittersweet moments.

───⊗───

One fine morning, Abi was surprised to see Guruma walk up to her after breakfast. 'Abi, will you please follow me to my room?' Abi nodded and followed Guruma. 'I need to congratulate you. You have achieved your goal!' Abi looked confused as she had no idea what Guruma was talking about. Guruma laughed gently. 'The seven magic steps – have you not realised it? You're there, my child, you've done it!'

Abi frowned and thought hard about what she'd done over the last few days. Nothing came to mind. 'But I could have hardly done something in the last few days. I've not had any adventures; I have not achieved anything!'

Guruma gave her an enigmatic smile. 'What makes you think that only having adventures makes you achieve things? The greatest things in life are often achieved by the slightest steps. Well, I can't tell you any more right now. Go and say your goodbyes to Sumathy, bring the magic sapphire, and come with me.'

Abi wanted to ask many more questions, but Guruma turned away and walked out of the room. Abi went back to her room and sat down with Sumathy, who looked anxious and apprehensive. But when she told her what Guruma had said, Sumathy beamed. 'Abi, that's fantastic. Isn't that what you've always wanted? You will get to see your mother now!'

Abi looked uncertainly at her best friend. 'But I will miss you,' she said, her eyes misting over.

Sumathy's eyes welled up, too, but she reminded her that this had been her goal for the last two years. 'You deserve this, Abi. This is another adventure, another phase in your life.'

Abi thanked her best friend earnestly. 'You've done so much for me. Thank you – what can I ever do to repay you?'

Sumathy gave Abi's hand a tight squeeze. 'Just stay my friend. And hopefully, one day, come back to Earth.'

Guruma was waiting for Abi in the courtyard. She smiled when Abi entered and asked her if she had said her goodbyes. 'Only to Sumathy. Where am I going?' asked Abi, unable to contain her curiosity.

'All in good time!' said Guruma, leading Abi out of the school and towards the forest.

After walking in silence for a while, Abi asked again: 'Guruma, where are we going?' She recognised this path – it took them to her secret stage where she practised her dance in front of the open sky and mountains.

Guruma did not reply but when they reached the stage, she asked a puzzled Abi: 'Are you sure you want to go to heaven to meet your mother?'

Abi nodded. The passion had ignited again in her belly. 'More than anything else!'

Guruma held her by her shoulders. 'Child, you need to know that it will not be easy. Your mother has the life of an *apsara*. She is not an ordinary woman. Bear this in mind and do not judge her harshly.' This made no sense to Abi but she nodded anyway. She wondered what would happen next. Guruma looked up at the cloudy sky above them. 'O Lord Indra, I have brought Abi here. Please grace us with your presence.'

Abi looked at Guruma in awe – it looked like there was light radiating from all around her. 'Child, hold up the magic sapphire so that it opens up the path to heaven.' Abi did as she was told.

The sky suddenly became very dark, and Abi could see lightning streak across the sky. In a short while, she heard a clap of thunder as well. In the midst of the clouds, Abi saw a sight that she would never forget. A majestic white elephant was walking towards them. There was a man riding the elephant – a man Abi had seen before and recognised from her textbooks, as well as her first flight to India. Indra, the King of Gods, the god of rain, storm and war, looked more amazing than any painting that Abi had seen. He was handsomely dressed in fine silks and wore a brilliant gold crown on his head. He carried himself with great dignity and elegance and gave her a dazzling smile. Abi remembered how she had seen this vision on her way to India on the plane and had thought that she was imagining things. Indra spoke to Abi in a booming voice that sounded a bit like the rumble of thunder. 'Abi, well done! You have managed to climb all the seven magic steps. That is no easy task!'

Abi looked at him in shock – she knew she had managed the step of courage in the forest but could not understand how she could have climbed all the others. Indra smiled. 'The seven magic steps are Courage, Patience, Sacrifice, Focus, Trust, Contentment and Goodness. You had already climbed Focus when you met Surya. There's no dearth of goodness in you, Abi. When you persuaded your schoolmates to help rebuild Krish's village, when you helped the wild dogs and the Naga in the jungle, and when you asked the Nagas to free Dhruva, you climbed Goodness several times over. When you were willing to give up your sapphire to save Sumathy's life, you climbed Sacrifice. When you made your way into the deep, dark, dangerous forest to reach the hidden temple and continued despite meeting creatures such as the *bhuta* and the *rakshasa*, you climbed Courage.' Abi shuffled her feet, feeling awkward. Indra continued, oblivious to her discomfort. 'When you listened to your friend Sumathy and jumped into the river, despite seeing those magical creatures in it, you climbed Trust. The fact that you did not seek out these steps every day of your school life and managed to control your mind and feelings is when you climbed a difficult step – Patience. And finally, the fact that you met with success and failure and made your peace with your situation and your environment and became happy in yourself is when you overcame the greatest challenge of all – Contentment!'

Abi stared at him in amazement. She understood what Guruma meant by saying that great things could be attained without grand adventures. Guruma spoke quietly behind her. 'Contentment is the hardest step of all, and there are very few people who can attain it, my child. The *asura* Varun knew very well that this was a step that he could never hope to climb, and that's why he left you alone and even helped you in your journey so that you could open up the way for him.'

Abi was still in a complete daze – she could not believe that she had achieved her dream. She looked at Indra and Guruma blankly as if she could not hear anything that they were saying. Indra rose, smiled and put his hand out to Abi. 'Abi, as the King of Gods, it is my pleasure to invite you to join me in heaven. You can stay there for as long as you like. Would you like to come with me?'

The clouds cleared around Abi and she was bathed in glorious sunlight. She looked at the sky and gasped as she saw a number of gods standing there to welcome her. She recognised Surya (the sun god), Chandra (the moon god), Agni (the god of fire) and Vayu (the god of wind) as she had seen them before, either in flesh or in her textbooks. There were many others that she could not recognise. A set of seven golden steps had appeared beside her to help her climb up on the white elephant, whose name Abi remembered from her lessons as "Airavat".

She turned towards Guruma and bowed to her before giving her a big hug. 'Thank you for everything. I could never have done this without you.'

Guruma returned her hug and smiled at her. 'No, Abi; you did it all with your own strength and qualities. You are an asset to this world. I am sorry to see you go, but I know that you would like to see your mother. Please remember what I told you earlier. Good luck!'

Abi climbed up the steps and sat down next to Indra. She looked at the other gods around her and was delighted to see them all beaming at her. She waved goodbye to Guruma and wondered with a thumping heart what heaven would be like. Indra pointed upwards and whispered softly to Abi, 'There's someone waiting to see you up there.' Abi looked up and saw nothing but a bright light – behind that light she tried to imagine the form of her mother. As they moved, Abi felt closer to her mother than she had ever felt before.

'Mother, I am nearly there with you,' said Abi to herself and smiled.

The
Destination

36

MOTHER

Abi pinched herself to see if she was dreaming. Three years ago, if anyone had told her that she would soon be travelling to heaven, seated on a white elephant, next to the King of Gods, she would have laughed in their face. Yet, here she was, doing just that. Airavat, the white elephant that she was seated on, walked gracefully through the clouds. Abi looked around and could see smiling faces of the various gods around her. Surya, the sun god, looked resplendent in his white chariot drawn by seven horses. He seemed to be lighting up Abi's path. There were other gods around her, but Abi was distracted – she sat almost in a trance, her heart full of hope and apprehension. She looked forward to seeing her mother once again. Abi had no memories of her mother, but she had seen various paintings on Earth. Her mother looked incredibly beautiful in the paintings – Abi wondered how lovely she might be in real life! Indra had said to her that someone was waiting for her in heaven. Abi's breathing became more shallow as her excitement grew, knowing that she was getting closer to meeting her mother with every step that Airavat took.

The elephant paused in front of a beautiful golden arch. The arch was decorated with pearls and precious stones and glittered away in the sunlight. Abi could not see anything beyond the arch except a bright light. *This must be the gateway to heaven,'* she thought, soaking it all up. Indra looked at her and smiled. 'You look very excited and tense, Abi. This is the gateway to heaven. Hold up your magic sapphire and the gateway will open itself to allow you to enter.' Abi held up the stone that she was wearing around her neck. It was shining a brilliant blue and the gateway seemed to melt away. As Airavat walked through the gateway, Indra spoke once again to Abi. 'Welcome to heaven. There are very few human beings who have entered this gateway alive, and you are one of the lucky few. You are welcome to stay here as long as you want.'

Abi was not quite sure how she should react and just gave him a smile as a response. Then she slowly perked up the courage to ask him a question: 'You said there was someone waiting for me here – where are they?' Indra smiled mysteriously and looked ahead. Abi followed his gaze immediately – she was hoping to see the graceful and elegant figure of her mother standing ahead, waiting for her. She could not hide her disappointment when she saw the figure of a man standing far away.

The male figure drew closer and Abi's face lit up suddenly in recognition. 'Father!' She felt ashamed that she had completely forgotten about her father, in her quest to find her mother. Of course, her father must have died and reached heaven! She mentally kicked herself at why such a thought had never occurred to her. This was even better than she imagined! She had a look of incredulous delight on her face as Airavat, the elephant, helped her down. For a moment, Abi was taken by surprise when she was set down on the "ground" – there was no ground beneath her and she felt as though she was floating on a blue sky. She ignored this feeling as she ran to embrace her father. It was amazing to see him and be able to touch him.

He held her in his arms and then stepped back to look at her. 'You look beautiful, Abi. I have been watching you grow up into this lovely young lady and a wonderful dancer,' said her father with a proud smile on his youthful face. He looked much the same as she remembered him. It seemed a bit incongruous that he was still wearing his usual crumpled jumper and trousers in heaven. Abi stared at him, spellbound. She felt very guilty about forgetting all about him – somehow she wasn't expecting to see him and did not know what to say!

'Abi, I am sure that you would like to talk to Hugh for a while. When you are ready to see the rest of heaven, just think of me and I will either come myself or send someone to take you round,' said Indra. Abi nodded and smiled gratefully at him and then looked on in awe as he disappeared.

'You'll get used to it,' said her father, taking her hand and leading her to a meadow. The meadow was beautiful – there were little white and yellow flowers all over the grass and clumps of golden daffodils scattered like stars in the sky.

'I never imagined there would be daffodils in heaven!' exclaimed Abi.

Her father chuckled endearingly. 'Abi, heaven is what means the most to you. That's the beauty of this place. It transforms itself to suit whatever works for the individual. You know how much I love the Lake District in the UK, and this is pretty much what heaven is for me. This and the magnificent lab that I have at my disposal.'

Abi looked at her father in wonder. 'A lab in heaven! That is amazing. I would never have guessed.' As her father laughed at her surprise, old memories came flooding back to Abi. 'I missed you so much, Dad! It was awful to think that I would never see you again.'

Dr Forbes gave her another hug. 'I missed you, too. It was a strange feeling. No one really wants to die, Abi; but when I died, I was happy that I had a chance to see your mother again but was so upset at losing you. Luckily, I could look down upon Earth and see you periodically!'

Abi and her father sat together for a long time, exchanging stories and talking about old memories. Then Abi hesitantly asked her father what she was desperate to know. 'Dad, where is Mum? Why isn't she here to see me? I want to see her so much!'

Dr Forbes gave her an understanding nod. 'Abi, you will see your mother soon; but I wanted to meet you first and wanted to prepare you a bit for that meeting. Your mother is not like other mothers on Earth. She is different – she is an *apsara*. And as a celestial being, she is not subject to the same kind of emotions and upheavals that we are. I just wanted to temper your expectations before I take you to see her.'

Abi was confused by her father's words but she wanted to see her mother so badly that she nodded. 'Guruma told me the same thing on Earth. Please let us go and see Mum.' Dr Forbes nodded, held Abi's hands and asked her to close her eyes. For a second, Abi felt that she had forgotten something. She shook her head to get her thoughts in order, but nothing came to mind.

When she opened her eyes, she was inside a beautiful palace with wonderful golden pillars and silken curtains on the large open windows. They were surrounded by beautiful women in exquisite clothes and jewels, adorning themselves by ornate mirrors. They smiled at Abi and her father as they walked past. Abi felt overwhelmed by the beauty that surrounded her. 'Are these *apsaras*?' she asked her father in a hushed voice. Her father nodded and pointed ahead. Abi started in wonder at the incredible vision in front of her.

She was totally stunned by the beauty of the woman who stood ahead – she was dressed in a rich white and gold outfit, wearing the most spectacular jewels around her neck, hands and head. She looked vaguely familiar – her large black eyes were almond-shaped and extremely alluring, and her smile was absolutely dazzling. 'Do you recognise her from her painting?' asked Dr Forbes. Abi shook her head slowly – could this be her mother? She was in shock. Abi was not sure what to expect, but she somehow thought that her mother would be much older than the gorgeous maiden who stood there. Her father's painting floated in front of her eyes – the girl in the painting had the same face and features, although this *apsara* was much more elaborately dressed.

'Welcome to heaven, Abirami!' Her mother's soft, gentle and melodious voice sounded soothing to Abi's ears. Abi stood there uncertainly, not knowing what to do next. She wanted to fling herself on her mother and give her a great big bear hug; but it seemed very inappropriate to do that to such a glamorous and perfectly dressed *apsara*. Her mother solved her dilemma by bending down and giving her a graceful and gentle hug. Abi held on to her mother for a long time – she felt a multitude of emotions sweep over her. This was the moment that she had dreamt of ever since she had found out about her. After a while, her mother disentangled herself and looked at Abi appraisingly. 'You look good and I know you've become a great dancer, Abi. Well done. Well, if you come to Indra's court in an hour's time, you will see us dance there. You need to go now; I have to practise.' Abi looked at her mother with a mix of hurt and disappointment. She was not expecting the dismissal so soon. Dr Forbes moved forward, gently held Abi's hand and walked out of the room.

Abi's eyes were swimming in tears when she reached the meadow outside. She sat down on the grass, put her head on her knees and started sobbing. Dr Forbes sat down by her side, pulled out a pristine white handkerchief and gave it to Abi. 'Abi, this is what I meant when I told you that your mother doesn't feel the same emotions as we do; but that doesn't mean that she does not love you. Stop crying, my dear – heaven's a happy place. Aren't you glad that you've seen me here?'

Abi wiped her face with her father's handkerchief and gave him a watery smile. 'Of course I am happy to see you – I was just taken by surprise by Mother. She's not quite what I expected.'

'That's totally understandable, Abi. But what are you comparing her to?'

Abi pondered a bit – she had not really given this much thought. 'It's probably to some of my schoolmates' mums. I have not met many in India, but I remember how some of my classmates' mothers would come to pick them up from school in the UK. I particularly remember Mrs Diana Hunt, my friend Chloe's mother. She was lovely – gentle, kind and very friendly to everyone. She really loved Chloe and it showed in everything she did or said. I knew my mum was an *apsara*, but somehow I thought she'd be similar to her and would love me and never want to let me go.' Abi was hurt and upset and also slightly embarrassed that her mother's indifference bothered her so much. 'Do you think I am being childish and silly?'

Her father's face was full of concern for her. 'No, of course not, Abi. This is the first time you are meeting your mum. Such emotions are to be expected. However, your mother is nothing like your friend's mum. You cannot expect her to behave like a normal human mother. You cannot change what she is – but you can try and understand it a bit more and accept her as she is.'

Abi tried to pull herself together. 'You're right, Dad. I have you anyway and I can't ask for any more,' she said, squeezing his arm. Once again, she had that feeling that she was forgetting something. She racked her brain but nothing came to mind. 'Oh well, what shall we do next?' she enquired, getting up on her feet.

'Would you like to have a look around heaven now? That will distract your mind – we can have a look around and then go to the court and watch your mother's dance.' Abi nodded with a smile. 'Would you like me to take you around heaven, or would you like a more divine escort?' asked her dad with a grin.

'You, without any doubt!'

Dr Forbes smiled. 'Well, then all you have to do is to close your eyes and let Indra know that you'd like me to take you round. Come, let's explore heaven!'

37

EXPLORING HEAVEN

Dr Forbes took Abi to his laboratory. 'This is the first thing I want you to see. I am so excited about it!' he exclaimed, sounding like a schoolboy who was showing off his latest gadget to a mate. Abi looked around, her eyes opening wide with amazement – it was an enormous room filled with all sorts of instruments and apparatus. There were racks of test tubes and bottles filled with chemicals of various kinds. Rows of preserved plants, fruits and seeds stood neatly arranged on shelves above their heads. There were fascinating charts on the walls and a variety of microscopes.

'I never imagined heaven to be like this!' exclaimed Abi.

Her father laughed. 'Heaven is a place that makes you happy. So it provides you with whatever takes your fancy, within reason. As you know, I have always wanted to study and experiment in a large lab and could not really afford it on Earth. So heaven has provided me with all the necessary equipment. Isn't it magical?'

Abi gave her father a loving squeeze. 'I missed you so much! It's great to see you happy here.' A frown creased her brow again. Every time she hugged her father, she had that feeling that she was forgetting something important.

Dr Forbes spent some time with Abi showing off all the paraphernalia in his lab and then decided that it was time for her to see a bit more of heaven. They walked out of the lab through a beautifully laid-out and immaculately maintained garden. There were magnificent multi-coloured flowers blooming everywhere, and Abi sniffed appreciatively at the delicate scent of the blossoms on the trees. Her father took her to the heart of the garden and they sat on a marble seat to enjoy the beauty and tranquillity around them. Abi could hear the melodious chirping and singing of birds and sighed happily. The seat was just under a beautiful tree that was blossoming profusely with white flowers that stood out due to their coral stalks. 'This is amazing – I feel at peace out here.'

'Abi, this is Indra's pride and joy. He loves this garden and you will see him come here and spend some time thinking and reflecting. The coral tree that we are sat under is absolutely beautiful – it flowers at night and the flowers fall down and scent the whole garden the next day. The *apsaras* come here, too; but at the moment, they are probably getting ready for their performance in Indra's court.' Abi was only half listening to her father. She was lost in the scents and sounds of the garden when she heard something vaguely familiar. She sat up straight as she heard the sweet strains of flute reach her ears. It sounded just like the tune that her young friend Krish used to play.

'Who's playing the flute, Dad?'

Her father gave her a mysterious smile. 'You will meet him soon, but I think it is now time for us to go to Indra's court. Surely you don't want to miss watching your mother dance?'

———✤———

Indra's court was more spectacular than anything that Abi could have ever imagined. It was an architectural marvel – she felt tiny as she entered the gigantic hall surrounded by intricately carved golden pillars. She looked up at the spectacular ceiling, painted elaborately in magical colours. She took a deep breath looking at the exquisite scenes painted in mesmerising blues and greens and inlaid with what looked like precious jewels. As she marvelled at the architecture, she felt that someone she knew very well would admire it too – but she couldn't think who. Another frown creased her brow again. Maybe earthly memories became fainter in heaven? At the head end of the hall was the most extravagant seating arrangement. There were layers of marble, gold and silk built up to support an ornate throne. The throne glittered and gleamed as if it was made of diamonds. Comfortably ensconced in the depths of the throne was a smiling Indra. 'Welcome, Abi. Come and sit here by my side!'

Abi walked apprehensively towards him. The seat that he was pointing to was high up above her, and she looked around to find steps that could take her up there. 'Keep walking towards it, Abi,' whispered her father from behind her.

But I have no more space to walk forward and I want to get up there! thought Abi. However, she trusted her father and took another step forward. To her surprise, she was now a level above the ground. She took a few more steps and found that she was walking on air, towards her seat. She finally reached her seat and looked at it – it was once again an incredible piece of art. It was carved out of granite or some such stone. Beautiful maidens adorned the sides of the stone chair, and the seat was chiselled to show off a fine example of a banyan tree. Abi looked thoughtfully at the seat. Beautiful though it was, it seemed very uncomfortable. She gingerly sat on the carved seat, taking care not to hurt herself on the hard stone. To her amazement, she felt as if she was sitting on a soft and fluffy cloud. Indra gave her a dazzling smile. 'You don't think that we would make our guests sit on hard stone, Abi,' he said. 'You will find that things are often not what they seem out here.'

From her vantage point high up, Abi could see everyone else in the court. The beauty and energy that seemed to emanate from the faces of the people in front of her took her breath away. There were many gods, dressed in splendid silks with beautiful gold jewels adorning their heads and necks. There were also many other people dressed as if they were from different parts of Earth. The one common thing that Abi noticed was that everyone looked happy and serene with a smile playing on their faces. She could see her father settling down on a seat a bit below her – he looked up at her and gave her a reassuring smile. The centre of the court was a wide expanse, and on the floor was an artistically painted pattern that reminded

Abi of the *kolams* that her friend Sumathy used to draw in the school courtyard. While Sumathy's *kolams* were made out of rice flour and paste, this design seemed to be painted with glimmering oil colour. She was taken aback by the beauty of the imposing courtroom and was lost in her thoughts when she realised that music had begun to play. The dancers were about to start!

Abi smiled appreciatively as she saw a golden orchestra play a variety of instruments in perfect harmony. She recognised some of the instruments, but there were many that were completely unknown to her. The orchestra carried on for a while, slowly hypnotising everyone. The tempo of the music began to rise and it soon reached a crescendo. As it culminated in a drumbeat that sounded like a clap of thunder, Abi saw the dancers enter the hall. The dancers' beauty was matched only by the perfect rhythm they commanded. They spread out in the courtroom, and before the audience could grasp what they were doing, there was a giant lotus made up of *apsaras* in the centre of the hall. The lotus opened and closed as the *apsaras* moved in unison. Abi was just admiring their incredible coordination of movement when the lotus opened up and the dancers formed a bird that seemed to flutter its wings. Abi knew that she was not the only one amazed by their skill as she could hear gasps and sounds of admiration around her. The bird transformed itself into a fish and then a deer. Abi had never seen such a magical group performance – she cheered lustily along with the rest of the audience when the group finished. She could see how the *apsaras* were way beyond any mortal dancers that she had ever seen or heard of.

Abi could feel the mood of the audience change – there seemed to be a strange apprehension that had befallen the hall. She noticed that the tempo of the music had also changed, to add to this electric atmosphere. Then she saw four exquisitely dressed dancers enter the stage. Her heart leapt up in excitement as she spotted her mother amongst them. The four dancers began their routine – it started off gently but very soon their dance became more complex and intricate than anything Abi had ever seen. They whirled and twisted and bent their bodies into impossible postures, in perfect synchrony with the music. She wondered if her mother would notice her in the audience, but she seemed to be very focussed on her performance. As the four continued dancing with immense passion, Abi realised that she was witnessing a fierce dance competition in heaven.

It was very hard to choose between the dancers – they all looked beautiful and had mesmerised the audience with their effortless style and grace. However, as the tempo of the music increased, the dance became more and more complex. Abi felt proud to see her mother's dance – she gave an exhilarating performance. Soon, one of the dancers stopped, bowed to the audience and stepped away from the stage. Abi was puzzled – why did she do that? She looked around her and noticed that Indra was indicating to one of the three remaining girls who also left. She understood immediately – Indra was judging the dance and now only the two best dancers remained on stage, and her mother Ananya was one of them. Abi started paying a bit more attention to the other *apsara*. She was beautiful – her face was perfectly oval, she had sparkling light green eyes and dark, shiny brown hair tied back into an elaborate bun. Abi noticed with a pang that her elegance and grace seemed matchless. All *apsaras* were brilliant dancers – better than any dancers that Abi could ever see on Earth. However, this one was something special. The audience seemed absolutely hypnotised by her performance. Abi tried to look at both the dancers objectively and dispassionately as a dancer herself, trying to forget that one of them was her mother. They were both amazing – clearly the best among the best. Ananya's dance was wonderful, but if Abi was being truly objective, she had to reluctantly admit that the other *apsara* was even better!

The dancers culminated their dance with some incredibly fast-paced movements that made them look as if they were dancing on air. As they finished, the whole of the audience gave them a rapturous standing ovation. Abi clapped in delight – it was such an honour to see these performances. Indra raised his hands and everyone went silent. 'Urvashi and Ananya – it is a real pleasure to see both of you dance. You had the audience as your slaves for the hour that you performed. However, this is a competition and I have to declare a winner! Ananya – you moved perfectly and showed mastery over your art. Urvashi – I have no words to describe your performance – it was inspired. While Ananya is a master of dance, you are clearly the grand master. I declare you the winner of today's competition. Well done!' The audience applauded once more as Indra presented Urvashi with a magnificent jewelled necklace for winning the competition.

Urvashi beamed at the audience as she held her prize in her hands, caressing the rubies gently. Abi's face clouded over with worry as she turned to look at her mother's face. Ananya looked thunderous and angry. She turned around without giving her daughter as much as a glance and stalked away from the courtroom. Abi's worried eyes sought out her father – he seemed to be taking it in his stride. He gave her an embarrassed smile and shrugged his shoulders. Abi realised that he had obviously witnessed such tantrums before!

38

TANTRUMS AND TRINITY

After the performance was over, everyone in Indra's court started mingling and talking to each other. Dr Forbes joined in and started introducing Abi to various members of the court. But Abi was very restless and kept staring at the doorway. Soon, her father noticed her discomfort and he turned and whispered to her, 'What's wrong, Abi? Why are you so distracted?'

Abi blushed in embarrassment. 'Sorry, I didn't realise that it was so obvious. I am just worried about Mother. She's rushed off in anger and she's not yet back to join everyone. I can see other *apsaras* in the crowd but not her!'

'Do you want to see her? Come, let's go and find her.' Abi nodded enthusiastically and took her father's hand as he walked out of the door. They walked into the magical garden that they'd been to earlier. Her father headed towards a corner that was filled with rhododendron bushes and walked purposefully through a narrow covered walkway. Abi tagged along, wondering where he was going. In a hidden corner, behind beautiful but overgrown jasmine creepers, there was a swing. Her mother was sitting on the swing, staring away into the distance.

Abi ran up to her mother and gave her a quick hug. 'You were brilliant! It was so great to watch you dance.' Ananya shrugged Abi away and turned towards Hugh. 'Once again, Urvashi wins! I don't know when she'll stop being Indra's favourite.'

Hugh gave her a boyish grin. 'Does it matter, darling? You're still my favourite! Why don't you concentrate on teaching Abi some dance? She's already a good dancer, and under your tutelage, she'll really blossom!'

Abi looked at her mother with excitement shining in her eyes. It would be a treat beyond compare if her mother were to teach her dance. But Ananya was still sulking after her defeat. 'She should probably ask Urvashi! After all, she's the grand master of dance... I am nothing compared to her.' Abi looked at her father with troubled eyes. She was really worried that her mother still felt so upset after the competition. Her father had just opened his mouth to say something when Ananya stopped him. 'Go away, both of you. I want to be alone right now. Go ask Urvashi if she wants to teach Abi – I don't care!'

Abi's eyes were swimming in tears as she walked away along with her father. Dr Forbes put his arms around her shoulders. 'Abi, cheer up. Your mother can often be like that. *Apsaras* are temperamental creatures. That's what makes them such brilliant dancers. It's not just the skill and techniques; it is also the passion that bubbles inside them. Sadly, the passion also bubbles up for the wrong reasons at times. They can behave like spoilt little children – petty jealousies come to the forefront. It's certainly not a quality I want you to learn from her. Your mother is devastated that she lost that competition. She practised a lot for it. Also, you were there in the audience – though she'll never admit that made a difference. She loves you and now she feels humiliated in front of you.'

'But I don't care if Indra crowns someone else! She's my mother and I love her anyway!' said Abi, indignantly.

Her father gave her an indulgent smile. 'I know, my dear; but her head's too full of envy, humiliation and anger to think logically. Don't worry about it. It's not you!'

They had been walking aimlessly through the garden for a while when they suddenly bumped into Urvashi. 'Ah, you must be Abi, Hugh and Ananya's daughter! How lovely to meet you!' Abi smiled shyly at the gorgeous *apsara*. Urvashi's light green eyes sparkled with interest. 'I hear you're a good dancer and Guruma's been teaching you. That must be wonderful. Even amongst us *apsaras*, Guruma's school is legendary. What did you think of the dance performance at Indra's court?'

Abi looked round instinctively, as if to see if her mother was around, and then answered hesitatingly. 'It was amazing. Everyone was so perfect – and you were spectacular to watch.'

Urvashi smiled with pleasure. 'If you have the talent, you'll be amazed what knowing the right techniques and a bit of practice can do. Would you like to learn some of these from me? I'd be delighted to teach you.'

Abi looked at the *apsara* with mixed feelings. She desperately wanted to be taught by someone like Urvashi. At the same time, she dreaded what it would do to the mother-daughter relationship if she did. Her father came to her rescue. 'I know what you're thinking, Abi; but this is a chance of a lifetime. Your mother is going to spend a few days sulking and she may never want to teach you. I'd suggest you do work with Urvashi and I'll manage your mother.'

Urvashi smiled at both of them. 'Yes, don't worry about Ananya for the moment. If I had lost, I'd probably be feeling the same as her; but don't let her moods get you down and let go of this chance. Meet me in the dance hall in some time.' She gave them a dazzling smile and sashayed away.

Abi was still feeling muddled and worried, but she couldn't help wanting to learn from the legendary dancer. Her father was very supportive – he told her how she could get her dance outfits and anklets by just wishing for them under the coral tree in the garden. He also kept telling her stories about Urvashi's dance prowess as they walked together through the golden palace where she had first met her mother, towards the dance hall. The hall was a wide open space with ornate golden pillars supporting a very high golden roof. There was an orchestra getting ready to perform. Abi marvelled at the number of instruments and musicians in the orchestra. Besides the usual artists playing the Indian drum (mridangam), cymbals (nattuvangam) and the vocalist, there were three stringed instruments – the veena, the violin and the tanpura. Abi was very excited as they did not always have a live orchestra for practice in Gurukul. Urvashi walked in and gave the orchestra a nod. To Abi's great surprise, they started playing a song that she had often danced to. Urvashi smiled and indicated that Abi should start dancing while she settled down to watch. Abi was more nervous than she had ever been before, but the familiar music seemed to calm her down and she started performing.

Abi was just getting really into her dance when Urvashi stopped her. 'Good. I have seen what you do. Let's go over it again slowly!' Urvashi performed the same steps that Abi had done just moments ago – but her grace and beauty of form took Abi's breath away. The *apsara* then started teaching Abi through suggestions, tips and demonstration. The class continued for a long while but Abi was thoroughly enjoying herself. Even the orchestra seemed to enjoy playing for her, and Abi forgot about her mother's petulance for the duration of the class. After a while, Urvashi sighed and called the class to an end. 'You've done well today – but you've got much more to learn. Come back tomorrow and we can do this again.'

Abi's eyes were shining when she went out of the hall to meet her father. 'It was great! I learnt so much – it was brilliant! She's asked me to come back tomorrow!'

She walked with her father towards the garden, talking for a long time, discussing enjoyable topics such as dance and some not-so-enjoyable ones, such as her mother's anger. She still kept getting the feeling that she was forgetting something, but she dismissed that, hoping that it would come back to her sometime soon. They were just walking on when they came across Lord Indra. 'Abi, I know your father has shown you around a bit, but there's much more to see. Don't you want to see the Trinity?' Abi stopped and looked at Indra with bated breath. The Trinity! They were the supreme gods in Indian mythology. Abi remembered Guru Mahesh's mythology lessons clearly – Brahma, the creator; Vishnu, the preserver and Shiva, the destroyer.

'Can I really get to meet them? That would be a tremendous honour!' said Abi, not believing her good fortune.

'They don't always appear in front of everyone. However, I think you are a special girl and they may choose to appear in front of you. Come, I'll take you to see Brahma today, and we can see the others later on!'

Abi was bubbling with anticipation as she travelled alongside Indra on Airavat, the white elephant. They passed through the clouds and the gates of heaven. The space around them was dark and mysterious and Abi could see stars sparkling everywhere. Planets revolved around them and she was sure she saw flashes of light – shooting stars – zoom past them in the distance. She held her breath in astonishment as a star travelled towards them – the twinkling ball of energy now transformed into a beautiful girl. She smiled sweetly at Abi and exchanged pleasantries with Indra. When she turned back into a star and disappeared amongst clusters of others in the sky over them, Abi could not hold back a cry of surprise. 'I did not know that the stars were girls!' she exclaimed, feeling a bit foolish.

Indra smiled knowingly. 'Why not? You have met Surya – so if the sun could be a god, why can't the stars be goddesses, too? That is Tara, one of my favourites.' Airavat walked slowly and majestically and Indra waved out to various celestial beings in the sky.

After a while, Abi could hear the sound of chanting emanating all around. It was an amazing feeling – she could feel the reverberations from the chants echo around them. Airavat stopped in front of a gigantic white lotus suspended in space – the chanting seemed to be louder than ever. The space around the flower was a deep inky-blue. There was a feeling of peace that filled Abi's heart with an amazing calm that could not be surpassed. She closed her eyes and instinctively brought her hands together in prayer position.

When she opened her eyes, to her amazement, the lotus unfurled its petals in front of her. In the centre of the lotus sat the god Brahma. Abi recognised him from his silver flowing beard, pristine white robes and the look of great wisdom in his eyes – exactly as he had been depicted in her books. As he smiled at her, a great white swan flew through space and sat down next to the lotus. The beautiful goddess Sarasvati, Brahma's consort, sat on the swan's back, dressed in a brilliant white sari, holding the veena in her hands. Abi stared at the two of them in awe – they were the source of all knowledge in the world, and she couldn't believe she was in their presence. The goddess of knowledge played the veena – the sweet strains mingled with the chants and made the moment more magical. Abi closed her eyes once again to appreciate the beauty of the sounds even more – she felt more at peace here than ever before! Abi completely surrendered herself to the moment. Her mind echoed with the chants, and although her eyes were closed, she could see the magnificent lotus suspended in black nothingness in her mind's eye. Her eyes were swimming with tears of joy. She was savouring every bit of it when she felt Indra's hand on her shoulders. 'Come, Abi; it's time for us to leave!'

When they got back to Indra's garden in heaven, Abi was excited yet peaceful. 'I felt so calm and the chants were so soothing!' she exclaimed.

Indra smiled knowingly. 'Did you know that besides being the creator of all creatures great or small, the god Brahma also gave birth to the dance that you are so devoted to?'

Abi shook her head in surprise. 'No, I didn't know that! I have only ever associated the god Shiva with dance.'

Indra shook his head. 'It's a pity that not enough is known or taught about Brahma on earth. That's a story for another time. I hear that Urvashi is teaching you dance – you are a lucky girl. She doesn't always share her talent and knowledge with everyone; make the most of it!'

As Indra walked away, Abi was left by herself, probably for the first time in heaven. She mulled over the events so far and wondered what the next day had in store for her!

39

MAYA SAMUDRA

Abi's classes with Urvashi continued at full steam the next day. She was surprised at the progress she was making. Urvashi seemed very pleased with her new student, too. Dr Forbes laughed at his daughter's amazement at her own abilities. 'This is Heaven, Abi. Unlike on Earth, where things take longer in order to build your patience and character, out here, both your mental and physical energies can be channelled towards a goal. You're clearly very determined to learn from Urvashi, and all your mental faculties and physical prowess is helping you attain your goal quickly!'

Abi found this piece of information very confusing, and she was just about to ask another question when she saw her mother walk past. 'Mother – wait!' Abi tried to run after Ananya but she disappeared around a corner and couldn't be seen anymore. Abi was bitterly disappointed and tried to fight the tears prickling her eyes.

'Abi, give your mother a bit more time, she'll come round!' said Dr Forbes, giving his daughter a squeeze around her shoulders. He was clearly used to this behaviour.

―◦◦◦―

Later, Indra was true to his promise and came back to take Abi to meet Vishnu. 'We're going down into the deep ocean – you will see many great and terrible things. But rest assured that nothing will harm you, and I will always be by your side. Will you be ok, Abi?' Abi nodded distractedly. Her mind was still on her mother, and she was getting worried that her dance lessons had harmed their relationship beyond repair. She was lost in her thoughts when she realised that they were now floating above a huge body of water, poised to enter. Her heart started beating more loudly in her chest. This was a huge ocean and she could not see the shore on any side for miles around. The waters were deep blue, calm and inviting. 'Do you remember my words, Abi? This is Maya Samudra – not everything is what it seems to be. Hold on to my hand and don't worry about anything!' Abi felt a sudden apprehension and almost resisted stepping into the ocean for a moment. Her time in the lake when she was attacked by the great fish came back to her mind. She felt Indra's strong hand hold her hand gently – she took a deep breath to calm herself. This was her chance to see Vishnu, one of the great gods – he was known as the preserver. Everything in the world survived thanks to him. Mythology said that he had appeared on Earth ten times in various guises. One of these guises, arguably the most famous one, was Krishna – a lovable, playful and mischievous cowherd who saved the world from a tyrant king and guided India through a difficult war. Her friend Krish was named after this great god.

Indra continued to hold Abi's hand gently yet firmly as they delved deeper and deeper into the dark blue waters. At first, Abi saw nothing except miles of shimmering blue water around her – then things started appearing. Beautiful fish started swimming past them, diving in and out of colourful corals that adorned reefs below them. The fish got bigger and more unusual as they moved further below – great big sharks, whales and others, that Abi had seen in her natural sciences books but could not even name, swam lazily past. Abi looked at them in thrilled amazement. Her initial fears had completely disappeared and had been replaced by a stunned wonderment at the beauty of the life around her. It looked as if a page from her favourite wildlife book had come alive; and although the predators and prey were swimming together, there was no tension, no animosity and no creature was attacking any other. Indra smiled and pointed at something in the distance. Abi looked on in surprise as a shoal of silvery fish moved away to reveal tigers, elephants and all manners of land creatures calmly passing by.

'How...?' began Abi when Indra gave his answer, already anticipating her question.

'Abi, all life begins in water – egg yolks are suspended in a sac with fluid, foetuses are suspended in water inside their mother's body. Water is a source of life and it preserves the living. This is Vishnu's abode – you will find all kinds of living creatures in this ocean – even those that don't normally live in the earthly seas.'

Abi was gazing in rapture at a ruby-throated hummingbird when the bird flitted away to reveal a dark shape within the heart of the ocean. Memories flashed in Abi's head – *This looks strangely familiar! Where have I seen this shape before?* She held her breath in suspense and anticipation as they moved closer to the centre. The shape became more lucid as a vagrant ray of sunlight penetrated deep into the ocean. Abi gasped as she recognised the coiled body of a gigantic five-headed snake. 'I have seen this in the waterhole near my school – that's where I found the magic sapphire. That snake saved my life!' The words tumbled out even though she didn't mean to say them aloud.

Indra nodded sagely. 'Abi, Vishnu is omnipresent and he is the great protector. So he was there to take care of you – you remember the grave danger that you were in?'

Abi nodded but was still unconvinced. 'But why? I am just an ordinary girl – why should he come down to save me?'

Indra gave an amused chuckle. 'Ordinary? Whatever one can accuse you of, Abi – that's not it! You are an extraordinary girl – not just because of your origins but because of the lovely, kind, gentle and passionate person that you are – there aren't many such people in this world, or it would surely be a better place! And clearly Vishnu thinks you're special enough for him to come down into the waterhole in the middle of the Himalayan Mountains to save you from a dangerous *asura!*' Abi felt very humbled and felt her cheeks warm up as she blushed a beetroot red – she could not believe that one of the greatest gods had come down to Earth for her.

When they descended to the floor of the ocean, Abi saw something that she could never forget, even if she tried. Resting on the coiled bed of a great serpent was the most magnificent god that she had ever seen. Vishnu's skin was a shimmering blue, standing out in a lighter blue ocean. He had beautiful eyes – almost shaped like lotus buds. But his most wonderful feature was his dazzling smile – there was mischief, fun, laughter and kindness all rolled into that smile. That smile reminded Abi of her young friend Krish. 'Welcome, Abi – it is wonderful to see you here. How are you finding your tour of the heavens?'

Abi returned his smile. 'It is great – I am really fortunate to be here. I also wanted to thank you for saving my life when I went into the lake to get the magic sapphire,' mumbled Abi awkwardly.

'Abi, you were protected by your friends and your own goodness. You have risked a lot for others – that makes you a very special person. I had very little to do with it,' said Vishnu with a twinkle in his eyes.

Abi couldn't help herself – she just had to ask him. 'You remind me so much of my friend Krish. I don't know what it is about him and you.'

There was a magical tinkle of laughter – as if bells were tolling in the distance. 'Look inside me, Abi. All living creatures are in here – including Krish.'

Vishnu got up and expanded himself to his true godly form. He grew larger and larger – his gigantic body spanned the whole depth of the ocean. Indra took hold of Abi's hand and they floated up to the level of Vishnu's face. It looked as if all the creatures in that ocean had merged in with his form – she could see all manner of living beings beneath his transparent skin. 'Do not be afraid, Abi – this form of Vishnu can be frightening as it is gigantic – but it is really a manifestation of life! It is something to behold with awe, not terror!' said Indra gently. Vishnu gave Abi a beaming smile and his humongous form vanished to show her a fleeting vision of her friend Krish. Then there was nothing to see except the lazy blue ocean and a single beautiful lotus that floated up to her. Abi picked up the lotus and closed her eyes in stunned wonder that she had been lucky enough to witness such an amazing sight.

―――⚬⚭⚬―――

When they arrived back in Indra's heavenly garden, Abi was very thoughtful and quiet. The meeting with Vishnu had changed her in some inexplicable way. She had matured inside. 'The final trip is tomorrow – to see Shiva, the great destroyer!' That perked her up considerably. Abi turned to Indra with shining eyes. The majority of her dance lessons were dedicated to Shiva. They said that even time stopped in wonder when Shiva danced along with his consort Parvathi.

'If you're going to see the greatest dancer of all, you better practise some more!' Urvashi's silky voice shook Abi out of her reverie.

'I would be delighted to dance some more,' said Abi and took Urvashi's hand to walk towards the dance hall.

They danced all night long – Urvashi was a hard taskmaster that night, and Abi was exhausted but exhilarated at her improvement. 'You have done well.

I wouldn't want any student of mine to come face-to-face with Shiva without preparing for it!' said Urvashi, pleased with all their effort.

'Is he really such a spectacular dancer? Tell me more about him, please!' begged Abi, wanting to learn as much as she could from her celestial teacher.

Urvashi's eyes gazed into the distance as if remembering something. 'The god Brahma created the Bharatanatyam, and we performed it for Shiva, who took it to another dimension. I have had the good fortune of being able to witness Shiva and Parvathi perform the cosmic dance. Abi, there are no words to describe it – watching them dance was one of the most wondrous moments of my life. I can only hope that you get that privilege.'

The next day, Abi was ready and overflowing with excitement as she waited for Indra to take her to Kailasa, Shiva's abode. Dr Forbes watched her with growing amusement as she kept pacing up and down. 'He'll be here soon. Why, Abi, I believe you're keener on this trip than going to Disneyland in Paris!' said her father with a laugh.

Indra was soon with them and held out his hand to Abi. 'Are you ready? It is the mountains today – Shiva rests on top of Kailasa. Abi, this is a rare treat – with this final meeting, you will have met and been in the presence of the great trinity!' Abi breathed deeply and took Indra's hand – this was an adventure that she was really looking forward to!

40

THE GREATEST DANCER OF ALL!

Abi and Indra descended from the heavens towards the towering Himalayan range of mountains. They could see one or two aeroplanes below them, transporting hundreds of people across the continents. 'What if the passengers see us?' asked Abi, feeling a bit silly as she asked the question.

'Abi, that's the magic of human minds – they have such colourful imaginations that we'll be passed off as a dream. Do you remember seeing me when you flew into India?' Abi nodded vigorously. How could she forget the sight of Indra riding on his beautiful white elephant! 'Did you tell anyone about me?' he enquired.

'Of course not! They'd say I was imagining it or else assume that I was mad,' said Abi sheepishly.

Indra nodded. 'That's what most people would do. So I wouldn't worry about being seen. Besides, people can only see gods when we want to be seen. And you're with me, so you're hidden away, too,' he said, with a smile playing mischievously on his lips.

They landed gently on a small plateau that held a stunning lake with blue-green waters. Mount Kailasa loomed majestically near them. 'Why did we not land closer?' asked Abi, as Indra started walking up the mountain.

'Abi, Shiva's anger can be terrible – I wouldn't dream of landing directly near him unless I knew that he was in a good mood. I haven't seen him in a while, and there was a big earthquake disaster recently, so I know he's been in a destructive mood. I can only hope he's come out of it now.'

Abi's heart was beating a bit harder – and it was not just due to the steep incline in the path. 'Are all earthly disasters caused by the god Shiva?' asked Abi tentatively.

Indra nodded solemnly. 'Sometimes, they are caused by humans themselves, but yes, often Shiva delivers his verdict in the form of some natural disaster or other.' They climbed up for a while and Indra stopped and looked around him. 'This doesn't look good. The snow is melting – that means that Shiva is still angry or that he hasn't closed his third eye completely.' Abi looked at him, puzzled. She knew from her lessons that Shiva could wreak havoc and even destroy the world if he opened his third eye, but she was confused about its significance to the melting snow. Indra explained very patiently: 'At times, Shiva opens his third eye to destroy something so that the earth can regain her balance. Once the destruction is complete, his third eye should close and everything gets back to normal. For some reason, if he's not closed his third eye completely, a lot of heat can continue to be generated around him, and although he's not destroying something knowingly, he can cause seasonal changes and global warming. I think the ice caps on this mountain are melting because of this. I foresee floods washing away the villages in the mountains soon.'

Abi silently tried to digest all this information as they continued walking. She had studied environmental changes and global warming as part of her natural sciences classes. She felt more confused than ever trying to apply Indra's interpretation to something that she had always regarded as a natural and scientific phenomenon. Is that what global warming was all about? The fact that Shiva had not closed his third eye properly? 'Stop, there he is!' whispered Indra, dragging Abi's hand to hide behind a large boulder. Abi peeked out cautiously. Shiva was sitting on a rock – he was exactly as she imagined. He had an incredibly handsome, chiselled face with high cheekbones and sharp features. His hair was matted – some tied up in a loose knot on his head while long, matted locks fell all around his shoulders. He was smeared with ash and was wearing a tiger skin around him. Snakes adorned his wrists and neck. Abi felt that she was watching an actor dressed up as the god in a play. Both his eyes were closed, but there was a slight opening of his third eye in his forehead. There was palpable heat being generated from it – the snow had completely melted in this area, and the few plants in the vicinity seemed to have dried and withered away.

Indra pulled at Abi's hand. 'Come, Abi; we must leave. He can be very dangerous in this state. If we disturb him, he can get incensed and destroy us. I still remember the time he burnt Kama, the god of love, for disturbing him. Poor Kama had to spend a lifetime on Earth as punishment, and it's only thanks to his wife's prayers and hard work that he is back in the heavens now!'

Abi hesitated. 'But we cannot leave him like this – the snow is melting fast – the rivers will be filled with excess water and flood. It will cause more destruction and possibly even death. Surely you won't let the wildlife and the people living around here suffer?'

Indra looked at her gravely. 'Abi, this doesn't just affect the life around here. It will have an impact on everything and everyone very soon. The air will become hot, the balance of Earth will shift, climates will change, the wildlife will find its habitat disappearing, and people will suffer everywhere. It will even reach Gurukul.'

Abi's worry was slowly turning into panic. 'Then we cannot leave! We must do something,' she said in a high-pitched whisper.

Indra placed his hand over her mouth to quieten her down. 'Hush, Abi! We cannot help anyone if we're both burnt to a cinder. There's one person who can help – Shiva's wife and consort, the goddess Parvathi.'

Abi brightened up slightly. 'Then all's not lost. Where is she?' she said, looking around as if expecting to see the goddess any minute.

Indra looked exasperated but then decided to indulge her a bit more. He sat down and explained in a hushed and hurried whisper. 'The gods visit Earth at times in human disguise. They spend some time there and normally have a mission to fulfil. The goddess Parvathi is down on Earth on one such mission. Unfortunately, we cannot just approach her or call her away from her purpose. We will have to pray to her and hope she comes back soon.'

Abi shook her head impatiently. 'But that's not possible – by that time, half the world could be destroyed!'

Indra gave her a tiny smile. 'Abi, you still have much to learn, and true patience is one of those things. At times, we have to leave things as they are – new life is often generated from the ashes of destruction. Come now, it's time to leave!'

Abi looked around her with tears swimming in her eyes. The snow was indeed melting quickly and she could hear avalanches in the distance. She thought of the river meandering by her dance school. The waters were probably breaking the banks by now. She thought of her friend Krish – his family lived in a village in the mountains. The river was their lifeblood and the mountain was the only home they knew. If their village got flooded, where would they go? They were not rich people, and life in the town or city would be even more impoverished and unbearable for them. She remembered what Lord Vishnu had said to her. 'I cannot let my friends suffer. I have to do something. They have saved me time and again – I cannot let them down.' Abi closed her eyes and tried to meditate as she did in the past to become calmer. She opened her eyes as an idea came to her mind. 'What does Shiva like? Is there anything that he is really fond of, besides his wife?'

Indra was getting slightly impatient and was keen to leave. 'Come, Abi; don't delay things. Shiva is an ascetic –

so material things would not impress him; but he's fond of dance, as you well know.'

Abi looked at Indra with shining eyes. 'Dance! Of course! Why didn't I think of it! If someone performs a great dance in front of him, maybe he'll calm down and then close his third eye.'

Indra hesitated slightly. 'It's worth a shot – but I'd suggest we go back and bring some of the *apsaras* here so that they can dance in front of him. Of course, getting them here would be a challenge – especially if they knew that Shiva's third eye was partially open. They are not the most generous of creatures, my *apsaras*…'

Indra started walking back and Abi followed him hesitantly. As she stepped on a puddle of water, she thought of Krish, Sumathy and all her friends in the mountains. This water would cause them no end of trouble – it would destroy their lives. She saw their faces in her mind – how could she leave them in danger! Abi made up her mind. She walked up to Indra and spoke quietly to him: 'No, I'll dance. Lord Indra – if you wish to leave, please do so. I don't mind being burnt – I have much less to lose than you. I am not a god – I don't have your depth of understanding of life to witness the destruction of people I love. I have to try!'

Indra looked taken aback. He gazed deeply into her eyes; there was a fire burning inside them. He sighed and smiled and sat down on a rock. 'I would love to see you dance – show us what Urvashi has taught you so far! I am the king of gods, Abi – I can hardly leave a young girl like you on her own to save the world!' Abi was delighted to know he was going to stay. She was nervous and Indra's presence comforted her in a strange way. She closed her eyes in meditation and thought of the music that she'd dance to. She could hear the strains of music in her mind. She got into the zone of the character whose dance she was going to perform. With a deep breath, she began.

Abi started to dance slowly and gingerly on the rocky surface of the mountain. The melting snow kept the noise low, but the rhythm in her feet caused gentle vibrations all around. As if by magic, music started playing in Abi's ears. She was surprised and couldn't see the source of the music but didn't miss a beat in her dance. Indra was nodding appreciatively and she became more confident. The music got louder and Abi began to dance as if nothing else mattered. She remembered all the tips and techniques that Urvashi had taught her. Her mind was now totally focussed on her dance, and she forgot all about her surroundings and circumstances. Her steps became more intricate as the tempo of the music started rising. She did not realise it – but she had now started attracting an audience. Animals and birds collected and watched her at a distance as if afraid of Shiva but still drawn to her dance. Some gods also joined Indra – Surya, the sun god; Vayu, the wind and Chandra, the moon god were among them; but Abi had eyes for no one. She was lost in a trance in her dance and in the music that was playing around her. She danced beautifully – her passion for the art poured out in the form of a raw energy and the *apsara's* lessons had given her an amazing grace. She twisted and twirled elegantly while an enthralled audience sat and watched with rapt attention.

Suddenly Abi sensed something change around her. There was a palpable tension in the air – a collective gasp that had not yet been uttered by the people watching her. She opened her eyes and, to her amazement, Shiva had risen and joined her in dance. They danced together in perfect harmony – she provided grace to his magnificent presence and energy. There was an indescribable power in his movements – it was like watching a great cat in action. But to her own surprise, she was able to match his performance and keep up with each of his very complicated steps. She became the Yin to his Yang. She danced with confidence, grace and joy – and these emotions were reflected in Shiva's shining face. They danced for a long time – their audience had increased many-fold. All the gods from heaven seemed to have descended to watch them dance. The wildlife had lost its fear and had formed a circle around them. The music had become even more enchanting as the goddess Sarasvati flew down with her stringed veena and added its sweet notes to the magical melodies in the air. Various *apsaras* appeared in the sky to appreciate their performance. Abi was feeling hot as she had been dancing for a while, but the air around her started becoming noticeably cooler. She looked at Shiva's face and realised the reason for this – his third eye had now closed completely.

As they completed their last dance, the audience stood up and applauded long and hard. Many of them were shedding tears of joy at having witnessed their unique and fantastic performance. Abi turned towards the tall, towering form of Shiva and folded her hands in deference. 'Well done, Abi. It's not a small feat to dance in front of such an audience. But it is an even greater achievement to dance so well that you got me to join you. Who is your teacher?'

Abi shyly raised her head and spoke in a quiet voice. 'There are three people who have created the dancer in me. My first one is Guruma – she taught me how to dance and much more. I have also been lucky enough to have been taught by the great Urvashi. Finally, my mother, Ananya – her talent runs within me.'

He was smiling now. 'You are a very lucky girl to have three wonderful gurus.' Shiva looked around him and understood the extent of the unplanned destruction that he had caused. 'Abi, you are very brave. I would like to give you a boon. What would you like?'

Abi was overwhelmed. 'I got what I wanted – I made you smile. I was worried for my friends down below – but I think they will be fine now. I don't need anything else.'

Shiva smiled – 'You are a lovely girl, Abi. You are always thinking of others. However, I would like to grant you a boon. If you don't know what you want just now, you can ask me anytime that it does become clear to you. A boon that you want for yourself and not for anyone else.' She could hear the cheers of her audience ringing pleasantly in her ears. What an amazing and fulfilling day this had been!

41

THE QUEST FOR VYDEHI

Abi returned to heaven with Indra and the other gods. She felt like a celebrity as everyone came to congratulate her on her bravery and her performance. Her eyes searched for Urvashi and finally found her in the crowd, beaming with pride. 'You were brilliant! I am so proud of you,' she mouthed in the distance. Abi saw her father standing a little away from the crowd, watching her with a big smile on his face. She broke off from everyone else to run towards him when someone held her back. A very shame-faced Ananya was holding her hand – Abi stopped and turned towards her mother.

'Abi, will you ever forgive me? You are such a courageous girl – I don't know if I'd have done what you did today. I feel so bad that you came to heaven in search of me and I treated you so indifferently. I heard you tell Shiva that I was one of your three gurus – whereas I hardly spent any time with you. I am sorry – will you forgive me?' Abi looked uncertainly at the tears welling up in her mother's lovely eyes. She had been very disappointed in the way her mother had treated her over the last few days – but she couldn't watch her break down and cry. After all, she was her mother and someone that she had yearned to meet for years. She gave her a hug – she would have to learn to forgive and forget.

After a while, the gods disappeared into Indra's court for a great feast. Dr Forbes and Ananya slipped out of the courtroom along with Abi and walked towards the garden. They wanted a bit of time together as a family – away from all the commotion and excitement. They strolled in the garden and talked to each other for hours. Abi felt happy and content – she was finally with her family. She watched her mother and father joke and laugh with each other and felt happier than ever before. Abi felt almost complete – though there was a strange niggling feeling at the back of her mind that she couldn't place. She wondered indolently if she should use Shiva's boon to remember what she'd forgotten but then chased away that thought. She couldn't use it for something so trivial.

The family spent time together and explored all the joys that heaven had to offer. Abi joined her mother in her practice and learnt more about the art. They would start their practice at dawn as Ananya felt that this was the most auspicious hour to practise creative art. Ananya opened her heart to her daughter and taught her without holding anything back. She was an amazing teacher, but she also seemed to know Abi really well. Not only did she teach her dance, but she also taught her how to look after herself by eating the right foods and resting her muscles appropriately after a tough practice. Abi blossomed more under her mother's guidance.

———∞∞∞———

One day, they were earlier than normal – the night was just fading and dawn had not yet broken. Abi, Ananya and Hugh wandered into Indra's garden, holding hands and enjoying the peace. They came across a large group congregated around the coral tree. *What are they looking at? Why is there a commotion?* wondered Abi.

Hugh tapped on the shoulders of a demi-god who was just in front of them and asked him the very same question. 'It is the Ashwini Kumars. They have returned after a long journey across the universe. We are just welcoming them.'

Abi stood on her toes and peered through the milling people to see two handsome gods seated on a bench under the tree. They looked exactly like a mirror image of each other – there was a bright light emanating from both of them. 'Abi, come, we need to go practise.' Ananya pulled Abi's hand to drag her away from the scene.

The twin gods heard her voice and got up and walked through the parting crowd towards Abi. 'Abirami – it is a pleasure to meet you. We heard about your dance with Shiva.' The twins even spoke in unison. Abi smiled at them – for some reason both her parents were tugging gently at her, as if they wanted to drag her away.

As the twins walked away with their admirers in tow, the niggling feeling at the back of Abi's mind resurfaced. The Ashwini twins reminded her of something. What was it? Suddenly it struck her like a bolt from the blue. The family wasn't whole – Abi's twin sister Vy was missing! Abi sat down on the ground, stunned by the enormity of her realisation. She hadn't thought of her sister in days – she was so lost in her quest for her mother that everyone else had slipped out of her mind. Ananya was the first to notice the change in Abi's expression. 'What is it, my dear? What's wrong?' she asked, with concern in her eyes.

Abi fought her tears and looked up at her parents. 'Where is Vy? Why isn't she here? How could I have forgotten about her! I have met Dad here – surely she must be here, too? Please tell me that she's not in hell...'

Hugh and Ananya exchanged distraught glances. Hugh moved forward to console Abi. 'Abi, no, she's not in hell, but she's not in heaven either.'

Abi looked at both of them miserably. 'I feel so bad that I've taken this long to remember her.'

Hugh looked embarrassed. 'That was our fault. We didn't want you to worry about her and we requested Indra that you forget about her. Indra wouldn't grant you total amnesia. He said that you'd not think about her as long as there were other things on your mind. However, if something or someone reminded you of her, your memories would come flooding back. The Ashwini Kumars did just that – and as we weren't expecting them here, we couldn't prevent it. Sorry, Abi – but we didn't want you to fret.'

'Dad, how do you know that she's not in hell? asked Abi, slowly digesting the information her father had given her. There was anger simmering inside her – but somehow in heaven, a negative feeling like anger couldn't last long. She knew they'd done it for her well-being – so she grudgingly curbed her feelings.

Hugh Forbes looked desolate. 'I remember the accident well. Our car rolled down the cliff – a door opened and you were thrown out. But Vy & I were still strapped in. The last thing I remember was the car blowing up! So, I thought Vy must have died at the same time as me. I searched high and low for her in heaven. When I couldn't find her, I pleaded and begged Yama, the god of death, to allow me to come into hell for a short while and search for her.' He stopped for breath and shuddered as if remembering something very unpleasant. 'Searching through hell was not a nice experience, but I did it. However, she's not there either.'

He stopped and looked at his wife. Ananya continued his saga. 'Hugh cannot go back to Earth, now that he's here. He can periodically look over someone he loves – so he could see you, but he couldn't see Vy anywhere. If Indra gives me permission, I can go back to Earth. He allowed me to go back for a short period to search for her – but I couldn't find her, Abi. I saw you in Gurukul, slowly settling in; but I couldn't find your twin sister anywhere at all. I am afraid we have no idea where she is now!'

Abi looked at her parents in dismay. 'Can the gods not help? Surely someone would know where she is!'

Hugh gave a little laugh. 'The gods are very different from us, Abi. They take things in their stride and are extremely philosophical about such things. They said to me that she'd appear before us when the time was right and when she wanted to.' Ananya shifted uncomfortably and looked at Hugh. Hugh turned to his daughter gravely. 'Abi, it is possible that she did die in the accident but then got reborn on Earth as another person! She will be impossible to find unless she remembers her old life and all of us!'

Abi had tears swimming in her eyes. She turned away in a huff. 'I need to be on my own for a while,' she said, walking off into the garden.

She was annoyed with herself that she had forgotten her twin sister, someone who was almost part of her. She resented her parents for making her forget about her in heaven but understood why they had done so. There must be a way to find Vy, if she was reborn on Earth. She was pondering this deeply when the Ashwini twins walked by. She noticed how they moved in perfect unison and felt a stab of jealousy and sadness. They must have seen the look in her eyes as they stopped and reached out to her. 'Are you ok, Abi? Something wrong?'

Abi told them about her twin sister and what her parents told her about being reincarnated on Earth. 'I would really want to find her – even if she were in a different person's body now! Can you not help me? Do you know where she is?'

The Ashwini brothers frowned in unison. 'No, my child. We cannot interfere with fate and tell you where she is. That would be wrong! But there may be one way... it's not easy... and your mother needs to be willing.'

Abi's eyes lit up in hope. 'Oh, tell me how, please! I would do anything to be with her again!'

The twins exchanged glances. 'Well, an aspara often leaves a jewel on Earth that can be found by a loved one and used to get back to heaven. We all know about your mother's magic sapphire. If she were to leave it again on Earth, in a difficult place, so that only you or your sister can reach it, that'll be the best way to find out who she is.'

Abi thought of her adventures in the waterhole to fetch the sapphire and then the arduous climb of the seven steps to heaven. 'Is there no other way? And how do I go about asking different people to jump in the lake to get the sapphire? Why would they even want to do it?'

The twins laughed heartily. 'Ah no, Abi. We don't suggest putting it in the waterhole. We can give your mother a magic bowl that's filled with fire. If she places the sapphire in its centre, only you or your sister can pick it out.'

Abi thought this through. It still seemed a bit tenuous, and she wasn't sure how many people she'd have to ask to try before finding Vy. 'Where do I even start? Where on Earth could she be?'

One of the twins winked at her. 'Have you read *The Alchemist*?' he asked.

'It's one of my favourite books,' exclaimed Abi, thinking how incongruous it sounded for one of the ancient gods to mention a modern classic.

'Well, you have your answer then. Your home is where your heart is, and what you seek is right there!' They grinned at each other and drew a golden bowl out of the air. It was filled with red and yellow flames, flickering prettily. 'Here's your bowl – good luck in persuading your mother!' The twins vanished just as Abi began to thank them for the gift.

———∞∞———

'No, I don't want you to go anywhere! Why can't you stay here with me? I'll teach you and you can have everything you want in heaven,' sulked Ananya, her lips pursed petulantly.

Abi fidgeted with the edge of her mother's sari, her hands shaking. 'Mother, I want to find Vy – and she's not here, is she? Please let me do this – help me, this is really important to me!' Abi had been trying to persuade her mother for ages but wasn't making much progress. Hugh sat watching the two of them argue. She finally turned to her father in tears. 'Dad, how can I leave Vy behind? Surely you're not happy about that? I have to find her… please…' she cried, with tears falling freely on her cheeks now.

Hugh looked at her for a while and then turned to Ananya. 'I know you and I have resigned ourselves to the fact that Vy doesn't exist anymore and she's now another person. But Abi hasn't. And she has to find peace in her own way. Do reconsider.' Ananya shook her head and walked off in anger, leaving Abi to her tears. Hugh gave his daughter a hug. 'Don't worry, I will persuade her. It will take several pleas but she will come round. But where are you going to start? Do you know where she is?'

Abi hesitated before replying. She had been thinking of what the twins had told her. 'Home is where your heart is…'

Her heart was in Gurukul. That meant that her sister must have been reborn in or around the area. How she was going to recognise her was a mystery. 'I have an idea where to start, but no idea how to proceed after that; but I think the way will come to me if I truly want it, Dad. And I am hoping that Vy will recognise me too – if she does, then surely she'll tell me or give me a sign of some sort?'

Hugh laughed without humour. 'I told your mother you'd want to do this! Ok, leave Ananya to me – I'll bring her round and get her to give you the magic sapphire to take back. But promise me this, when you feel that your work on Earth is over, please use the sapphire and come back to us!' Abi gave her dad a loving hug – and willed him silently to persuade her mother.

42

BACK TO EARTH!

Ananya finally came round and placed her magic sapphire in the centre of the fire-filled bowl. It had taken her father more time than he anticipated to persuade her, but he finally did. Her mother looked like a child about to cry as its favourite toy was being taken away. Abi suppressed the need to laugh at the irony – she felt as if she was the adult and her mother the child in this relationship. 'Mother, it will be ok. I know you and Father are fine in heaven. Don't you wish to know how your other daughter fares? She must be all by herself on Earth. I have got to go and find her – please understand.' She squeezed her mother's hand affectionately. Her parents sat with her for a while before going back to the palace.

Abi sat back in the garden and watched her parents walk away, leaving her alone for a short while. She knew she had to say her goodbyes to Indra and the other gods soon, but she wanted to mull over the events of the past few days and her incredible adventures in heaven, and also think about her plan of action when she got back to Gurukul. She could hear the birds singing in the trees, and the subtle fragrance of the flowers in the garden enveloped her. The sun was throwing a warm ray of light on her. She savoured every moment of her time left and closed her eyes with a smile on her face. The peace around her lulled her into sleep. In her dreams, Abi was transported back to Kailasa where she and Lord Shiva had just finished dancing. A tall, graceful and imposing lady walked up to her – she was dressed in plain white robes. Her long, shiny hair was tied loosely and she had adorned it with the heavily scented temple flowers. Her angular face was radiant and beautiful. Abi realised that this was the goddess Parvathi and walked up to her. 'Well done, Abi. It is not easy to soothe Shiva and get him to close his third eye. You are a brave girl and have done something that not many others could or would have done. You have a lot of strength within you – and in this instance, you looked inside to find the answer. When you are in deep trouble, remember that all the *shakti* or power that you need, lives inside you. When no one else can help you, you must know that your inner strength can. Believe in yourself, Abi.' Abi looked at the goddess in wonder. As she stared into the goddess's intense grey eyes, something stirred inside her. Where had she seen her before? Abi woke up in shock as the realisation hit her like a bolt of thunder. She had looked into those deep, unusual grey eyes many times before – Guruma was the goddess Parvathi!

Abi had no time to reflect on what she had seen in her dreams as she saw Indra approaching her. 'Abi, I hear from your parents that you want to go back to Earth. Are you sure? You are welcome to stay here as long as you want – you will not be touched by pain, hunger or true grief out here. There are indescribable treasures that you can uncover while you're here.'

Abi stood up and smiled gratefully. 'That is so kind of you, but I have to go back and find my sister. My parents have each other and they are happy here. I have to find Vy – she may be all alone. I am all she has on Earth. She's more precious to me than any treasure.'

Indra nodded in understanding. 'Well, if you want to wander around heaven and say your goodbyes, do so. And then come back to me. I will need to take you back to Earth. If you go back unescorted, you will find that time moves very mysteriously and you'd land back several thousand years in the future.' Abi was puzzled to hear about the time difference between heaven and Earth, but she knew she hadn't uncovered all the mysteries in heaven and should make her peace with that. She thanked Indra and walked purposefully towards the *apsaras'* palace to meet up with Urvashi.

Abi spent a long time meeting all the celestial beings that she had befriended in heaven. Urvashi was sad to see her go but was delighted that Abi had every intention of continuing her dance.

Loads of hugs, good wishes and farewells later, Abi strolled back through the garden to Indra's court. On her way, she noticed a dark lady standing under a coral tree, as if waiting for her. Her hair was peppered with grey but tied back elegantly. She was wearing many jewels on her hair and neck. She couldn't be called beautiful, but there was a dignified grace about her personality. She smiled at Abi to reveal perfectly formed teeth. There was something vaguely familiar about her, but Abi couldn't place her at all. 'I hear you are on your way back to Earth, my child,' said the woman in a gentle voice. Abi nodded in affirmation. 'Well, I wanted to wish you good luck. If you take the magic sapphire back, you may find your sister. But you may also attract evil. I came to warn you about that.' Her green eyes glazed over and looked towards the earth as she spoke these words.

'Are you talking about something specific? What sort of evil?' asked Abi, guessing that the woman had not told her everything.

'You are a good girl – and brave. But you are very young – and wisdom only comes with age and experience. At the first flush of youth, the world is filled with romance, and everything seems rosy or golden, even if it is not.'

Abi looked at the woman, puzzled. She had no idea what she was talking about. 'You and I both care for someone out there, Abi. Someone who doesn't always deserve the love he gets from people. He is my son and I desperately want him back here. But I do not approve of the shortcuts he wants to take to get back to heaven and to his family. Please be careful of him!' Abi's eyes widened with dawning comprehension. This was Varun's mother! And she had come to warn her that she may be in danger if she took the jewel back to Earth. After all, Varun had tried to return to heaven before, using her and the jewel as his means. 'Be careful, Abi – don't let your heart rule your head. The only thing that can save you is your kindness – remember that, always!' said Varun's mother before she vanished.

Abi stood for what seemed like an eternity, staring at the spot where the woman had vanished. Could she really take her advice and control her feelings for Varun? Would she be in danger again? Abi then remembered the soothing gaze of deep grey eyes – Guruma would always protect her. She thought about Gurukul, Sumathy, Krish and baby Vi, and her heart filled with delight. Yes, that's where her heart was. She shook her head and decided that it was time to go back.

∞∞

Abi's eyes were closed shut as per Indra's instructions. She felt movement in and around her body even though she was still sitting cross-legged. It was as if they were travelling at great speed through space. She felt (or imagined) that lights were flashing past – could these be stars and planets? At times, she felt as if she was moving through water – but had no problems breathing. Indra had warned her about the vagaries of time, and although she did not understand the reasons behind it, she dutifully followed all the instructions that he'd given her. He'd specifically asked her to keep her eyes closed, whatever happened. She found it hard to do so and tried to distract herself by thinking. She remembered learning about Einstein's theory of relativity and wondered what the great scientist would say if he had the opportunity to travel through time and space as she was.

'You can open your eyes, Abi. We are here!' Indra's deep voice shook Abi out of her reverie. To her great surprise, they were both sitting cross-legged on the rocky ledge near her school. This was her secret hideout and she used to come here to practise her dance. This was where she met Indra before making her way to heaven to see her mother.

She looked around her hesitantly. The sun was shining in a cloudless blue sky, and a gentle breeze ruffled her hair. 'What date is it?' asked Abi, feeling very foolish – she had no concept of time travel and couldn't fathom whether they were back to the same day that she departed for heaven.

Indra flashed a magnificent smile. 'Time is a strange thing, Abi. I could have brought you back to the exact same moment in time that you left. However, that would have taken me longer and been a bit more complex. Besides, you have spent much time in heaven with your parents – you have to pay for that privilege in some way. It is probably a year or so after you left, by my estimate. Things will have changed on Earth – but not so much that you will not recognise them.'

Abi stood there trying to absorb all the information Indra gave her. He laid a gentle hand on her shoulder. 'It has been a pleasure having you in heaven, Abi. You have proved yourself really worthy of the magic sapphire.'

Abi looked at Indra with a tinge of regret. She had formed a real bond with some of her celestial friends – she would miss them a lot on Earth. 'Thank you for letting me visit your wonderful kingdom. You spent a lot of time with me – I will always treasure that!' She looked on wistfully as he disappeared into thin air.

Abi started walking back towards her school through the forest. She was surprised that she remembered the path very well. She was just midway through her journey when she spotted a familiar figure at a distance. 'Abi – is that you?' Sumathy squealed in delight and ran towards her to give her a big hug. 'I can't believe you're here. How are you? Did you meet your mother? How was heaven? Tell me all about it!'

Abi grinned as she gave her friend a hug and looked at her in amusement. 'Let me take a breath! I'll tell you everything. First, let me look at you properly. You look great.' Sumathy blushed at the compliment. She was always conscious of her looks – she thought she was not very pretty as her teeth protruded slightly and she was skinny enough to be a supermodel. The year had been kind to her – she seemed to have put on a little bit of weight which suited her a lot. Her face had filled out a bit and her teeth did not look so prominent. She gave Abi a wide smile and goaded her to tell her about heaven. 'It was strange,' said Abi. That was the only way she could describe it. 'It was not what I expected – but then, I didn't really know what to expect.'

They sat down underneath a tree and Abi told Sumathy all she could remember. Sumathy held her breath as Abi described the dance incident with Shiva. Her eyes were shining when Abi finished the tale. 'Abi, that's so wonderful. I always knew you were special – but to dance with Shiva! What an honour! But it's really well deserved. I missed you so much and thought of you often.' Abi felt quite guilty about not missing Sumathy as much while she was in heaven. It was probably because nothing was the same there and there was so much wonder to fill her mind. Changing topics, she asked to hear about what was happening at school. 'I have pretty much finished my studies. I am now helping Guru Uma and teaching the younger students,' said Sumathy proudly. 'Many of our classmates have left school, now that they have graduated. Pooja has become very famous – she has moved to New Delhi and is a well-known dancer there. Oh, and Kala has got married! Can you imagine – she's too young – but she wanted to.' Abi digested all the news slowly. Sumathy carried on excitedly and told Abi about all their classmates. Baby Vi had been very sad since Abi had left and had still not begun speaking – everyone thought she'd never speak. It seemed that only Sumathy and Jayalakshmi had stayed back at school. Jaya wanted to study more and become a dance scholar. Abi thought about Guruma – she hadn't mentioned how the goddess Parvathi had appeared to her in her dreams, in Guruma's guise. That piece of information was too confusing to share at the moment.

After a while, the two girls made their way back to Gurukul. Abi felt butterflies fluttering in her stomach. However, her fears were put to rest as she walked into the courtyard. 'Look who's here – it's Abi!' A number of girls rushed towards them to greet Abi joyously. Some of the teachers came along to welcome her as well. As everyone clamoured around, Abi had a sudden thought. What had Guruma told everyone about where she had gone?

A worried look appeared on her face and her eyes sought out Sumathy, who was standing a little away, smiling at all the excitement. She understood Abi's fears immediately. 'Girls, let her breathe. She's just come back from the UK; she's really tired!' said Sumathy loudly, giving Abi a significant look.

Guru Uma nodded vigorously. 'Sumathy is right, girls. She's only been away for a year and all of you are making such a fuss. Abi, you probably want to go have a wash and then rest in your room. Come back at dinnertime. I will bring baby Vi to meet you then.' Abi took her offer up gratefully and waved a cheery goodbye to the girls as she and Sumathy walked towards their room.

Sumathy had left everything exactly as Abi remembered. All her belongings were neatly kept in their usual space. Her mother's painting was still hanging up on the wall above her bed. She realised how much her best friend would have missed her and gave Sumathy a sudden hug. 'Thank you for looking after my things.'

Sumathy blinked away tears and sat down on her bed heavily. 'So much has happened – you've been away for so long! But I am really happy that you're back. I was not sure if you'd ever come back.'

Abi nodded. 'I wasn't sure either. But I realised that my sister is still on Earth. I have to find her, Sumathy – she'll be all alone! Will you help me?'

'Of course I will. Do you even have to ask? Guruma always told me to have faith and you'd be back!'

Abi listened to her friend in amazement. Guruma was indeed incredible. 'Where is she? I should go and pay my respects to her,' said Abi, getting up.

'She's away for a few days. No one really knows where, or if they do, they refuse to tell us. Some say she's gone to meet a sage in the snowy mountains – but that's only a rumour.' Abi thoughtfully mulled over this piece of information. Could that sage in the snowy mountains be Lord Shiva?

43

ATTRACTING EVIL!

Abi enjoyed being back in school. As they sat down on the well-swept floor to eat their dinner off banana leaves, she thought about the feasts in heaven. Although no one really felt any hunger or thirst out there, they would have magnificent feasts to celebrate and socialise. She was amused to note that she was feeling peckish – so she was a normal mortal once more! The smell of stir-fried vegetables and creamy dal wafted towards her, and she sighed with pleasure. Eating on Earth was much more fun than in Indra's palace, even if the food was less exotic. She tucked into her meal happily and didn't talk or pay attention to anything else for a while. Once satisfied, she looked around her and noticed some new faces. Sumathy turned to her and whispered, 'The new girls are a mixed bunch. The one in yellow is very good, but one or two of the others are quite appalling. I have to teach them tomorrow.' Abi looked at her friend's face in mild wonder. Things had changed since she'd left school – it was odd to see her best friend as a teacher.

Suddenly someone tugged at her hair and she turned to see the shining eyes of baby Vi looking at her. The child had grown a lot since she left. She had short, curly black hair and dark coffee brown skin. The resemblance to Guru Uma was there to be seen. Vi hugged Abi in delight – she held on to her tightly, as if she would never let go now that she had come back. 'She hasn't been this happy since you left, Abi,' Guru Uma said, coming up to their side.

'I hear she hasn't started speaking yet, Guruji. Have you shown her to a doctor?' asked Abi, her eyes full of concern for her favourite toddler.

'It's very odd – there's nothing wrong with her. The doctors say that she just doesn't want to talk. She's been very sad since you left – maybe now that you're back, you can coax her to say a few words…' said Guru Uma, looking at her daughter affectionately and then turning to look at Abi with new hope in her eyes.

———⁂———

That night, Abi lay in bed wide awake, thinking of baby Vi. The child's birthmark had become very pronounced and looked exactly like Vy's scar. What if this was her twin sister? But how could she have the heart to get the child to put its hand into the magic fire! 'What are you thinking, Abi?' Sumathy's voice was clear and sounded loud in the silent night. Abi hesitated for a while, but she had always shared all her secrets with Sumathy and it felt churlish to not tell her this one. She sat up and poured her heart out to her – including her suspicion that baby Vi was Vydehi, reincarnated, and how she felt that she couldn't really test the child by asking her to put her hand in the magic fire to verify she was indeed the right person.

Sumathy sat silently and listened to the whole story. 'You may be right and this may be your sister. But I agree; getting her to put her hand into the fire doesn't sound like something a loving sister would do. Let's wait and see what Guruma says when she's back. I am sure she will have a suggestion; she always does,' soothed Sumathy. Reassured, Abi went into a deep sleep that night, hoping for the best.

———

She woke up early next morning and got into the Gurukul routine. After bathing in the stream, she and Sumathy went up to the school's main courtyard to attend to some chores. Sumathy busied herself with drawing a beautiful and elaborate *kolam* on the floor, in the centre of the courtyard. Abi watched in admiration as her fingers flew over the wet ground, drawing complex patterns with powdered rice. *Kolams bring prosperity and happiness. Every morning, one should clean the floor and draw a kolam outside their dwelling.* Abi remembered Sumathy's words from the first time she came to Gurukul. How time had flown!

After a while, Abi stopped watching her friend and went into the kitchen to help the cook prepare breakfast. She stopped in her tracks in surprise when she recognised a plump face among the pots and pans. Dhanya, her classmate, was wearing the cook's robes and barking out orders cheerfully. 'Dhanya – what are you doing here? Are you the chef? Sumathy didn't tell me about you!' exclaimed Abi joyously.

Dhanya always had a penchant for good food and had once beaten Abi in a cooking competition. 'Abi, welcome back!' Dhanya's round cheeks dimpled into a wide smile. 'I finished training and decided that my career was in cooking. I plan to open a large restaurant in the city, in a few years' time. Our cook had to go away for a year, attending to his family. So, I thought this would be a good place to practise before I start my own business. So, what would you like for breakfast?'

Abi had a splendid time working and chatting with Dhanya. The chores were followed by a lip-smacking array of dishes at breakfast. After finishing off the last crumbs on her banana leaf, Sumathy turned to Abi with a serious face. 'Abi, I have to teach – I can't let Guru Uma down. Why don't you see if Guruma has returned? I saw Kaliram clean her room this morning and that's a good sign.'

Abi nodded and made her way to Guruma's room in the courtyard – she could feel her heart beating faster. It looked much the same – the pictures of gods in the corner with flowers, and an oil lamp, throwing soft light on their faces, was a reassuring sight. Abi hesitated in the doorway as the room looked dark and uninhabited. 'Come in, child. I cannot wait to see you!' a gentle voice called out from inside.

Abi rushed in and was delighted to see Guruma occupying her favourite chair behind her desk. Guruma stood up and hugged her fondly and stood back to inspect her. Abi could see new frown lines on Guruma's face, and there was clearly a troubled look in those deep grey eyes. But Guruma wanted to hear all about Abi's adventures and listened to everything she had seen and done in heaven with great interest. When Abi had finished her story and told her about the magic sapphire and her suspicions about Vi, Guruma's eyes flickered thoughtfully. 'You are quite right, Abi. It would be a cruel way to test the child. And if she's not your sister, she is definitely going to get burnt. But I have another idea. Whether or not she's your twin, she has a great affinity to you. Why don't you try and teach her to speak? Doctors have said there's nothing wrong with her – maybe once she starts speaking, she will say something you can recognise.' Abi stared at her guru with a mix of excitement and disappointment. Excitement because the idea sounded plausible but disappointment because it sounded like it would take a few days, weeks or months before she would even know.

Guruma seemed to understand her turmoil. 'I know it's not going to be easy, child. But you, of all people, will remember that nothing can be accomplished without hard work and patience! *Udhyamena hi sidhyanti karyani, na hi manorathaihi,*' said Guruma, quoting Abi's beloved Sanskrit *shloka*. Abi nodded, trying to convince herself that it would be fine. 'There's a bit more, child,' said Guruma, with a strange glow in her eyes. 'Abi, I am required elsewhere. If you hadn't been where you were and saved the world by dancing with Shiva, you know there would have been disaster. I am worried that it can happen again. I have to get back to my home.' Her deep grey eyes looked over the horizon, towards the snowy mountains in the north. Guruma had answered Abi's question without her asking it. Abi stood back, dumbfounded that her suspicions were true – Guruma was indeed the goddess Parvathi!

Abi was rooted to the spot in shock, gazing at Guruma in awe. 'It's ok, Abi. I am still the same person, even if you know the truth about me. There are only two things that worry me. One of them is Gurukul. I know that Guru Uma will be able to take over and run it as well as I do – but she's distracted, worried about her child. If you can take that worry away from her, by teaching her and getting her to speak, Gurukul will have its new Guruma.'

Abi looked at the pleading look on her face and felt ashamed that she was hesitating. 'Of course! I will absolutely do everything in my power to get that child to talk. And Guruma, you have to go back to your home – it's unfair that you have already spent so much time away from it for us.' Guruma smiled – her grey eyes filled with hope and the twinkle came back into them. 'What's your second worry? Maybe I can help there, too?'

Guruma smiled – 'My second worry is you! Abi – you have brought back the magic sapphire. This will attract evil – Varun will once again have another chance to try his luck. Given you've already earned your way up the seven steps to heaven, it will be even easier for him to get hold of you and make you take him there. I worry that if I leave, you will be all alone to face a very dangerous *asura*.'

Abi looked pensively out of the window. She remembered what Varun told her the last time they'd met and she had saved him from the Nagas. She wondered about his innate nature and hoped that he would have overcome it by now and he would not harm her, but there was no way of being sure. However, she certainly didn't want to keep Guruma with her instead of her rightful place in Kailasa. She looked back into those grey eyes with new-found conviction. 'You will just have to trust me, Guruma. I will be absolutely fine. I will study more, learn more mantras, martial art and other sciences to protect me from danger. I will have Sumathy and all the other gurus here to look after me. I know how well they can fight when needed – I remember the dacoits well. Plus, with Krish and Bal in the village, I don't think we are short of friends and supporters, do you?'

Guruma looked torn – she wasn't convinced that Abi could tackle Varun, but she also knew it was time for her to return home, to her husband Shiva. She took Abi's hands in hers and studied her face for a few moments. 'I know you can find *Shakti* inside you, Abi. Promise me that you will do all that you said – learn more, keep your friends close and not take any silly chances. I will not forgive myself if you come to harm. But I know that if I don't return, you and the entire world will be open to risk. My Shiva needs his Parvathi besides him to function properly.' She smiled as she said these words.

Abi bent down and touched Guruma's feet. 'I have your blessing – I will be fine, I promise!'

Guruma spent the next few days making various arrangements and announcements before getting ready to leave. All the teachers and students were upset, and although they didn't know who Guruma really was, they finally accepted that she needed to return home to her family. Before she announced her move, she made sure that Abi had started taking Vi under her wing and started teaching her. As predicted, Vi thrived under Abi's care and was now starting to utter simple words like "Ma", "Abi" and "Guru". Guru Uma was relieved that her child had finally started to speak and was very grateful to Abi. So, when Guruma asked her to lead the school, she accepted without reservation. Her biggest worry, her daughter, was now developing like a normal child. Before she left, Guruma drew an intricate *kolam* outside Gurukul's courtyard. 'As long as this *kolam* is uncovered and unspoilt, it will protect the school and no evil will be able to enter.' Her eyes flashed at Abi, who understood that Guruma was adding this protection for her specifically, to ward off Varun. As her last act as Guruma, she drew up an entire syllabus of studies for Abi and gave strict instructions to a number of the teachers on what Abi needed to master and by when.

'I will be here in spirit to watch over all of you! Guru Uma is now your Guruma. Good luck, children – look after yourselves and each other!' There wasn't a single dry eye in the school when Guruma left. Guru Uma decided to convert her room into a memorial for Guruma. Abi brought her bowl with the magic sapphire and flames into the room and left it burning brightly next to the pictures of the gods – this was her little tribute to the great guru.

44

GURUKUL BURNS!

Life carried on in Gurukul much the same way as before, even without Guruma. Everyone followed their routines religiously; and dance, music and studies were taught and learnt as before. Abi was very careful to start her syllabus and spent a great deal of time meditating, as per Guruma's explicit instructions. She enjoyed it all, but most of all, she enjoyed spending every single free minute with baby Vi, who was now getting to be relatively chatty.

Krish would visit the school regularly and would also teach Vi how to sing. She couldn't yet string full sentences together but kept trying her best to talk and sing with broken words, which pleased Abi more than anything. 'I have a feeling she is Vy, really,' said Abi to Sumathy one day. 'She just feels so familiar and is so comfortable with me. She's also really good with animals. Why do I need to prove to myself that she's my sister when I am happy to accept her as it is?' Sumathy agreed with a smile. She was secretly worried about having the sapphire back in the school and constantly watching out for Varun. She wasn't sure how Abi could get rid of the gemstone and fervently hoped that Guruma's *kolam* offered sufficient protection for everyone in and around the school.

Guru Usha called out to Abi, asking her to come to the doorway of the courtyard. 'What is it, Guruji, you look worried?' said Abi, stepping out.

Guru Usha pointed to the tree that stood majestically outside the doorway. Its leaves offered shade to all who stood underneath and it acted as a beautiful canopy to Guruma's *kolam*. 'The tree is sick – it seems to be dying!' Abi looked up in surprise and indeed all the leaves seemed to be drooping and losing their green colour.

'That's odd,' said Abi, 'I could have sworn it was absolutely fine yesterday. What could have caused this?'

All the teachers came out to inspect the tree, but no one could find anything obviously wrong with it. 'I am going to the town and fetching Mr Basu from the school to have a look at it,' said Guru Usha finally. 'He's a keen botanist and I am sure he will know what to do or at least know someone who can help us with this.' With apprehension, Abi watched Guru Usha and Guru Rama leave together for the town. Something seemed odd with the way the tree had suddenly started dying in a day!

The teachers would not be back until the next day as they had only left in the afternoon. Abi and Sumathy continued their classes and then got busy with dinner and preparations for the next day's studies without giving a second thought to the teachers and the tree. It was Amavasya or no-moon, and the girls went to bed, commenting to each other about the stillness and the darkness that night. There was not a single star to be seen in the sky, and the atmosphere was murky and humid – as if it was just going to rain. Abi had just fallen asleep when she was woken up by a rustling sound. She sat up as if an electric shock had gone up her spine. She couldn't see anything obviously wrong inside the room, and Sumathy was still snoring gently in her bed. Then it hit Abi. There was an eerie glow outside and it was getting brighter by the minute. She rushed out of her room and stood horrified as she saw giant flames leap up the courtyard. Gurukul was burning!

'Sumathy, wake up! We are on fire!' screamed Abi and ran towards the courtyard, followed by a disoriented Sumathy. Some of the teachers had just reached the doorway and they were trying to fill buckets of water, but the blaze was too strong. Normally, everyone vacated the inner courtyard at night. Previously, Guruma would have slept in her room, but as Guru Uma had kept her old quarters outside the courtyard, there was no one likely to be inside. However, they needed to be sure. Abi acted on instinct and jumped into the courtyard through the blazing doorway before anyone could stop her. All the rooms were blazing, but as she searched, she couldn't find anyone trapped there. The fire was getting worse and finally Abi came back out, having satisfied herself that there was no one in trouble. 'What on earth were you thinking!' chided Guru Uma, pulling Abi away from the fire. 'The fire brigade have been informed, but it will take them a while to come from town. Please don't put yourself in danger in the meantime, Abi.'

Abi nodded meekly and watched in horror as more and more trees caught fire – the entire forest was getting destroyed. Sumathy came up to Abi and pointed at the doorway silently. Abi followed the direction of her finger and her heart missed a beat. Guruma's *kolam* was nowhere to be seen; it was covered by a heap of dead leaves that had fallen down from the diseased tree. The girls exchanged dark looks – this didn't seem like a coincidence. 'Was the bowl still inside Guruma's room? Did you see it?' asked Sumathy, echoing the thoughts that were forming shape in Abi's mind. She thought back to her frenzied search inside the courtyard. She didn't remember seeing a bowl there – but then she couldn't be absolutely sure. The two girls looked at each other, panic written all over their faces! This felt like Varun's doing!

They didn't have much time to react to their realisation as Guru Uma was organising the teachers and students to collect in a safe place so that she could take attendance and make sure everyone was ok. Luckily, all the girls and the orchestra were accounted for, when Guru Uma had a shock. Her baby was missing. She nearly fainted from the realisation, and it was lucky that Guru Mahesh was close by to catch her before she fell to the ground. 'Where's my child? Where's Vi – I left her in my room…' she shouted hysterically. There was a mad scramble as everyone went round all the outer rooms, searching and calling out for the child, but she had indeed disappeared.

Abi and Sumathy were searching one of the rooms furthest away from the school when Abi was startled by an owl that took off from a nearby tree. She remembered her peacock feather and fumbled at it frantically. 'Please… please warn the villagers that the fire is spreading! And tell my friends the Nagas that we are in trouble… maybe

389

they can help us,' she shouted at the bird, hoping that it would hear some of what she said. She collapsed in tears into Sumathy's arms, blaming herself for the predicament that Gurukul found itself in.

'Oh dear, please don't cry,' said a deep voice behind her. Abi and Sumathy turned to find Varun standing nonchalantly, one hand on his hip and another holding baby Vi. The child seemed unharmed and was playing with something in her hands.

Abi looked into his glowing green eyes with distaste in her narrowing eyes. 'Why do you have to destroy the forest and all its creatures to get what you want? Let that child go!'

Varun gave her a dazzling smile. 'Oh, don't worry about the forest. I have the power to stop the fire, and I have a nectar that will help all the trees grow back. I can't help the people; but hopefully they can get out of the way!'

Abi nearly spat with disgust – she couldn't believe that she once had a soft spot for him. 'Well then, use it!' she shouted, loud enough to be heard over the burning noise.

'Not so fast, my dear. I need you to do something for me in return. Baby Vi, show Abi what you're playing with, be a good girl!'

Abi's eyes widened as she saw the magic sapphire glint in the child's hands. 'Ah, Abi, that's how the fire started. I was watching you and knew that you suspected young Vi here to be your reincarnated sister. There was only one way to find out. I made the tree lose its leaves and stole the bowl of fire and the baby and got her to fish out the sapphire from inside the bowl. You were quite right; she is your twin. Sadly, I knocked over the bowl by mistake and the fire spread like... like wildfire...' he guffawed, pleased with his choice of words. Vi looked at Abi with her big black eyes and Abi felt several emotions go through her at once. She felt joy; she had been right about Vi all along. She also felt fear for her sister and the entire forest. Finally, she felt repulsed, as if something creepy was crawling on her skin – she could not believe that Varun was so casual with so many people's lives to get what he wanted!

'But the sapphire is no longer my objective! Ever since I found out that the seven steps to heaven needed to be climbed through a mix of good deeds, I knew that I wasn't cut out for that way. But you – you've already earned your place. You have the credentials to go up the seven steps again. Except, this time, you will need to take me with you.'

'Never!' shouted Abi, her voice hoarse to be heard over the blazing fire.

'Never say never, Abi.' Varun's voice sounded dangerously silky. 'Even Lord Shiva cannot save you now!'

45

LIKE A PHOENIX
FROM THE ASHES

When things go badly wrong, you can always panic and make them worse! Guruma's words echoed in Abi's ears. She closed her eyes and tried to make sense of everything that was going on. The entire world was falling apart. She had no choice; she would have to do what Varun wanted to save the forest and save her sister. As he said, even Lord Shiva could not help her now! She opened her eyes and gave an involuntary shudder, as if she'd got an electric shock. Of course Lord Shiva could help her! She still had her boon from the time she'd helped close his third eye. Varun was playing with baby Vi in the meantime, throwing her up in the air and catching her. 'You don't want me to miss, do you? I may land up throwing her into the fire by mistake,' he said with a maniacal grin.

Abi flashed a look at Sumathy, hoping that she would understand what she wanted her to do. She needed time.

Sumathy seemed to understand the unspoken words and started pleading to Varun. 'She's just a baby! How can you do this to her? Varun, you have to stop this fire. If it spreads to the village, they will lose everything. The fire brigade will take too long to come here, and even if they do, they can't save us as well as the village!' Varun was visibly getting increasingly exasperated, but Sumathy went on, without even pausing for breath.

In the meantime, Abi closed her eyes, took a deep breath and prayed to Lord Shiva. Using the power of her mind to put the fire, the fear and concern aside, she was able to meditate with full focus on the god. Shiva soon appeared in her mind and smiled at her. 'Please, Lord Shiva, can I ask for my boon? I need to save the forest and my sister from this demon.'

Shiva had a gentle smile on his face. 'Which one is the boon, my child? You can ask for one. I can either get rid of the fire and save the forest, or I can kill Varun and save your sister. I cannot do both. You have to make a choice.' Abi stared at the god in dismay. How could she choose between these two things? Whatever the choice, she would lose something precious. She was about to protest when she remembered that gods could be mercurial and also strangely philosophical about life and what they will or won't do. Guruma's advice came back to her: *Seek Shakti inside you, child. You have all the answers inside.* She could have Varun killed and her sister would be safe – but it was also likely that the child and everybody else would perish in the fire. She needed to do what was right, not what was easy. She hardened her heart and made the choice.

Varun lost his patience with Sumathy's incessant whining. He was getting tired of Abi's inactivity. With a laugh, he threw the baby towards a burning tree. Abi opened her eyes as Sumathy screamed at the top of her lungs. The child had fallen with a thud into the fire. Abi stared at Varun and felt that time had stalled. All the noise around her became fainter. Suddenly orange haze around her disappeared. She turned around to look – the fire had vanished. Shiva had given her the boon!

Varun stared in horror, his eyes wide with disbelief, as the fire went out. Abi and Sumathy ran towards the tree where he had thrown baby Vi. She had fallen on top of a nest and looked uncomfortable but totally unharmed. 'How did she escape the fire? I saw her go into the flames,' asked Sumathy, in surprise.

Abi knew the answer. 'The fire was started from the magic flames in the bowl. Vy and I are the only two people in the world that this fire wouldn't harm. So that's why she's safe.'

'Not for long,' said Varun, who had recovered from the shock of the fire going out and was standing before them, with a knife gleaming in his hand. 'This blade can definitely harm your sister, and it will, unless you take me back to my home,' he shouted. Sumathy and Abi looked at each other in the desperate hope that one of them would think of a way out. Abi blinked a tear away when she realised that Sumathy's face was blank – they were both out of ideas.

Abi resigned herself to her fate. It looked like he would get what he wanted. They were lucky that no one had got hurt yet; and although much of the mountain was destroyed, life would grow back. Abi nodded in acquiescence and took the magic sapphire from Varun's hands. She took a few deep breaths to calm her beating heart, closed her eyes and got ready to invoke Lord Indra. Before she could utter a prayer, she was stopped by a hiss and a loud rustle on the floor! She opened her eyes to see that they were surrounded by snakes. A couple of the snakes coiled themselves soundlessly around Varun's ankles. The Nagas had arrived!

Varun stared around him in terror. She could see him trembling. He had been scared of the Nagas ever since the time previously that they had taken him captive. One of the snakes raised its hood in front of him. As they watched, the snake grew into an enormous serpent, towering above them all. Its hood was as wide as a dance stage, and venom dripped from both its fangs. The snake opened its mouth wide, ready to swallow Varun whole as Abi, Sumathy and Vi stared at it in shock. Varun seemed broken – there was fear in his eyes, but there was also a terrible sadness. He had, at last, given up and resigned himself to his fate. Abi looked at him and realised what she saw in his eyes was what she had felt every single day after she had left her home in the UK. Homesickness! A horrible gnawing feeling that she could never return home and it would never be the same. She suddenly felt sorry for him and understood why she related to him so well before. They were two of a kind in terms of missing their homes and their loved ones, though that's probably where the similarity ended.

'Stop!' screamed Abi, throwing herself between the gigantic serpent and Varun. 'Don't eat him! His main fault is that he misses home. And he's already undergoing punishment for that. It's not right to kill him for wanting to get back home.'

The serpent looked at her in surprise. 'He has tried to harm you so many times! How can you trust that he will not do so again?'

Abi looked at Varun and then shrugged her shoulders. 'I don't know if I can trust him again. In fact, I probably can't. But I also know that I cannot allow a person to be killed because he tried his best to get back to his home and his loved ones... that is something I cannot do!' The snakes hissed at each other as if asking each other what to do next.

The great serpent changed into a Naga and looked at Varun with narrowed eyes. 'Abi has asked me to stop and so I will not kill you. But if you ever try to harm her or any of these girls again, I will not stop even for Abi.'

Abi called out to the Naga before he turned away. 'Please... I need another favour; will you take this magic sapphire with you? I will always feel in danger while I have it in my possession. But no one will dare to steal it from you, and I hope you'll accept it as a token of my thanks!'

The Naga accepted the gem and looked at Abi thoughtfully. 'Do you realise that this means you will not be able to go back to see your mother and father until you die?'

Abi nodded. 'My life is here in Gurukul, with my friends and my sister. My parents will always be part of me. I am sure I can wait a human lifetime to see them.'

Varun looked contritely at the floor as the snakes released him from their grip and slithered away into the burnt forest. 'Abi, I am glad you didn't allow a living being to be killed, even if he was horrible,' said Vi, speaking impeccably. Abi laughed and hugged her baby sister with tears glistening on her cheeks. Sumathy was still looking at Varun suspiciously, wondering what he would do next.

Varun fell down on his knees and looked at Abi with tearful eyes. 'I cannot believe you saved me! My mother once told me that nothing matters more than goodness. I never believed her until now.'

Abi gave him a sad smile. 'I recognised that awful feeling of homesickness in you and related to it totally, but I don't agree with the path you follow. I hope you can find peace with yourself one day.'

Varun reached out into the air and pulled a pitcher out of nothing. 'Here, take this and use it to resurrect the forest. It is nectar and is very potent on plants. This is the least that I can do for you.' Abi accepted the pitcher gratefully. 'I am going to go away and learn some of the qualities that you display so effortlessly. Patience, contentment and selflessness. Good luck, Abi, and thank you for sparing my life.' Abi watched in silence as Varun disappeared into the air. Sumathy's eyes stayed narrowed.

⸻

After a while, the girls went around the trees and sprinkled drops of nectar liberally. The trees shot back to life, much to their pleasure and amusement. They made their way, growing the forest all the way back to Gurukul. There was no one there as everyone had gone to the village to warn them and find a safe place to save themselves from the fire. Abi looked sadly at the burnt buildings. While they could bring the trees back to life, it would take a lot of hard work to rebuild the school. Abi then looked at Sumathy and Vi – she had a lot to be grateful for. And she had a new purpose in life. They had to rebuild the school and bring it back to its former glory. She smiled as Sumathy squeezed her hand. 'A new life and a new beginning! After all, from the ashes rises a phoenix!'

ACKNOWLEDGEMENTS

This book is a product of love, and my love for books was passed down to me by my father. I also want to thank Steven, my much-loved husband, for being my first audience for this book, listening to every chapter with infinite patience and querying each twist in the tale with relish. And thanks to my mother, Smt. N. Krishnaveni; and my mother-in-law, Audrey Hunt, for their encouragement.

The next love this book represents is my love for dance. I would like to thank my Guruji Smt. Saroja Vaidyanathan and her dance school Ganesa Natyalaya as what I have learnt there has defined me and made me who I am today. A big thanks to Rama Vaidyanathan, another brilliant dancer, who has been my inspiration since my teenage years. Her foreword means more to me than I can ever express.

I have been very lucky to have some brilliant and talented friends who have contributed to this book. A big thanks to Tina Rajan, the amazing artist, for her wonderful drawings and cover sketch. Thanks to John Cogan and his daughter Tara for believing in me and giving me confidence and feedback as I wrote. I also want to thank Srishti and Gayathri Sikka and Joe Picard for being my first few reader-advocates of the book.

Last, but not least, a big thanks to the whole team at Matador Publishing for all their help and support in bringing this book out into the market.